LOST RIGHTS

LOST RIGHTS

The

MISADVENTURES *of a* STOLEN AMERICAN RELIC

David Howard

HOUGHTON MIFFLIN HARCOURT
BOSTON   NEW YORK
2010

For information about permission to reproduce selections from this book,
write to Permissions, Houghton Mifflin Harcourt Publishing Company,
215 Park Avenue South, New York, New York 10003.

www.hmhbooks.com

Library of Congress Cataloging-in-Publication Data
Howard, David, date.
Lost rights : the misadventures of a stolen American relic / David Howard.
p. cm.
Includes bibliographical references.
ISBN 978-0-618-82607-0
1. United States—History—Civil War, 1861–1865—Confiscations and contributions.
2. North Carolina—History—Civil War, 1861–1865—Confiscations and contributions.
3. Lost articles—North Carolina—History. 4. Theft of relics—North Carolina—
History. 5. Manuscripts—Collectors and collecting—United States.
6. United States. Constitution. 1st–10th Amendments. I. Title.
E480.H847 2009
973.7′8—dc22   2009018046

Book design by Brian Moore

Printed in the United States of America

DOC 10 9 8 7 6 5 4 3 2 1

FOR ANN

Freedom is a hard-bought thing.
—PAUL ROBESON, actor, cultural scholar, political activist

Contents

Introduction

CHARLENE BICKFORD DIDN'T GIVE the appointment a moment's thought. The notion was too far-fetched to merit even a blip in her daily schedule. Her colleague, Ken Bowling, had mentioned it in passing the day before: A man had called wanting to come to the offices of the First Federal Congress Project in Washington, D.C., and have the staff authenticate a document. He'd claimed to have an original copy of the Bill of Rights. Bickford and Bowling had heard such unlikely boasts before. Their response was, in essence: *Uh-huh. Sure.*

The caller had chosen the ideal experts. Bickford and Bowling were preeminent authorities on the first-ever United States Federal Congress, which convened from 1789 to 1791. Combined, they had more than sixty years of experience examining documents from that era. Bickford, the director and coeditor, was in her mid-fifties and stood just over five feet tall, with short-cropped brown hair and glasses with large, round frames that exaggerated the size of her eyes. She spoke softly and in a measured voice, as if permanently habituated to hushed, scholarly spaces.

The project, run under the auspices of George Washington University, had an audacious goal: to collect all documents relating to the inaugural Congress and publish them in twenty-two volumes. This task had occupied most of Bickford's professional life. On the day of the appointment, she'd spent more than half her life studying the political maneuverings of that two-year period. She knew the handwriting of the First Congress's three clerks like she knew her own.

Which was why the Bill of Rights authentication request was so implausible. Bickford had never seen such an esteemed document outside an official setting. The parchments on which the three clerks carefully inscribed the fourteen copies of the Bill of Rights in 1789 are among the rarest and most treasured artifacts in American history. Of the manuscripts that President George Washington sent off—one for each of the thirteen original states, and another for the new federal government—only nine remain in official custody. New York's copy was believed to have burned in a fire. Georgia's either went up in flames or was simply lost. Three others were stolen, but the thefts—all unsolved—happened more than a lifetime ago. One was snatched during the Civil War and hadn't been seen since. No original had appeared on the historic-manuscript marketplace for almost sixty years. For this reason it would be difficult to assess the value of such a document—but it would likely be in the tens of millions of dollars.

Bickford had seen only two genuine originals: Delaware's and the federal government's. The latter is on display in the dimmed and filtered light of the Rotunda for the Charters of Freedom in the National Archives, where hundreds of thousands of visitors view it annually. Archivists call such sovereign documents "holy relics."

Because such broadsheets are so rare—and so stratospherically valuable—Bickford and Bowling occasionally fielded requests exactly like this one. The story was always the same: The breathless caller had just sifted through the possessions of a recently deceased relative—a grandparent, say—and had found what appeared to be a valuable artifact, perhaps an official-looking document bearing a date from the 1700s. Heart thrumming, the heir began making phone calls to figure out whether it was real, and if so, how much it might be worth. Sometimes one of these people found their way to Bickford and Bowling.

The two experts usually played along, even though the First Federal Congress Project's staff has more than enough to do and was not in the business of authenticating historical documents. The documents were rarely what they appeared to be. Countless copies and counterfeits had bubbled into the marketplace—some of them extraordinarily convincing forgeries on paper that was expertly aged and faded. Bickford and Bowling could quickly flush out a flaw that was invisible to a novice: The paper was too new, the handwriting not quite right.

More often it was a case of mistaken identity: "People will buy one of the copies of the Constitution that they sell at the National Archives—you know, they sell these reproductions—and stash it away in their papers," Bickford says. "When they die, somebody in their family finds this thing and thinks it's the original."

"Put it this way," says Bowling, coeditor of the project and Bickford's longtime colleague. "We've been shown a printed, footnoted version of the Bill of Rights and told that it was an original copy. So one never expects much."

The notion that someone in Topeka might unearth a priceless relic beneath a nimbus of attic dust was mostly sheer folly. And so, unlike tourists charmed by the cherry blossoms or moved by the Vietnam Veterans Memorial, these types of guests of the First Federal Congress Project often left Washington disappointed.

The day of the Bill of Rights appointment—February 24, 2000—was typically prosaic. Bickford had a new graduate intern who needed her ears and eyes as he built the project's first website. The staff faced the ongoing task of assembling and editing volumes fifteen through seventeen of First Congress documents. Bickford confronted the usual mélange of paperwork necessary to keep the project in the black—no small task for one of the tiny quasi-governmental entities struggling to stay afloat in the backwaters of the nation's capital. At times the project barely had enough funds to pay staff salaries, and in lean years it was in peril of getting "zeroed out," as Bickford termed it. The suite of offices was often cluttered with cases of spring water and soda purchased at Costco.

Although the project would eventually produce the most thorough documentation ever of the federal government's creation, it wasn't particularly sexy. Few outside a small circle of fellow academics and history buffs—Bickford called them "our groupies"—would notice.

Still, Bickford loved the job. She initially studied French history in graduate school, then landed a job as a clerk-typist at the First Congress Project to help pay her tuition. She never left. If you ask where she grew up, she'll reply, "A place called Adams, New York. In Jefferson County." If the listener hasn't caught on, she might add, "Sort of apropos—we work with people named Adams and Jefferson all the time."

Bickford built her life around routine and continuity. She moved to Arlington, just across the Potomac, when she arrived in Washington in 1967. For more than thirty years she'd had the same commute: She walked to the Metro for the seven-minute train ride to the Foggy Bottom–GWU stop. When you devote your life to a cast of characters who lived more than two centuries ago, there aren't a whole lot of surprises in your day-to-day existence. But the steadiness of her world agreed with her.

For the people who had called for the appointment that February afternoon, the relative anonymity of the First Federal Congress Project was no doubt a selling point. At the National Archives or the Smithsonian, they would have encountered uniformed officers and security cameras. By contrast, there was nothing official about Bickford's workplace. The visitors would simply walk past a concrete school playground and Classic Floor Designs store before pushing through the glass doors of the Gelman Building at 2120 L Street, NW. Inside, a guard at the front desk might have asked them to enter a name in the logbook. No ID was required. Up on the second floor, Suite 255 was locked, the entry buzzer broken; a handwritten note taped to the door read "Please knock loudly."

Inside, the absence of the marbled and crenulated grandeur so prevalent in Washington is striking. The main conference room, a windowless rectangle with low-hanging drop-in ceilings, seems frozen in the LBJ era: the chipped Formica-topped tables and desks, the wall of heavy steel file cabinets, the ceiling-high shelves of reference volumes. The cluttered rooms emit a vague perfume of aged paper. Thumbtacks attach replicas of antique maps to the walls.

When the knock came at around 3:00 that afternoon, three

men and a woman crowded through the door and into the dimly lit lobby. Something immediately seemed odd about the visitors. As they shuffled into the conference room, Bickford and Bowling introduced themselves. The guests shook hands with them but did not offer names. They gathered close to the conference table, actually a set of four smaller surfaces pushed together, seeming vaguely uncomfortable and avoiding eye contact. The group lacked the usual twitchy energy of people hoping to strike it rich. In fact, none of the four seemed interested in even basic niceties. An awkward feeling settled over the room. Bickford later recalled that two of the men were heavyset and wore trench coats, and they gave off a vibe as if they might be bodyguards; they seemed to be watching the historians. It struck Ken Bowling that the person who had called to set up the appointment also hadn't offered a name.

One of the men laid a large cardboard art carton on the table. The entire First Congress Project staff—Bickford, Bowling, handwriting expert Helen Veit, and Chuck diGiacomantonio, plus the intern—gathered around. Two of the men carefully lifted the flaps off the box and pulled out an ornate but chipped wooden frame. They laid the frame on the table. Inside was a creased and faded document that looked very old.

Charlene Bickford leaned close, stared for a few seconds, and felt the air leave her body.

An art expert might comb the globe for a lifetime and never find a lost masterpiece such as *The Taking of Christ,* the Caravaggio painting discovered in 1990 after being missing for four centuries. A rare-books dealer might dream of stumbling onto a sheaf of unpublished Mark Twain journals wedged behind a shelf in a remote stack, but never experience the exhilaration of that discovery.

For passionate scholars who do experience such revelatory discoveries, the moment can be euphoric. When Henry Stanley finally located Dr. Livingstone, he wrote that he wanted to "vent [his] joy in some mad freak, such as . . . turning a somersault." There is the story of an expert bird watcher—one of the top five in the world— who for decades had pursued the rare flame-crested manakin. After years of globetrotting, Peter Kaestner, a buttoned-down, high-ranking foreign-service diplomat, finally spotted the bird in the Brazilian jungle and unleashed a stream of jubilant expletives that reverberated through the canopy.

The First Congress Project staffers avoided such histrionics despite the exhilaration they felt. The stilted situation and their own reserved personalities made any sort of outburst unlikely. Though they'd spent thousands of hours staring at ancient documents, they rarely saw originals. Even if their budget had allowed them to buy manuscripts—which it didn't—the historians would not do so; they were not collectors. When they came across a stray document for sale, they asked a groupie to acquire it and send a copy.

Staring at what was almost certainly an authentic, original Bill of Rights, the scholars initially said nothing at all. They took in its unusual broadsheet dimensions—the document is twenty-six and a half by thirty-one inches—and the elegantly curved *s*'s and *f*'s that grace the script of that era.

Bickford leaned close. The word *the* at the top was a perfect match: a very tall, thin *t* with an *h* that's shaped like the previous letter, both of them crossed—probably the handiwork of William Lambert. She studied the tidy cursive rendering of the familiar passage "Congress shall make no law respecting the establishment of a religion, or prohibiting the free exercise thereof; or abridging the freedom of speech . . ." That looked right. Down at the bottom, the signatures—Vice President John Adams; Frederick Augustus Muhlenberg, Speaker of the House; and John Beckley, Clerk of Congress—were perfect.

As the shock wore off, the editors launched a barrage of questions: Where did their visitors get this document? What did they know about its history? What did they plan to do with it?

The inquiries went nowhere. The visitors responded with variations of "I'm not at liberty to say." Long, awkward silences smothered the room as the scholars and their visitors took turns looking down at the document and then back at each other.

When it comes to many events beyond the late eighteenth century, Bickford struggles with a spotty memory. When she recounted the story later, she described the woman as having blond hair. She remembered that the two "bodyguards" seemed to study the editors more closely than the Bill of Rights and that they looked "thuggish." She wondered whether they were armed. Beyond that, though, her memory was blank. "It made me think I wouldn't be a very good witness," Bickford said, "if somebody mugged me."

After a few minutes of the stonewalling, diGiacomantonio and Veit walked off in frustration. Bowling soon followed. He'd experienced such clandestine behavior before: Anonymous requests for information. Furtive phone calls. For decades Bowling had been obsessed with chasing after letters and documents written by or to members of the First Congress that had long since been scattered among collectors. On several occasions he'd located long-lost missives, only to be refused access even to copies. Some collectors believe that exposing the documents' contents reduces their value. After almost forty years of such episodes, Bowling merely shrugged. Collectors can be quirky. "It's their hobby," Bowling said, "their porn."

This time, though, he was irked. "It was absolutely and completely obvious it was an original, unless it was a masterful forgery," Bowling said. "But these people were creeps, they seemed to be armed, they refused to identify themselves, and clearly they had stolen property and didn't want anybody to know who they were."

Suddenly, Charlene Bickford was alone with the group. She'd had little preparation for this sort of experience. There had been only one prior incident during her thirty-three years on the job in which an authentic First Congress document had suddenly bubbled to the surface: an original version of the Lighthouses Act. But she'd seen that relic in a catalog—a far different experience from having it unexpectedly appear in the middle of her office.

Bickford felt just as annoyed as her colleagues with the eccentric visitors, but she found herself unable to walk away—as if the amazing artifact was exerting some kind of magnetic pull, despite the uncomfortable circumstances. So she did what was most natural in a room filled with prickly silence: The reserved historian started talking.

"This is a document that looks very much like one of the original fourteen copies of the Bill of Rights," she began, stating what her reaction had already made obvious. "They're really fourteen originals and not fourteen copies, so this is a singular document. But you should have other experts examine the material it's written on and make a complete study of it to finally authenticate it."

She paused and looked around. "The fourteen copies were made, one for the federal government, and one for each of the states. Under order of Congress, Washington sent them out to the states with a letter to each governor. Five of those states have lost their copies: Pennsylvania, New York, Maryland, Georgia, and North Carolina. That means that if you tried to sell this, you would have to deal with some of those states, and maybe all five of them, taking an interest in trying to claim it."

Bickford hoped this would spark some conversation, but again, the guests simply nodded. "You should be trying to find out which state it belongs to," she said. "And the way to potentially find out what state it belongs to is to have it taken out of the frame and have this backing taken off." She pointed through the glass cover at the cardboard to which the document was glued. "Then we, or someone, can look and see if there's any docketing on the back."

Docketing is a useful tool for determining the history of two-hundred-year-old records. In the eighteenth century official papers were often stored in long, narrow boxes. In order to get a document such as the Bill of Rights to fit inside, a clerk would fold it several times; he would then write a brief notation on the outer fold summarizing its contents so he could quickly identify the record later. The clerk might also note the date on the document, or the date it arrived. But since he made the notation *after* doing the folding, the docketing always appeared on the backside.

"You'll need to find a highly skilled conservator to take it out of this frame," Bickford said, "and remove it from this backing."

Then she made one last bid for their cooperation. "When you're doing authentication on a document, you need to have some of the background on it: where it came from, who the seller was," she said. "If you would give us that information, or tell us how to contact you, then we might be able to have a conversation about this. We could do some research, and we could tell you more. It's difficult to be helpful without the facts."

At this, two of the men Bickford believed to be bodyguards started packing away the document. Bickford regretted not taking the appointment more seriously; she hadn't prepared for the eventuality that a holy relic might actually come through the door. Or worse, that it might just as suddenly disappear again. She regretted that she didn't spend a little more time studying her visitors. "I was so focused on the document itself, the fact that we had an original Bill of Rights on our conference table," she said. "It just really took your breath away."

Faced with no better option, she simply offered a warning. "I will tell you this," she said. "If the document is what it appears to be, it has tremendous value, but the state that it belongs to could claim it. There are laws that apply to getting it back. It's priceless, but it's also worthless."

The guests nodded and thanked her, then walked back out through the lobby. She never saw or heard from them again.

Priceless.

That word gets bandied about frequently in conversations involving sacred American relics. People like Charlene Bickford use the term literally: an item without price, since by definition it can't be bought and sold. To her, selling a Bill of Rights—a document owned by the people—would be like pawning the Liberty Bell, or the Statue of Liberty.

The historic-document market, though, operates under a different mindset. Most dealers and collectors don't willingly buy and sell stolen materials. But often an item's provenance is unclear. Sometimes a document's history can be obfuscated, or rewritten. Landmark historic documents frequently appear for sale at auction houses such as Sotheby's and Christie's. The marketplace for old papers connected to America's history, and its greatest historical figures, has never been more robust. Tens of millions of dollars flow through the market every year. In December 2007 a group of investors paid $21.3 million for a copy of the Magna Carta. A few years earlier two collectors had doled out more than $8 million for one of the 1776 copies of the Declaration of Independence.

Priceless? Not to collectors. If a buyer and a seller come to terms on a sale amount, no object is priceless.

That's why, a little more than three years after the strange meeting in Washington, Robert Clay stood at a window thirty-two floors above downtown Philadelphia, soaking in sweeping views of the city awash in bright, late-winter sunlight.

Clay was due any minute to walk into the adjacent conference room and introduce himself as a dot-com multimillionaire prepared to write a $4 million check for an original Bill of Rights. He mulled over the final details of the transaction and in his mind played back the brief speech he planned to give to the small assemblage next door. In a few short words Clay hoped to capture the magnitude of the moment. How many people in their lifetimes had the chance to acquire a truly iconic piece of American history?

Even under normal circumstances it was a daunting task, to harness such remarks. And this situation was anything but normal.

In fact, nothing was as it seemed. Clay wasn't a multimillionaire, and he had nothing at all to do with Internet commerce.

Robert Clay was actually FBI agent Bob Wittman, and the speech, which would be recorded by a hidden wire, was the final act of an elaborate piece of theater—a sting—staged to lure the document and its sellers to downtown Philadelphia.

This is the story of one holy relic's 138-year journey away from official custody, an odyssey that began in the ruined South in the waning days of the Civil War and climaxed in the upper reaches of that Philadelphia skyscraper, steps away from where the nation was born. This is also the story of the people responsible for this relic's odyssey, and the toll its passage took on their lives.

Priceless might, at least, be one way to describe the moment when "Robert Clay" turned and began walking toward the conference room next door. Even he couldn't have guessed the high cost of what would happen next—or how, in the quirky and colorful world of people who buy, sell, and study historical papers, nothing would ever be the same again.

1

A Break-in

NO ONE WILL EVER know exactly what happened on the morning of Thursday, April 13, 1865, just after General William Tecumseh Sherman's army marched into Raleigh, North Carolina. The citizens of the state capital were well aware of the mayhem that Sherman had inflicted on the cities and towns of Georgia and South Carolina, and officials in Raleigh, keen to avoid that fate, had surrendered the previous day. Still, Raleigh's residents were wary. They locked doors and blockaded windows against his arrival.

Sherman's troops, by contrast, felt hopeful about the coming day. When reveille sounded at 4:00 a.m., the soldiers of the Ninety-fourth Ohio Volunteer Infantry quickly broke camp and fell in. After years of war, their early-morning movements were rote, and on this day their steps felt lighter despite the chill and the patter of light rain. They hoped to be the first into Raleigh. The troops strode down muddy, eerily silent streets, past shuttered homes.

There was ample reason for optimism. They'd heard persistent whispers that the war was nearly over, an eventuality that—after all that had transpired—felt both impossible and inevitable. Robert E. Lee had surrendered at Appomattox four days earlier, accelerating the death rattle of the Confederacy. An exhausted and bitterly rent nation was tilting toward the uncertain place between all-out war and whatever came after.

There was no way to anticipate the chaos that was coming. The very next day, John Wilkes Booth would fire a pistol ball through Abraham Lincoln's head, and the North, on the verge of cathartic celebration, would instead convulse in horror. Several thousand of Sherman's enraged and vengeance-minded troops would gather to torch Raleigh, and the city would be saved only when a Union officer threatened to fire cannons on the blue-clad mob.

The city would be saved, but the South would be doomed to a bleak Reconstruction. But all of that would come later. All that Sherman's soldiers saw before them that April morning was a clear path to victory. They planned to claim the spoils of the victor and vanish into the fog of a fading war.

Rue P. Hutchins felt the turmoil of that most tumultuous week in United States history. Three years earlier, Hutchins, a loyal supporter of Lincoln and the Union, a schoolteacher turned whiskey distiller, and a decorated major, had led much of his small Ohio town into battle.

No one would have blamed Hutchins for being an unenthusiastic combatant. His ancestors were southerners, from Virginia and North Carolina. They were Quakers, too—people whose religion prohibits violence.

But the Hutchins clan had a defiant streak, an inclination to do things differently. Hutchins's grandfather, Meredith, joined the great westward movement that accompanied the opening of the Ohio Territory in 1795. He married an Irish woman, Susannah Fitzgerald, from outside the Quaker faith, resulting in his expulsion from the church. On the frontier the couple started over, opening the first inn in Little York, Ohio. One of their sons was also named Meredith. The younger Meredith married and had an only child, Rue, in 1833.

He eventually settled in Tippecanoe, population 949, the town's name a transliteration of the Native American word for a river rapid.

Western Ohio in the 1860s was a place of tall corn and robust wheat and barley crops and deep Union loyalty. During political rallies leading up to Lincoln's election two years earlier, there were fes-

tive barbecues and torchlight processions with brass bands and fireworks and well-heated oration. But by mid-1862, as the news of the
horrors of Bull Run and Shiloh and Fort Donelson filtered back,
the festivities ebbed. Talk of quick and decisive victory gradually
blinked out. In July, Lincoln issued a call for three hundred thousand more volunteer troops to smother the uprising.

Within weeks, a month shy of his twenty-ninth birthday, Hutchins
began enlisting the men of Tippecanoe. Recruiting could not have
been pleasant just a month or so short of the stout fall harvests,
but there was an air of inevitability to the proceedings. Confederate
forces were raiding neighboring Kentucky, only about seventy miles
to the south. Hutchins signed up a hundred or so men, including
three relatives: Benjamin, Tanzy, and William Hutchins.

The outfit was absorbed into the Ninety-fourth Ohio Volunteer
Infantry and named Company D. Rue Hutchins was made captain
and commanding officer. He had no military experience, and training was not an option. The 1,010 men of the Ninety-fourth Ohio
were sworn in at Camp Piqua, in southwestern Ohio. A few days
later they were issued guns and three cartridges each, but no uni-
forms, backpacks, or canteens. The next morning they marched
south in street clothes. That night they were in Kentucky.

The Ninety-fourth fought its first real battle in Perryville less than
three weeks later. Colonel Joseph W. Frizell, in his field report, told
how "a most murderous and incessant fire from infantry was opened
upon me." At Stones River, near Murfreesboro, Tennessee, on New
Year's Eve 1862, the men charged the enemy through a cedar forest
during a ferocious daylong battle, Hutchins out in front of Company
D. That frigid night the thoroughly spent opposing armies lay down
with their weapons in close proximity. The troops of the Ninety-
fourth hunkered in the mud and standing water without food or
fires. Stones River cost the regiment fifty-four men—including much
of Rue Hutchins's family. Cousin William's sons, Benjamin, Tanzy,
and William, were all injured; all three later died in hospitals.

A photo of Hutchins from that era shows the grim-faced officer
in profile wearing a thick, droopy mustache, his wavy hair receding.

After Stones River, many of the badly fatigued troops, exposed to wet, frigid nights, contracted typhoid fever and measles. One March day alone, five men of the Ninety-fourth Ohio died in camp.

The months unfurled in a blur of hardship. In September 1863 the Ninety-fourth Ohio fought at Chickamauga, the war's second-bloodiest battle: "So close were the enemy," Hutchins wrote in his report, "that we could plainly see into the barrels of their muskets at each discharge."

After Chickamauga, the army's "Report of Effective Forces" showed the Ninety-fourth Ohio had 193 men ready to fight—fewer than a fifth of its original number.

In October 1863 Hutchins, now a lieutenant colonel, led his men into battle on Lookout Mountain, Tennessee, and on the grand charge on Mission Ridge. In 1864 the Ninety-fourth joined Sherman's elite army for the march into Georgia. The Ohioans were now hardened veterans—survivors of two years of Confederate gunpowder and bayonets, and disease.

Sherman stormed Atlanta and launched his iconic March to the Sea, slicing the Confederacy in half. His army fought at Buzzard's Roost and Resaca and Kingston and Pumpkin-Vine Creek and Kennesaw Mountain and the Chattahoochee River and Peachtree Creek and Jonesboro. In the first months of 1865 they crossed into North Carolina.

The Ninety-fourth Ohio, like much of Sherman's army, virtually consumed the South. Sherman adhered to the doctrine of total war—war not just on enemy soldiers, but on the general population. The army stripped the landscape. This was the original shock and awe. "Sherman's bummers," as they became known, seized every chicken and pig and vegetable garden and any other object of desire in their path, and they burned and destroyed the rest. Many took Confederate documents—which were light to carry but proof of their far-flung travels—as trophies.

Sherman once watched a soldier march past him carrying a chair on his back, according to a newspaper account. "Yes," the general said, "I see, but they can carry what they please, just so they carry enough ammunition to fight with."

One embedded reporter noted that the soldiers had invented a euphemism for their smash-and-grab tactics. "'*Piruting*' is the term employed to note a certain complexion of raid common upon a grand scale in Sherman's latest march," he wrote, "and the name '*Piruter*,' (an eccentric compromise with *pirate*) vividly describes that wild, erratic, impromptu cavalry who took the lead in the last great expedition."

They would tear the country apart in order to keep it whole.

Nearly a century earlier another young man had struggled to bind together a fragile union of states.

The year was June 1789. James Madison, with Alexander Hamilton's help, had just pushed eleven of the thirteen states to agree to a Constitution—enough to create a federal government.

This was a remarkable feat. In the years following the colonies' rejection of British rule, the euphoria of newfound freedom had given way to pessimism about the Revolution's success. What emerged post-1776 was a deeply divided infant of a country. The states had little in common and—outside of war operations—no history of working together as a cohesive unit. Slavery was a divisive issue. There was no reason to believe that creating a single republic out of a hodgepodge of states would work.

The Constitution made many new citizens uncomfortable. Anti-Federalists feared the new government would merely create a new form of tyranny. They believed the Constitution was not the answer to any present-day crisis; it was the flash point for a future one. Opponents noted that the document did not explicitly guarantee fundamental human rights such as freedom of speech and of religion. North Carolina and Rhode Island declined to accept it, citing the absence of such pledges.

When the new Congress convened, Madison—under intense pressure back home in Virginia—began agitating for the inclusion of these liberties. Most of his colleagues opposed the idea. They wanted to give the new government a chance to drop roots before they started tinkering, and they bombarded Madison and his constitutional amendments with ridicule. Some accused him of proposing flimsy bromides; others thought his fixes went too far, representing the worst kind of micromanagement.

Summoning all his political heft, Madison dragged the amendments in front of Congress for debate in August 1789. For six days the polemics raged in New York City, the nation's first capital. Madison delivered impassioned speeches about the need for the new nation to seal its newly built windows and walls against the persistent seep of tyranny. On one blistering-hot Saturday, the vitriol grew so intense that some congressmen challenged their colleagues to duels.

The argument in favor of the amendments was unmistakably powerful: Humans are inherently flawed. And when power corrupts, people need to be saved from their own darkest impulses.

After days of bruising debate, Congress passed James Madison's amendments. There were sacrifices: The Senate reduced the number from seventeen to twelve. And Madison couldn't write the changes directly into the Constitution. The amendments would stand alone in a separate document.

William Lambert, Benjamin Bankson, and an unknown third clerk penned copies: one for each of the eleven states, two others for Rhode Island and North Carolina, another for the federal government. They stooped over parchments in Federal Hall, in lower Manhattan, writing fluidly in black iron-gall ink.

Senate President John Adams and House Speaker Frederick Muhlenberg signed each copy. On October 2, 1789, presidential secretary William Jackson penned cover letters to each state's governor, and George Washington signed them.

North Carolina's copy arrived in Raleigh on the desk of Pleasant Henderson, engrossing clerk of the general assembly. Henderson was an old hand with such papers, having served previously as private secretary to Governor Alexander Martin, among other posts. Henderson creased the parchment in half, and then in half again, and then trifolded it, so he could slip it into his filing box. Then he scrawled on the back:

1789
PROPOSED AMENDMENTS TO
THE CONSTITUTION OF THE
UNITED STATES——

Back in Virginia, Madison eagerly awaited word on the amendments' reception. The nation's leaders wanted North Carolina to join the union. Though the state still harbored a strong anti-Federalist current, the amendments made the Constitution far more palatable. And North Carolinians, already marginalized by remoteness, didn't want to be isolated, an island of holdouts.

On December 22, 1789, North Carolina joined the United States.

The remainder of the Ninety-fourth Ohio reached Raleigh before 10:00 that morning of April 13, 1865, breaking their marching speed record on the way. They headed straight for the Capitol, a Greek revival building that housed the state government and the Supreme Court and State Archives and Museum, and served as a military supply depot. Former Governor David Swain, a member of the delegation that had surrendered to Sherman the day before, had returned to the Capitol that morning to await the despised general's arrival. Swain had strolled through the empty building, footsteps echoing in the gloom, until he found a caretaker.

Together they assessed the Capitol's ravaged state. The process of emptying the building of its secrets and treasures had been a chaotic affair. The floor of the rotunda between the Senate and House of Commons was thick with discarded papers and documents. Glass museum cases had been smashed, their specimens removed. The state's prized rock collection had been scattered. In the houses of the General Assembly, inkwells were dumped over, papers flung with abandon. Someone had doused a bust of John C. Calhoun in ink. Bound documents coated the floor of the state library.

Union General Judson Kilpatrick's cavalry arrived first, in pursuit of the retreating Confederates, who had set fire to a railroad depot. They paused only to dispatch a rogue Texan and raise the flag over the Capitol, and then left the town in the hands of the Fifth

Ohio Cavalry. The men of the Ninety-fourth Ohio rolled in shortly thereafter, the headwaters of a dark blue torrent of Union infantry.

Three days later William Anderson of the *Philadelphia Inquirer* toured the Capitol building and reported chaotic scenes that resembled what Swain had witnessed. "Curious hands have been busy with the Secession records," he wrote, "and many of them strew the floor."

The numbers were too vast—ninety thousand Union troops in Raleigh in the days after the city's surrender, including twenty thousand from Ohio regiments—to put a name to the thief. Many were camped on Union Square, right near the Capitol. Scores also had business inside the building: work details or social or military meetings. And they were all allowed to do as they pleased when they were off duty.

Sometime soon after arriving, a group of Ohioans walked through the State House, trophy hunting, exploring the building's north wing. They were Sherman's bummers. At least one of them was from Tippecanoe—quite possibly one of Rue Hutchins's recruits. After entering the secretary of state's office on the first floor, they rifled through files.

The soldier from Tippecanoe found a folded parchment. On the outer surface, for filing purposes, there was a notation:

1789

PROPOSED AMENDMENTS TO

THE CONSTITUTION OF THE

UNITED STATES——

More than a century later, historians and archivists would ponder that moment of discovery. Did the soldier know he had just bagged a magnificent relic—one of the nation's seminal founding documents?

The answer is almost certainly no. The strange journey of a priceless parchment began with a simple, anonymous act of vandalism and theft—of "piruting"—just like thousands of others committed during the war. Smash and grab. Nothing less, and nothing more.

2

The Natural

WAYNE PRATT WAS A hulking man, well over six feet tall, with a lineman's shoulders and barrel chest that rounded into a pronounced paunch. His trademark mustache had gone fully gray, and at sixty-three he was mostly bald on top, only a few tenacious wisps levitating above his skull. Pratt's dark eyes danced impishly—except when the subject turned to his troubles, and then they went as dark and impenetrable as obsidian.

Pratt spoke with a heavy Boston accent—not the Brahmin, upper-crust, Julia Child *toh-mah-to* variety, but the gritty Southie brand, generously peppered with profanity. The word *dollar,* for example, came out of his mouth as *daw-lah.* He was known for spinning elaborate tales that sounded wildly embellished and insisting they were true. Pratt was also an expert juggler and had sharp comic timing, telling ribald jokes, then loosing volcanic eruptions of laughter. He was a relentless extrovert and had a Clintonian need to be around people, and to win them over. Many businessmen compartmentalize employees, clients, and friends, but in Pratt's risible orbit, these categories frequently and seamlessly overlapped.

Pratt bought and sold antique American furniture. In particular, he specialized in New England high-style furniture, especially Boston and Rhode Island block-fronts. But he also featured folk art and primitive portraits and Nantucket lightship baskets and weathervanes and American and German toys, including pinball machines and mechanical banks. His multimillion-dollar business, Wayne

Pratt, Inc., which featured shops in Woodbury, Connecticut, and Nantucket, Massachusetts, allowed him to argue that he was one of the nation's top five Americana dealers.

This, he said, was because he could spot the mostly invisible differences that separate truly great furniture from pieces that are merely excellent. "I like beautiful things," Pratt said. "And the difference between something that's really beautiful and has all the aesthetics and is perfect, and something that's just very good, is very subtle. They might have the same line and design, but there are small things.

"A block-front chest, for example. You might find one that's perfect, absolutely spectacular, and another one that's great but has some minuscule flaw. That second one might be a $50,000 or $100,000 piece. Knowing the difference between a chest being worth that amount and one being worth $500,000 to $1 million— that's where I make my money."

He was sitting in the attic office of his sprawling Woodbury store on a low-hanging, rainy day in January 2007, the kind of day when the sky leaks out so little light that when afternoon gives way to dusk, you hardly know the difference. Pratt's desk was empty except for a calendar planner he unconsciously fiddled with and a phone that rang roughly every ten minutes. He answered maybe one in four calls. Pratt had agreed to talk about his troubles, which he'd never spoken of publicly, but just then he was explaining how he'd managed to do so well in life, rising from poverty to the throne of his eponymous empire. "I don't think that's training," Pratt said of his abilities, leaning back and raising his upturned palms in a kind of apologetic shrug. "I think you either have it or you don't. You can be trained to tell whether something is right or wrong, but to know what's truly great—that's something that's born into you."

Pratt was at the point in his professional life where he didn't particularly like working with customers who lacked this bred-in-the-bone acumen. "I like to enjoy my clients' collections," he said. "I don't like to have to bullshit with them over a piece of shit. I don't like to get into situations where you have to say, you know, 'Isn't that interesting? You must really love it. Did that come down through your family—is that why you have it?'"

One thing that was startling about Pratt's particular talent was that, unlike many other top dealers, he didn't grow up around great objects. He hailed from a blue-collar family in South Easton, on Massachusetts's south shore. Pratt's father, Eldon, sold cars and worked at Simpson Springs, bottling birch beer and a carbonated Yankee concoction called coffee soda. His mother, Vera, was a post-office employee and drugstore clerk and did as many other odd jobs as she could handle between debilitating bouts of manic depression. Pratt's grandfather, a semipro baseball player back in the day, sold knickknacks out of a shed behind the family house—old medicine bottles, replicas of Noah's Ark, and the like. The family struggled mightily to pay the bills.

The Pratts lived next door to the Morses, owners of Brockton Tool. The Morses were good to the Pratts. One day young Wayne became enamored of a cast-iron toy steam shovel made around the 1870s. Mrs. Morse gave it to him for a nickel. The toy steadily grew in value until it was worth hundreds of dollars, but Pratt never sold it, even into adulthood; the steam shovel was one of the few pieces to which he remained sentimentally attached. And the fascination with old things that the object sparked—that turned out to be worth far more.

As a child, he said, he began saving money for antique toys by doing chores for the Ameses, another wealthy local family. Working around the house, he stopped to gaze, awestruck, at the antiques he encountered: Boston-made chests, dressing tables, and chairs from the 1700s. His fascination growing, he volunteered to clean up neighborhood barns and attics for free. The deal was that he got to keep whatever he found.

As an adult, Wayne Pratt wove rich and elaborate yarns from the penury of his childhood. Like many other people who have built successful businesses from nothing, he is attached to a rather elaborate mythology. According to the Pratt legend, he bought his first piece of furniture, a Windsor chair, at age seven. He peddled antiques throughout his childhood, his sales rising from $20 items to pieces worth ten times that. "When other kids were working for $2 an hour, I could sell a chest or a weathervane for a couple hundred," he said.

His parents were so financially on the edge they never bothered opening a checking account, he said. As Pratt told the story, his business grew so quickly he decided to get a checkbook rather than carry rolls of cash. But when he arrived at the bank, the teller encouraged him to open a savings account, which seemed more befitting a child. Wayne insisted, though. "I have a business," he said. "I buy antiques."

The teller sent him to the manager, who again tried to talk some sense into the precocious boy. Again, Wayne persisted. After finally giving in, the manager asked Pratt how much money his parents would deposit to open the account.

"Oh, no, I've got money," Wayne said, and pulled a wad of bills totaling $2,400 from his pocket. The manager immediately called the police. But the responding officer recognized Pratt. "He bought a clock from my wife for $300," the cop said.

The book *Objects of Desire*, about high-end antiques and the people who handle them, built eloquently on the Pratt legend. "In high school he ran the 100-yard dash and the 440 not so much for the thrill of victory as for the economic rewards that ensued from team bus trips to neighboring schools," Thatcher Freund wrote.

After completing his races, Pratt often knocked on a couple of doors, found a chest or a couple of antique chairs, and tied them to the back of the school bus. By his senior year he owned a '55 Plymouth whose trunk lid and backseat he had removed. He made a habit of registering as a peddler with police in surrounding communities. He drew elaborate street maps and formed a strategic plan to knock on every door in town . . . Pratt kept elaborate records in thick books—"Mrs. Jones has highboy. Called on her. Offered $200"—and every six months returned inquiring to

Mrs. Jones's. He sometimes came across a rare object for which he knew he might get tens of thousands of dollars. Because people grew suspicious at large numbers, he found that an offer of a few hundred dollars was more likely than one of a few thousand to result in a sale. Old people made the best prospects . . . He could tell from the old lace curtains and the neatly trimmed yard whether a house promised treasures.

Pratt at first couldn't reconcile this passion with his working-class background. The culture of his family was to make a steady if modest living. Thinking that was his prescribed path, he went to Bryant and Stratton Business Institute in Boston, earning an associate's degree. He found a job at Savin Business Machines, the precursor to Savin Corporation, selling photocopiers.

Soon he rose to national sales manager at Savin, and not long after that he left to cofound his own photocopier business, Method Consultants. He was in his mid-twenties and was married and had two daughters. He might have spent decades enduring the vicissitudes of the photocopy industry if he hadn't had a knack for old things.

Even with his day job, Pratt found spare hours to hunt for objects he could buy at bargain prices and sell for profit to antiques retailers higher up the chain. He was what antiques dealers call a "picker." After doing this for a few years, he was no longer able to ignore the siren song of antiques. In 1969 he fled the workaday business world and opened a dealership in his home in Marlborough, Massachusetts, about twenty-five miles west of Boston. He began driving around the Northeast, buying and selling furniture. It was a heady time. He often traveled in a dilapidated van with John Walton, an antiques dealer legend who had a shop on Park Avenue in New York City. Haunting auctions and flea markets, they often finished their days with a load of Victorian furniture tied to the vehicle's roof.

Pratt sold to Walton and other prominent dealers such as Israel Sack in New York and Hymie Grossman in Boston. He made $100 one day, $5,000 the next, and soon he grossed more than $100,000 a year. He ditched his business suits, operated on his own clock, and plunged headlong into the chase. Every day held the possibility of a great new find, and Pratt was a relentless optimist.

He had another unique attribute. As a child, he had been diagnosed with dyslexia, which made reading difficult—but he had an astounding memory. "He could look at a picture and remember every detail—like he had a photographic memory," said Pratt's sister, Cindy Pratt-Stokes.

Antique-furniture dealers—especially the elite ones—never forget a great piece: where they saw it, what its strengths and flaws were, how it compared to others like it.

When Wayne was a teenager, he said, he accompanied antiques dealer John Walton into a Massachusetts home to look at a highboy. The piece was perfect. Later in life, he walked into a different residence, in Boston, and immediately identified the highboy as the one he'd seen more than two decades earlier. He could even tell the owners what room it had been kept in, and how it had been positioned. "They couldn't believe it," Pratt said.

Wayne made a big impression. "Pratt will never forget," Thatcher Freund wrote, "that Walton called him 'the greatest picker that ever lived.'"

Over the next twenty years, Pratt doggedly clawed his way upward. He began specializing in certain items—carved breadboards, Windsor chairs, block-front chests—until he became an expert known for having the best of those pieces. His house, open by appointment only, became a mandatory stop for bigtime dealers doing the New England circuit. Part of Pratt's appeal was his epic congeniality, and his talent as a raconteur. Massachusetts-based dealer Ron Bourgeault often intended to make a quick visit, only to have his stops descend into a sort of Mediterranean torpor. There was food and glasses of wine and Wayne spinning his tales, and several hours often passed before Bourgeault finally stumbled back to his car.

Beneath all that Yankee bonhomie, Pratt was a fierce competitor. As his cachet grew and he started handling better objects, he began bidding aggressively at auctions and traveling hard, broadening his exhibition schedule to twenty-five shows a year. He also recruited top-notch help. In 1978 Pratt approached Marybeth Keene, a dealer based in Rochester, New York, about joining his business. They complemented each other perfectly: Pratt enjoyed roaming around, buying things; Keene liked working the booth. Pratt had big, unwieldy ideas; Keene was adept at separating the wheat of his brainstorms from the chaff and handling the details. He could find great things, and she had a knack for making everything around them look appealing.

By 1983 Pratt was ready to jump the fence from the vast shantytown of pickers and midlevel dealers onto the manicured lawn of the antiques-world elite. He placed his first advertisement in the *Magazine Antiques* and soon afterward attended a show on Long Island. A woman in a fur coat walked up, pulled out the ad, and bought several objects. "Our business took off after that," Keene said. They began dropping lower-level shows and accepting invitations to better ones.

Pratt opened a second shop on Nantucket in 1991, specializing in nautical antiques and accessories, Ralph Cahoon paintings, and Nantucket baskets. Two years after that he made his biggest, most ambitious move: He relocated his Marlborough operation to Woodbury, Connecticut, where he bought a sprawling, fourteen-thousand-square-foot store. One of the top antiquing towns in the Northeast, Woodbury boasts some forty dealerships lined up along the edge of Main Street. Pratt suddenly owned one of the largest.

The antiques world took notice. Around that same time he received his first invitation to show his wares at the Winter Antiques Show in New York City, held in the Seventh Regiment Armory on Manhattan's Upper East Side. This is the stamp of greatness in antiques. Of the hundreds of dealers in American antiques, fewer than three dozen get picked to exhibit there. A committee of experts vets each piece on display.

Pratt's first year there, he sold a Newport kneehole desk for an amount rumored to exceed a million dollars. A few years after that he became a guest appraiser on the hit PBS television series *Antiques Roadshow.*

A big part of being a successful antiques dealer is honing your instincts. You have to know which doors to knock on and be able to calculate how much money to offer without making a customer wary. The longer you keep at it, the more your instincts sharpen. When Pratt first heard about the Bill of Rights, his instincts told him it was a hoax.

The year was 1993 or '94, and he was chatting with Leslie Hindman, owner of the Chicago-based Leslie Hindman Auctioneers. Pratt had long been divorced, his marriage having ended after eight years. He and Hindman had been dating for a while, long-distance, hop-scotching half the continent, alternating weekend visits between Chicago and Nantucket. She was a blue-blooded midwesterner and he a rough-edged New Englander, but they were both self-made entrepreneurs. They were their own brands. They had plenty to talk about.

Hindman told Pratt she was working with an Indianapolis family looking to sell an original Bill of Rights. Yes, she said, *that* Bill of Rights, the one from 1789, freedom of speech and all that. Pratt wouldn't have heard of the family; they were regular, middle-class people.

Pratt said the story sounded ridiculous. How many copies of the Bill of Rights could even exist? And what were the chances that one of them was sitting in the home of some anonymous Hoosiers?

Hindman insisted it was true—she'd gone to Indianapolis and seen the document herself. There was a lawyer who represented a couple of old ladies who'd grown up with it. They'd inherited it from their father, who had inherited it from *his* father, who had owned it since the 1800s. "There's a whole story about where it came from," Hindman said.

The family lawyer had approached Hindman about auctioning the document. The family wanted to sell because the market for historic manuscripts had recently exploded. But there was a problem: The document had been snatched from North Carolina during the Civil War, and if Hindman held a public auction, the state might demand its return. The Indiana family was talking about a seven-figure price tag—Hindman had heard everything from $1.5 million to $3.5 million—and clients got skittish about spending that kind of money on objects with thorny histories. Hindman wondered whether Pratt had any customers who might be interested.

If Pratt had heard the story from almost anyone else, he would have waved it off. But Hindman was not someone to be dismissed lightly. Once she plugged in the details, Pratt could see a framework of plausibility. After all, hadn't he found great objects in surprising places? Didn't he of all people—an underprivileged kid from South Easton—know that Boston Brahmins didn't have a monopoly on great American furniture?

The longer you worked in antiques, the more this axiom proved to be true. On *Antiques Roadshow* he would see it over and over again. At a filming in Tulsa, for example, Harold from Kellyville, Oklahoma, brought in an old bureau he used as a TV stand.

Harold knew little about antiques, but the bureau looked, well, *old*. Pratt had no clue about Kellyville, Oklahoma, but was erudite about old things. Together, they made good television. "The *fiihst* thing I do when I get a chest like this is stand back and look at it," Pratt said, his accent ramped up a notch for his television segments. "The last man who touched that *suhface* was the man who made it. It's absolutely *puhhfect*."

Pratt spotted the handiwork of John Cogswell, a Boston crafts-man who had probably built it around 1765. "If you look at the drawers all together, you can see the perfect undulation of the wood that gives the front its curved appearance," Pratt said. "The drawers were all cut from the same piece of wood, the same tree."

He pointed out the inspired craftsmanship, from snug dovetail joints to beautiful ball-and-claw feet. And then, the climactic mo-ment: Pratt pegged the chest's value at $125,000 to $150,000. Har-old rolled his eyes, let out a nervous chuckle, then steadied himself on the piece of artistry formerly known as a TV stand. "Whoo," he said. "I can't believe that."

"Don't do a thing to this chest," Pratt said. "It's 100 percent *puhh-fect*."

In Denver another participant brought in a bowl from his aunt's Ohio farm. "When the farm was sold, my father took this and passed it down to me," he said.

"It's a wonderful early burl bowl," Pratt explained. "A burl is a nodule that comes off the side of a tree. This bowl was hand-turned from one particularly large nodule that came off a tree around 1790, 1800."

The owner had thought the bowl was oak, but Pratt corrected him: It was actually maple, as was the matching pounder. "I can tell that it goes with the bowl," he said, "because it's made of the same wood and has the same coloring." The only flaws were the handles, attached around 1860, and the fact the bowl was round and not oval. "But with its magnificent size, color, condition, and the marvelous pounder," Pratt said, "I'd value this at $35,000."

So, if Pratt's world is one in which Harold from Kellyville can possess a television stand that's actually a $150,000 chest, and another man can own a $35,000 bowl without knowing whether it's oak or maple, couldn't an anonymous family from Indianapolis secretly harbor a Bill of Rights?

Pratt thought maybe. If the manuscript was authentic, it would be an extraordinary find, worth huge sums of money.

Pratt knew nothing about historic documents or the world they moved through. But he knew Americana, and he knew old things.

How hard could it be?

3

The $4 Treasure

NOT LONG AFTER that conversation, Leslie Hindman bowed out of the quest to sell the Bill of Rights. But she had piqued Wayne Pratt's interest, and as she exited from the negotiations, she connected the antiques dealer with Charlie Reeder, the lawyer representing the family in Indianapolis.

Pratt called the attorney and was intrigued enough to book an airline ticket to the Midwest. He viewed the trip as a fact-finding mission—and maybe more. Maybe, if all went well, he would find his way into a major transaction. It was an adventure of sorts. Maybe it would turn out to be something like the story of the $4 Declaration of Independence.

In 1989 an anonymous bargain hunter from Philadelphia was trawling at Renninger's, a country antiques market in Adamstown, Pennsylvania, when he stopped in front of a beat-up painting. It wasn't the canvas that grabbed him—a murky, amateurish rendering of a country landscape—but the nice, if battered, frame. The shopper thought it might be salvageable. The asking price of $4 was a worthwhile gamble.

When he returned home and removed the painting, though, he found the frame was crudely built and in far worse shape than he'd realized. It was a piece of junk. But while taking it apart he found something intriguing: Hidden behind the canvas, folded to the size of a business envelope, was a crisp, well-preserved copy of the Declaration of Independence.

The bargain hunter considered it a nice find—perhaps it was an antique reproduction. The Declaration has been reprinted many times over two centuries, in newspapers and elsewhere. The farther removed the facsimiles are from 1776, the more their value drops.

The bargain hunter showed the document to a friend, who became animated about the find and urged him to investigate. So he called Sotheby's. David Redden, head of the auction house's rare-books and manuscripts department, identified the document as an "unspeakably fresh" first printing—the most valuable in existence.

That particular printing took place the night of July 4, 1776. That day, of course, the Continental Congress had adopted Thomas Jefferson's landmark opus, making official the new nation's plan for sovereignty. The manuscript went straight to John Dunlap's Philadelphia print shop, where Dunlap spent a sleepless night cranking out 250 copies so that word of the colonists' audacious declaration could be transmitted immediately to local officials and military leaders, including General George Washington. The British subsequently burned some of the documents; others were lost over the centuries. Just twenty-four of Dunlap's broadsheets survived into the late twentieth century, a mere four of them remaining in private hands, at least until that unlikely find in 1989. (The original Declaration, signed by fifty-six members of Congress, is in the National Archives.)

The Dunlap Declaration was every tag-sale shopper's fantasy find—and the timing was exquisite. A few months later, in January 1990, a different Dunlap sold at Sotheby's for a record $1.59 million—more than double the auction firm's high estimate of $600,000, even with the country wallowing in a recession.

Early the following year Sotheby's experts pronounced the $4 Declaration genuine. And in June 1991 the firm put the broadsheet up for auction, sparking a bidding war. One of the bidders, predictably, was New York–area dealer Seth Kaller. Though still only in his mid-twenties, Kaller was the exclusive broker for Richard Gilder and Lewis Lehrman, two successful financiers who as collecting partners had recently begun spending aggressively on big-ticket manuscripts. Kaller squared off that day against Donald J. Scheer of Atlanta, president of Visual Equities Inc., a year-old fine arts investment company looking to expand into historic documents.

When the bidding was over, Scheer emerged as the winner at $2.42 million, establishing a new high-water mark for historic documents—and providing an exclamation point to one of the more fanciful tales to emerge from the antiquities world in recent memory. "This is a record for any printed Americana," said the auctioneer, David Redden. "It was far and away the highest price for historical Americana ever."

Scheer said he believed in the document's greatness—so much so that he was prepared to pay considerably more.

Pratt knew that the Bill of Rights was a far different story. This Indiana family already knew they had a rare treasure, so this was no thrift-store bargain. Pratt wasn't at all sure how things would work out. He would put himself on display, see what he could learn, and offer to broker a sale. You always have to be curious, and you always have to ask. Pratt planned to stay for just a few hours and then return home.

Attorney Charlie Reeder met him at the airport, and the two men sat down to talk. Pratt studied Reeder. A medical-malpractice lawyer in his mid-fifties, Reeder had a fairly noticeable stutter and the flat, twangy accent that's long been a staple of native Hoosier David Letterman's comic repertoire. Reeder was a full-fledged midwesterner: He was born in Dayton, attended nearby Miami University, earned a law degree from Indiana University.

Reeder laid the whole thing out: He represented two sisters, both over fifty. The story was just as Hindman had said: The sisters' grandfather, one Charles Shotwell, had bequeathed the document to his son Grier. When Grier died back in 1972, his widow had kept it. And when she died in August 1990, her daughters had decided to sell the old parchment. Anne Shotwell Bosworth and Sylvia Shotwell Long had no plan in place for sharing the document, and no means of protecting it. Plus, they had five children between them, so there was no fair way to hand it down. Now that its value appeared to be peaking, they'd decided to unload it. Sell high, as the saying goes.

Fine, Pratt said. But where did the document come from?

That, Reeder replied, was ancient history. Family lore held that a Union soldier had snatched it from Raleigh, North Carolina, during the Civil War, then sold it to Charles Shotwell after returning home. There was some family correspondence to support that story.

The document was beginning to fade—the Shotwells knew nothing about conservation—and the family wanted to sell it to a museum or public institution where it would be professionally preserved.

And the price? Less than a year had passed since the $4 Declaration of Independence had sold for $2.42 million. So Pratt was not at all surprised to hear Reeder's asking price: $2 million.

They chatted; Pratt spun a few stories and told Reeder about his successes with antiques. Leslie Hindman had spoken highly of Pratt and told Reeder he could trust him. Reeder agreed to Pratt's offer to broker a deal.

The two men shook hands and left it at that. There would be no formal agreement until Pratt lined up a customer.

But before he got on the airplane home, Pratt told Reeder that he thought the family was asking for too much money—especially given the questions about the document's history.

Pratt didn't consider himself a potential buyer. He didn't have a couple of million dollars to throw at anything. He'd just made the biggest move of his life in relocating to Woodbury. He'd purchased the historic Marshall House, a 1752 structure and surrounding buildings last occupied by Kenneth Hammitt, a longtime antiques dealer who had recently died. Pratt had then ordered a sweeping overhaul to create fourteen thousand square feet of floor space. He'd also brought along a core group of employees from Marlborough, including Marybeth Keene and her husband. Pratt had fifteen to twenty employees, ten trucks. His extensive inventory included folk art and paintings along with the usual assortment of furniture. The move to Woodbury had solidified his standing in the industry—he now had a marquee business in a legitimate antiques destination—but financially it was a precarious stretch.

Even in flush times Pratt wouldn't have tied up $2 million on a Bill of Rights. He much preferred to tap into his network of customers—people accustomed to spending huge sums of money on old things. Pratt thought he might even develop some new clientele. He'd heard that Bill Gates, for example, was building a collection of historic documents and had recently spent $30.4 million on Leonardo da Vinci's illustrious notebook, the Codex Leicester. Who wouldn't want Bill Gates as a customer?

Pratt was particularly adept at moving objects through his web of buyers. Say a client came looking for a top-of-the-line, six-figure block-front chest. Pratt wouldn't go out and try to find one; that would be too time-consuming and expensive. Instead, he'd look through the list of block-fronts he'd sold over the years and call their current owners to ask whether they'd be willing to sell them back.

Every time Pratt sold a great object, he told the buyer he'd like a chance to reacquire it. Pratt usually offered to swap one antique for another—he guaranteed he'd take back anything he sold in exchange for any similarly priced piece—but he also bought objects back for cash. He was known for not so much selling antiques as leasing them. He thought of antiques as an extended family with which he had a lifelong attachment.

In 1972 he paid $3,200 for an excellent Windsor washbasin stand. He sold it soon after for $5,000. In June 2007 Pratt agreed to buy it back for $75,000. Pratt knew the object hadn't been on the market for thirty-five years and thus would be fresh and exciting to a new generation of collectors. He figured he'd get $100,000 to $125,000. Years later he might buy it back for $150,000.

That was why he never charged exorbitant rates, Pratt claimed. For one thing, Pratt wanted his customers to keep buying things. Overextend clients on one piece, and you limit their ability to acquire others. But Pratt also priced objects so he could afford to reacquire them later. "Some clients I've sold $30 to $50 million worth of furniture, and I've done that by taking things back, trading," he said. "I've always done that, and it's always been a benefit.

"Sometimes you lose a client, but 80 to 90 percent of the people I deal with sell me things back," he said. "It's a wonderful way to keep relationships. If you've done good by them, and they like you, they'll sell it back to you. As people get older, or send their kids to college, their situations change, and there's always a possibility of getting things back. I've got stuff in Minneapolis, California, even southern England."

This also allowed him to be a little sentimental even as he honed his mercantile instincts. You could love an object but still sell it, figuring you haven't seen the last of it. The Bill of Rights was different: He would never buy it back. The likely destination was a museum or institute—a place with permanent collections. But that was a good thing in one sense: Unlike with the Windsor washbasin stand, he didn't have to be careful about the price. This time Pratt could ask for as much money as the object would possibly bring.

Everyone knew the story of the $4 Declaration of Independence. Fewer people knew it had ended messily. When Donald J. Scheer said he believed in the document's greatness, he apparently meant its greatness as an investment. He didn't want the Declaration on his wall. Less than two years after paying the record sum of $2.42 million, he tried to resell it. Antique furniture and documents are similar in one sense: People tend to get more excited about something new and unknown—something "fresh to the market," in the parlance of the trade.

In 1991 the Declaration was fresh, came with a fascinating backstory, and happened to go up for sale just as the nation was basking in the afterglow of the first Persian Gulf conflict. It was an auction-house perfect storm.

In May 1993 everything broke differently. Seth Kaller showed up at Sotheby's again, but this time he had no deep-pocketed adversary. Bidding fizzled at $1.75 million, short of the $1.8 million reserve. The auction was a flop. An hour after it ended, Sotheby's tried to convince Scheer to sell the Declaration to Kaller for $1.5 million. Scheer balked.

Sotheby's officials, however, claimed Scheer *did* agree to $1.5 million and moved ahead with the sale to Kaller. The geyser of litigation that erupted as a result was as predictable as Old Faithful: Scheer's firm filed a restraining order to stop the transaction. Sotheby's lawyers countered that Scheer had reneged after the deal was done, amid an internal disagreement among Visual Equities' principals. "They were not misled or defrauded," Marjorie E. Stone, Sotheby's general counsel, told the *New York Times*. "What they are trying to do is wriggle out of an offer that they accepted." Visual Equities eventually retained ownership.

But all that anyone in the antiquities world remembered—including Wayne Pratt, a fixture at Sotheby's—was that a piece of junk art had yielded a multimillion-dollar prize. The great tearing sound reverberating across the countryside after each retelling of that whimsical tale was thousands of junky old oil paintings being knifed open. "Recently we've seen about a dozen Declarations found in picture frames," Linda Ries, of the Pennsylvania State Archives, told the *Maine Antiques Digest* after one twenty-four-hour news cycle involving the Declaration. "But they were all replicas."

When things were quiet in his antiques shop on Nantucket, Wayne Pratt plunked down outside, on a bench he called "the office." Sitting in the sun, he alternated between talking on a cell phone—sometimes he carried two of them, in case he had to work out a complicated deal involving multiple clients—and chatting up tourists strolling the island's main drag.

Lots of money swaggers around Nantucket on any given summer day, and Pratt pursued it as lustily as he chased a great Windsor chair. If he spotted someone carrying a Nantucket basket—one of the many types of antiques he had championed—he would offer to buy it, just to start a conversation. Pratt had found that people are more likely to relax standing outside than they are in the store, where they might feel a tacit pressure to buy. And once they loosened up and started chatting, they were more likely to eventually walk inside and buy something. Unlike some antiques dealers, who can seem starchy and intimidating, Pratt had a plainspoken charm that was disarming. He might unleash a couple of jokes or start juggling.

Pratt was perched on his bench one late-spring day in 1995 when his plan for the Bill of Rights began to coalesce. One of his customers, John Richardson, happened to walk by with his wife, Peg. The couple from Washington, D.C., was vacationing on Nantucket.

Pratt had met Richardson, a lawyer, more than ten years earlier at the Washington Antiques Show, and over the course of many conversations about early American furniture they'd become friendly. Pratt knew he'd need an attorney to sell the Bill of Rights. The negotiations would likely be intricate, the tax implications complex. Then there was the question: Was it legal to sell a Bill of Rights?

To people who handle centuries-old furniture, the notion didn't seem so far-fetched. "We've had chairs that belonged to George Washington," said David Schorsch, Pratt's friend and a prominent dealer who occupied the next shop over in Woodbury. "I currently own a chair that belonged to Benjamin Franklin. It was his; it's documented. These are national treasures that we are allowed to own. So the idea that something like that could be obtainable isn't that crazy."

As Pratt gabbed amiably, it struck him that John Richardson would be ideal for the job. Richardson, who was in his mid-fifties with a medium build and graying hair, had for several years been a partner in the firm Richardson, Berlin & Morvillo, which had primarily represented transportation entities—mainly railroads and small airlines—in labor disputes and routing and regulation battles. Richardson, who specialized in the airline industry, had just made a career move about six months earlier, joining another D.C. firm to run its airline regulatory practice. This fairly esoteric corner of the law rarely landed him in the spotlight.

True, antique documents didn't exactly fall within Richardson's legal purview; like Pratt, he knew much more about antique furniture. But he was a seasoned Washington lawyer with more than twenty-five years on the job. He was also a political insider, a fundraiser and Democratic operative in Washington.

Better yet, Peg—known inside the Beltway as Margaret Milner

Richardson—was a longtime tax attorney whom President Clinton in May 1993 had appointed commissioner of the IRS. Peg had taken time off from her job with a top firm to work on Clinton's campaign; she was also a good friend of the First Lady. John Richardson was known to joke that it was a conflict of interest for his wife to pay income tax.

To Pratt, this was an elegant nexus: The Bill of Rights was a government document, and the Richardsons were government people. John Richardson was intrigued. "How do you know it's real?" he asked.

Pratt said he didn't—not yet. But the Indiana attorney had said that Pratt was welcome to get it authenticated.

Pratt floated an idea: He probably couldn't afford the attorney's fees involved in researching and selling the Bill of Rights; would Richardson do the legal work on contingency—for a cut of the profit? If they lined up the right client, they could sell it for millions. Richardson said he would think it over and investigate further when he returned home.

Not long after he touched down in D.C., Richardson called Pratt. He'd spoken to Charlie Reeder. Richardson said they would need to dig deeper into the document's provenance, but he was ready to sign on.

On June 23, 1995, Richardson faxed Pratt a two-page letter laying out their agreement: "You have asked us to determine the lawfulness of the purchase and sale transaction you contemplate; to counsel you with regard to the legal risks involved in proceeding with that transaction; and to assist in completing the purchase and sale transactions in an effective manner in the event you decide to proceed with it."

Payment would be contingent on a sale. Richardson wrote that after "appropriate research," he might advise Pratt not to go through with the deal. If that happened, and Pratt bailed out, Pratt would have to reimburse only Richardson's expenses—travel, photocopies, telephone, and so forth. If the sale happened, Richardson would charge his normal hourly rate times three, plus 30 percent of the profit.

Although that would be a hefty sum, Pratt wouldn't have to pay anything out of pocket. And if everything lined up right, they would both do exceedingly well. The standard brokerage fee is between 10 and 20 percent. On a sale of $4 million, that might mean $800,000.

Some in the antiques industry view such arrangements as inherently risky: A lawyer hired to provide objective advice should not have a selfish reason to bring a sale to fruition, the argument goes. As Richardson noted in his letter, "We recognize that this arrangement may inherently appear to create a bias, and we are prepared to seek third-party advice if needed to resolve any conflicts or apparent conflicts of interest that may arise."

But Pratt figured the benefits of including Richardson far outweighed the risks. The lawyer had political connections, and his wife was the IRS commissioner—those were strong selling points. They would make potential buyers feel comfortable. Pratt didn't mind taking a calculated gamble here and there anyway. He believed that if you didn't take chances in pursuit of the great stuff, you wouldn't get anywhere at all.

Pratt began to compile a list of potential customers. He aimed high: Bill Gates. Bill Ford, chairman of Ford Motor Company. Yale president Richard Levin. He contemplated selling it back to the state of North Carolina—a motivated buyer, for sure.

Richardson, meanwhile, began digging. Pratt said the attorney eventually compiled a thousand-page notebook filled with Bill of Rights research. By digging into the history of the fourteen Bill of Rights manuscripts, Richardson undoubtedly found much more than he had anticipated. And much less.

Five of the original parchments had vanished from official custody, some under highly suspicious circumstances.

This alone might have served as a red flag—a reason to stop and recalibrate. But Wayne Pratt was not one to be easily dissuaded.

4

The Grain Man

MAY 10, 1897, was a modest day for the newspapers of Indiana's capital city. The top of the front page of the *Indianapolis News* delivered word that lawyers had argued over a hostile insurance company takeover. A girl had died after jumping from a window of the Home of the Good Shepherds. And a historic document hung on an office wall in the Board of Trade building.

It was a slow news cycle. The last story in that bunch seemed particularly unlikely. There was nothing otherwise newsworthy about the occupant of office number twenty-three in the Board of Trade. Charles Shotwell hailed from somewhere else, for one thing—a transplant from back East. For another thing, he was a grain broker—just one more opportunist tapping into the heartland's seemingly limitless fertility. He bought grain, sold it for a little more, and went home to his family. Went to church on Sunday.

By 1880 Indianapolis was one of the nation's largest inland cities. In the past decade its population had more than doubled, to more than one hundred thousand. It was a key crossroads, its vast array of railroad lines connecting every corner of America: grain from the West, cotton and tobacco and hogs from the South and Southwest, and manufactured goods from the East. More than eighteen hundred freight cars rolled through the city every day.

Reporters in Indianapolis, or anywhere, really, don't just go looking for stories about grain brokers. But somehow the reporter wound up in office twenty-three, wound up scanning the walls. Wound up seeing a document hanging there.

Most of today's prized relics didn't get treated as such in the nineteenth century. Furniture and paintings and documents now thought to be precious and rare were often junked or consigned to the shadowy maws of attics or basements.

Those objects were not valuable, not yet at least. As years passed, tastes changed, collectors became more educated and selective. Curators and aficionados passed judgment on what was great and important.

The Bill of Rights was like that. In the nineteenth century it was not yet a proper noun. It was "a nothing document," in the words of historian Ken Bowling of the First Federal Congress Project. Outside of a few collectors, few saw its inherent value.

What is an object worth? A person might prize an otherwise worthless piece of art because his or her grandfather painted it. That same person might give away an important piece of the nation's history because it means nothing to him or her, because it's a nothing document.

The Civil War soldier from Tippecanoe didn't have much need for a folded parchment. Perhaps he'd carried the document home from Raleigh only to find that folks back in Ohio were more interested in flags and muskets. The document was hardly even historic; it wasn't even eighty years old yet.

Until one day, the year after the war ended, the soldier ran into a friend, a young man named Charles Shotwell.

Shotwell was born into a restive family. His parents, Eli and Emeliza, were New Jersey natives of Dutch and English origin. After marrying in Somerset County in 1840, they moved to New York City to open a grain and flour business. It was the beginning of a long-term family fascination with grain. Charles was born in 1846, the fourth of seven children. He was eight years old when Eli packed the family up and moved to the blown-wide-open expanses of western Ohio, where he purchased 160 acres of farmland a few miles west of Tippecanoe.

The city folks did well there. They had a maid and a farm hand,

and business exploded in town during the war. Prices shot up as southern crops became increasingly scarce, and hog farmers and whiskey distillers started making small fortunes. Corn and wheat, always in demand, were Miami County's top harvests.

But then something changed. Maybe Eli couldn't leave New York behind. Within a few years he sold the farm and moved back to the city.

The war had started when Charles was thirteen, and the Ninety-fourth Ohio Volunteer Infantry had formed a year later. Shotwell had been old enough to go if he'd wanted to. The recruiters didn't ask for birth certificates. Instead, he decamped for New York with his parents.

In 1866 Charles returned to Ohio to visit a sister who had married a local man and settled in nearby Troy. One day he stopped off in Tippecanoe. "I hoped to meet some of my boy friends of the days when I was a resident of the town myself," he later recounted.

> I went into one of the stores of the town that day, where I met one of the boys that I had known before the war. He told me of several of his experiences as a Soldier, one was, of his being in Sherman's Army when it marched "Thru Georgia" to the sea. He told me of that Army going into the City of Raliegh [*sic*], North Carolina (The Capital of the State), and said that the City had been set on fire by the retreating Confederates before the Union Army entered the City. The Union Army, he said, throughly [*sic*] sacked that City, and he was one of a Company of Soldiers, that went thru the State House and helped themselves to whatever they pleased to take. They went into the Office of the Secretary of State and forcibly took what they thought was worth carrying away. On opening a vault there, they found several boxes locked, which they proceeded to open and from one of them he took the parchment . . . After he had shown it to me and related his story about it, I became very much interested in it . . .

After a little discussion, Charles and the unknown soldier reached a deal. Charles handed over $5.

• • •

After buying the fancy broadsheet, Shotwell embarked on his own wanderings. Like his father, he found it difficult to stay put. There was a job in New Jersey, as a salesman for the Lambertville Spoke Manufacturing Company. Then he was a partner of Marble Mills in Greenwich, New York, north of Albany. But eventually Shotwell made his way back to New York City. There, on February 16, 1878, he married a Brooklyn girl, Ann M. Van Bokkelen. Then Shotwell did his peripatetic old man one better: He headed more than seven hundred miles west, all the way out to Indianapolis, and started from scratch again.

Shotwell arrived in this futuristic boomtown with his historic relic packed among his things. North Carolinians would have shuddered to think of the miles he'd put on the parchment already. But even in Indianapolis, Shotwell still didn't stop moving. The 1879 Indianapolis city directory listed the family address as the Remy Hotel, 20 Circle Street, opposite Circle Park, in downtown. In January 1879 Ann gave birth to a son, Charles, and the 1880 register shows the growing clan at 378 North Meridian Street, Indianapolis's central north–south artery.

When the second son, Van, arrived in 1881, the Shotwells lived at Dorsey Place, on Bethel Pike. Not long after that Ann died, and Charles kept moving. Between 1881 and 1894, the city directory lists at least nine different residences (the volumes didn't specify his street address in the city's Irvington neighborhood for several of those years). The only apparent constants were the boys, the parchment, and the grain. Shotwell worked in the Chamber of Commerce Building, later renamed the Board of Trade. He took a partner not long after arriving in Indiana, but that lasted less than a year. Shotwell was soon on his own again, even moving from office to office within the same building.

In 1893 Charles remarried, and everything changed. Clara Moore was eleven years younger than Charles, but she settled him. They moved to Irvington and stayed put, and he kept office number twenty-three. Their son, Grier, was born in 1896. Charles served as chairman of the Grain Appeals Committee. He was a founding member of the Republican-leaning Columbia Club.

Charles Shotwell was forty-eight years old. He had arrived wherever it was he had been trying to go. Somewhere along the line he had unfolded the document and glued it onto a piece of cardboard and put it inside a wooden frame. Once folded, parchment is difficult to flatten. Glued to a backing, though, it remained smooth and legible. It may have been a nothing document, but all that fancy writing—he described it as "a remarkable piece of penmanship"—meant something to him.

This was remarkable, too: the condition of the document after all of Shotwell's ramblings. Late in life he reported the parchment "has been kept with little exposure to the light and is still in splendid condition . . . [E]very line of it is almost as legible as when it was first written."

The painful reality of American government in the late nineteenth century is that the document was probably as safe with Shotwell as it would have been in the possession of most states, or even the federal government. Most public officials didn't grasp the importance of safeguarding the stories of the country's past. The concept of public archives was just winking above the horizon.

Wars and religious strife have been rough on historical writings. When Rome fell, barbarian tribes overran the crumbling empire, destroying libraries. Vandalism, invasions, floods, and fires wiped out many early libraries in ancient Greece. In the seventeenth century early Egyptian documents began to surface: stories written in fantastical characters that scholars didn't recognize. Islamic leaders, however, viewed the remains of their pagan ancestors with repugnance and destroyed everything they could find. One traveling dignitary learned of three hundred rolls "written in an unknown language" found in nearby Damietta; the local sheik had ordered them burned.

John Covel, one of the first English scholars to hunt for documents in Eastern monasteries, plunged into the archives at Mount Athos and other locales. He wrote of seeing "vast heaps of manuscripts . . . of the Fathers, or other learned authors . . . all covered over with dust and dirt, and many of them rotted and spoiled."

On Mount Sinai's St. Catherine monastery, the German researcher Constantin von Tischendorf wrote of "infamous negligence" so profound that one manuscript he held "teemed with fattened white mites."

While overthrowing the regime of Louis XVI and Marie Antoinette, French revolutionaries seized the state records and pointedly used them to wrap fish. More entrepreneurial-minded Parisians simply grabbed papers and sold them, and the appearance of so many captivating documents signed by early French kings spurred a collecting craze in Europe.

When his army took Simancas in 1809, Napoleon issued orders for his soldiers to loot the Spanish archives, which dated to the sixteenth century and were the first created by a nation-state. Marshal Kellerman personally directed the removal of more than two hundred wagonloads of historical papers to the imperial library in Paris; in all, crews removed 7,861 bundles of documents dating from the 1300s to the 1700s. When the French withdrew in 1811, Spanish peasants took their turn overrunning the archives, grabbing whatever Kellerman had left behind. When Napoleon's army fell, the Spanish ambassador to France demanded the return of the looted papers but had little to show for the effort. Louis XVIII had major issues with Napoleon's geopolitical stances, but he approved of the general's taste in historic papers; he sent back only the less notable documents.

Napoleon's army also raided the Vatican, carrying out loaded, heaving oxcarts of papal bulls and ecclesiastical documents. For much of the rest of the twentieth century, more antique papal documents turned up in France than anywhere else, including Italy.

In England, after the imperial estate of the East India Company was sequestered to the Crown, the new heads of India House wiped out most Indian naval records. In the United States the Civil War scattered many seventeenth- and eighteenth-century papers. "Many old court houses in the South," the prominent dealer Mary Benjamin wrote, "were emptied of their contents during the Civil War, and it was said by contemporary witnesses that the path of the Union forces could be traced by following the old family papers strewn along the road."

World War II tore away another chunk of collective history. The Nazis seized many historic items, and Allied bombings destroyed others. Countless documents were lost from European repositories—the archives at Monte Cassino, the Ateneo de Manila, the State Archives of Naples, and the Columbaria library at Florence.

What's harder to understand was the unvarnished neglect that accompanied the peaceful, fin-de-siècle United States in which Charles Shotwell resided.

Around that time a man named J. Franklin Jameson began to investigate how successfully America was safekeeping its records. A wiry, whiskered, distinguished-looking man, Jameson was a teacher, writer, editor, researcher, and administrator. He was also one of the nation's first historians: In 1882 he obtained one of the first two doctorates in history granted in the United States. Fourteen years later Jameson convened a team to investigate the state of the nation's historic documents.

What they found was appalling. There *was* no record keeping— not in any organized sense. In a country fully focused on its future, the past was mostly an inconvenience. There were virtually no government-supported archives. The rotating casts of politically appointed toadies who ran clerical offices had no sense of how to handle stacks of old records; many simply took home what they liked.

"Hardly any State possesses at present complete files, either in manuscript or in print, of its own records," Jameson's researchers tartly reported in a 1900 memorandum to Congress. "Some of the records appear never to have been systematically preserved. Some have been lost. Some are in the possession of other States or of the National Government. Large portions still exist in manuscript only, while others, the originals of which have disappeared, are in printed volumes now scarce and virtually impossible of replacement."

The report spells out crimes and misdemeanors in graphic detail. "A typical case of the loss of important records through ignorance and carelessness is found in Nebraska . . . [T]he janitors at the capitol, in the course of their cleaning, found a box of manuscripts, and concluding that they were of no value, burned them. As near as can be made out, the entire records of the constitutional convention of 1875 went up in smoke."

In Pennsylvania, history repeated itself. In 1851 a legislative committee had investigated the commonwealth's archives and reported widespread negligence and loss. "Humiliating as it is to expose the neglect of which we have been guilty," the committee wrote, "let us hope a good result; and that State pride may be sufficiently aroused to remove the evil, in a judicious selection (by some competent person) and publication of what remains."

It didn't happen. Jameson's report found that many of Pennsylvania's valuable historical papers were stored in "attics, cellars, or any other nooks and corners in the capitol buildings" where they were "not only practically inaccessible and liable to destruction by fire, but were also exposed to the ravages of rats, dampness, and dirt, or to mutilation and theft by unscrupulous persons who had access to them and realized their commercial value."

In North Carolina, Jameson discovered, "The office of librarian has always been given to party men as a reward for party faithfulness, and this has had the usual effect."

Squirrels had nested in records stored in barrels in a Massachusetts town. New York City's public records were "indiscriminately heaped together in a large pile on the floor and covered with dust." Curious, an investigator poked through the mess. In one pile were reports of health officials' struggles with a deadly "malignant fever" in 1798. Another held records of testimony taken during an 1842 probe of a political scandal during which party leaders had freed convicts from Blackwell's Island to vote illegally. In yet another he found an index to riot claims during Civil War recruitment drives. Much of the city's wildly colorful history was buried in the grime.

The federal government did no better. Fire heavily damaged the records of the War Office and Treasury Department in 1800 and 1801. Throughout the nineteenth century, "water, theft, negligence, insects, rodents, chemicals, extreme cold or heat, and mold led to the loss of or damage to many federal records," historian Donald R. McCoy wrote.

Things began to change after the Civil War, during a period of rapid governmental growth. After a fire razed part of the Department of the Interior building in 1877, officials spoke in favor of a general, fireproof repository for important national records. But it wasn't until 1933—in the depths of the Great Depression—that workers laid the first cornerstone of the National Archives.

Jameson's report stands out as a scabrous indictment of government neglect. "It is a matter of common observation, also, that manuscripts of official documents, especially those of the years prior to 1861, are constantly appearing at auction sales in the large cities, and . . . are being scattered in this way about the country," his committee wrote. "The United States has itself bought, at a cost of many thousands of dollars, various collections of papers, many of which were of an official and public character.

"It may be doubted if in any country in the world archives of relatively so much value are so lightly regarded or so carelessly kept."

Charles Shotwell carefully safeguarded his nothing document. His wife, Clara, was descended from a family of Revolutionary War heroes, and the handsome broadsheet reminded the Shotwells of the nation's goodness and generosity. Its presence in their home or Charles's office, where it sometimes hung, broadcast something similar about the Shotwells: They were on the right side of history.

Shotwell's broadsheet became part of the family fabric. It connected the elderly man to his young self. He kept it for so long, it was easy to forget that the nothing document still might mean something to somebody else.

And so, when the *Indianapolis News* reporter walked into his office on that spring day in 1897 and admired the 108-year-old parchment, Shotwell didn't hesitate to explain the story of how he came to possess it more than three decades earlier.

He told the story innocently, proudly even, with no notion whatsoever of the trouble he was about to cause for himself.

The article ran under the headline "A Historical Relic: Original

Copy of One of the Twelve Constitutional Amendments." At the time it didn't occur to anyone involved, least of all Charles Shotwell, that it might cause an uproar nearly seven hundred miles away. "Hanging upon the wall in an office in the Board of Trade building in this city is an interesting historical relic of undoubted authenticity," the story began.

> It is no less than one of the thirteen [*sic*] original copies of the twelve amendments to the constitution. One of these copies was sent to each of the thirteen States, that formed the compact. This document is a parchment twenty-eight inches wide by thirty-two inches long. It is perfectly preserved, the ink in some places still a jet black, but for the most part a rusty brown; the handwriting is admirably plain, free from all flourishes, and as even and regular as copper plate.

The story quoted the document's preamble and described the signatures of John Adams and the rest. And then:

> This document belongs to Charles A. Shotwell. Explaining how it came into his possession, he said: "I was living at Troy, O., at the close of the war, thirty-two years ago. I got it off a soldier in an Ohio regiment. I believe it cost me $5. He took it from the State House at Raleigh, N.C., when that place was pillaged by Sherman's army."

That was where the story ended. But it was only just the beginning.

5

Best Friends

THE FIRST THING Charlie Reeder noticed was the airplane. The twin-engine eight-seater was a blue Piper Chief with the word *Matthews* painted in white on the side.

Reeder was at the Indianapolis airport to meet Wayne Pratt again, a couple of years after their first visit in the mid-1990s. There had been no developments since that initial meeting. Pratt had struck out with everyone on his dream list. But Pratt wasn't discouraged; he remained enamored with the idea of arranging a sale, and he knew deals of that magnitude took time. To let Reeder and the Shotwell family know he was still serious, he had recently wired $50,000 for an option to purchase the Bill of Rights. This was a firm expression of the antiques dealer's dedication to the cause— though it was also refundable if Pratt couldn't make a deal happen.

As further proof of his enduring interest, he had returned to Indianapolis with reinforcements.

Bob Matthews was Pratt's best friend, godfather of his son James. A real estate developer in his early forties, Matthews was about fifteen years Pratt's junior and looked even younger. He had a bantam physique, a giant, toothy smile, and an edgy, high-voltage comportment. Matthews spoke in gushing, roiling torrents of words. He couldn't sit still for more than two or three minutes at a time.

The antiques dealer and the developer shook hands with the medical malpractice lawyer. Pratt explained that Matthews was interested in buying the Bill of Rights to turn over to a museum or library, and that Bob wasn't just his friend but also a major client.

Bob was a top buyer of antiques, Pratt said. That airplane? They flew back and forth between Nantucket and Connecticut on that aircraft, often carrying loads of pricey furniture. Bob was a wealthy, influential, and politically connected businessman who would add prestige to any deal involving the parchment, Pratt explained. Add in John Richardson—the Beltway lawyer whose wife, Pratt always hastened to mention, was commissioner of the IRS—and what you had was a Bill of Rights all-star team. They had the clout to do this right, and do it big.

Taking the cue, Matthews began talking about President Clinton. Reeder didn't need his lawyerly skills of deduction to gather that both men were strenuous name-droppers. Two years earlier, Matthews said, he'd attended a "White House coffee"—one of the awkwardly named and lamely conceived affairs at which the president schmoozed major contributors. After that, Matthews said, the Clintons couldn't get enough of him. Democratic Party bosses had invited him to a private movie screening with Bill and Hillary last year, but he'd declined. Matthews was a Republican, after all. He had his standards.

Reeder was not a big Clinton fan and felt twinges of annoyance at the pair's oleaginous sales pitch, but it was still hard not to be a little awed. Matthews pressed on. Did he mention that he was a Republican? Right: He also knew Bob and Elizabeth Dole. And Connecticut's popular governor, John Rowland, was Matthews's pal going back twenty years; Rowland had spent time on Matthews's yacht, the *Bon Vivant*.

So no, Matthews said, instead of seeing the movie with the Clintons, he asked how much *not* to go to the movie. And he sent the Democratic National Committee a check for $50,000 to leave him alone. "It was one of those things where, you know when things feel too good?" Matthews once said, describing his need to brush off that pesky White House. "You're like the moth getting caught in it?"

• • •

Bob Matthews was born in France, the fourth of six children; his father was a career government-service officer. They lived in Turkey and Morocco, among other far-flung locales, before finally settling on Cape Cod.

The family was not well off despite the exotic settings of his early youth—all those kids on a government paycheck—so young Bob was a scrapper. At his father's urging, he spent his senior year of high school at a vocational-technical school, where he learned carpentry and other skills. But Matthews knew very early on that a workaday, clock-punching trade would never fulfill his searing ambitions. Much like his buddy Wayne, Bob came packaged with his own hagiography—a gregarious tale of pluck and derring-do honed through many tellings. In one chapter he works his way up from dishwasher to cook at a Cape Cod lobster house, saving every penny, so he could buy a red convertible when he turned sixteen. But Bob wasn't about to stop there. He planned to become a millionaire by age twenty-two, his lucky number.

Somehow, the legend holds, after high school he earned a community college degree, traveled out West and worked as the foreman of a coal-crushing team in Wyoming, hitchhiked through Central America, briefly attended music school in California, and returned home for a year at the University of Massachusetts—and *still* earned his first million by that enchanted age.

The path to his outsized aspirations led down the gilded pavers of real estate development. While Matthews was attending UMass, studying economics, he and his brother Gerry scraped together $2,000—they saved cash by hiding it in a freezer, under a turkey— for a down payment on a beat-up four-family colonial in Belchertown. They refurbished the house themselves, Bob's carpentry skills proving handy, and upped the rent from $80 a month to $400 for the college students living there—"spoiled kids," as Matthews put it.

Matthews refinanced the property and made $45,000, just like that. "I said, 'What can beat this?' I just made forty-five grand," Matthews later told the *Hartford Courant*. "Economics major? Forget about it."

He took that money and moved to Waterbury, Connecticut, where another brother, David, was already embedded as an insurance agent. A city of 108,000 situated in the winding Naugatuck River valley, Waterbury was an intriguing landing spot for a mogul in waiting. During the early and middle twentieth century, Waterbury boasted the nation's largest brass factories, and the explosive demand for the metal brought immense prosperity. Downtown featured an expansive green and elegant, stately buildings; mansions loomed in the hills above. But as other metals replaced brass, and labor became cheaper on foreign soil, the mile-long factories began to close. The last of them had been shuttered by the time Matthews alighted in 1980.

When the local economy cratered, the real estate market went down with it. Everything was a bargain when Matthews arrived. He and his brother started by scooping up several derelict apartment buildings and presciently converting them into low-price condominiums. These were the first such conversions in town, and they went on sale for $29,900—with $300 down—just ahead of the incipient condo boom. That project was the first of a string of emboldening successes. "Interest rates were above 20 percent in some cases," Bob Matthews said later, "and popular wisdom had it that you couldn't make a dime in real estate. 'Popular wisdom' had it all wrong; you can always make money if you choose your projects carefully. I look for undervalued properties that could stand with a bit of improvement."

Such cocksure pronouncements were a Matthews staple. Still only in his twenties, the young developer was brash and cartoonishly arrogant. A former employee recalls meeting Matthews and his brother in an elevator in the office building where they'd set up headquarters. Just after exchanging introductions, the Matthewses began detailing the properties they'd bought and the profits they'd reaped. "They were saying, 'We're from Massachusetts, and we're gonna take this one-horse town and fix it up,'" the ex-employee recalled. "I thought, You guys are assholes, is what you are."

In a typical moment of bombast, Bob and David Matthews threw a party at the downtown Mattatuck Museum and invited the city's power brokers. The brothers flew in on a rented helicopter, timing the landing so they could stroll off the bird, like dignitaries at Camp David, just after all the guests had arrived.

Mayor Edward D. Bergin Jr. was serving his third term in office when the Matthews boys arrived in town. At their first meeting the brothers strode in and demanded federal rent-assistance money for a building they'd recently purchased. "They thought the subsidy had been assigned to their building, but that was not the case," Bergin said. "For two out-of-town guys, that was highly unusual behavior. It wasn't the normal way developers acted in Waterbury. Usually you'd come in *before* you bought the building and ask if it's eligible, or can the city do something here to help." Bergin, who lasted fourteen years in office in a famously bruising political environment, sent them packing.

Banks were there to fill the cash void. The Reagan renaissance was ideal for go-getters in need of extended lines of credit. The Matthewses acquired major historic properties like the Rectory Building, a grand example of Richardson Romanesque architecture. Striking out on his own, Bob Matthews bought the Frederick Buildings, situated on either side of the historic Palace Theater, and the Farrington Building—both of them downtown landmarks. By the end of the eighties, Matthews controlled nearly a quarter-million square feet of commercial space. People began calling him the Donald Trump of Waterbury—a moniker he did not discourage.

Matthews endeared himself to longtime Waterburians for his judicious renovations of prized edifices. "I think he's brilliant," said the ex-employee who first met Matthews on an elevator. "He's way beyond lucky. He really was all about quality; he didn't do anything halfway."

To the wider world Matthews projected a Horatio Alger–like quality: the scrappy and ambitious young go-getter, building an empire out of smarts and ingenuity, almost a little wide-eyed at his own success. In 1986 the *New York Times* bestowed on Matthews partial credit for Waterbury's rebound from the brass collapse, noting that he "has been buying up buildings along East and West Main Street like adjacent spaces on a Monopoly board." "He was the star of the scene," a city official recalled. Waterbury officials could scarcely get the attention of state leaders in Hartford, but Matthews and his brother David flew in U.S. Senator Bob Dole and his wife, Elizabeth, to attend the launch of a side business.

In postindustrial Waterbury, where hope drained away like an ebb tide, people bought into the wunderkind. Between the prolix narrations of his nearly superhuman feats, Bob loved to throw a good party, which he often did at the Brass Horse, a restaurant he'd acquired on the Green. In a city fascinated by, and in some ways stuck in, its own history, Matthews was a gust of fresh air. "I love old buildings," he told Charles Monagan for a book about the city's history. "Restoring them to what they used to be—that's our niche. If it means digging into the pockets a little deeper to save a stained-glass window, it's still worth it."

Wayne Pratt and Bob Matthews met in the early 1980s at a huge flea market in Brimfield, Massachusetts, where Pratt was selling antiques. Matthews, walking the grounds with a girlfriend, approached Pratt's booth and introduced himself.

Once they started talking, they recognized how much they had in common. They were both eastern Massachusetts guys who'd started out with nothing but dreams and boundless energy. And they both begrudged the trust-funded gadabouts who sometimes outbid them for an object or property. "We both came up the hard way," Pratt said, pronouncing the word *hahd*. "I could understand how he felt about people having money who didn't have to work for it."

They were natural salesmen who could talk their way into almost anything. Pratt was struck by the younger man's incandescent charisma and catlike intensity. Matthews couldn't sit still; he was constantly prowling the room during conversations. "He was outgoing, flamboyant, and a bit of an asshole," Pratt said. "But I liked him."

As their careers blossomed, Matthews became a regular at Pratt's shop. Eager to emit the scent of affluence, Matthews chased the traditional trappings of wealth—antiques included. In the late eighties he bought a small plane and started riding horses and playing polo.

He purchased a gated estate, complete with bridle trails, in Middle-bury, the wealthier town on Waterbury's western border.

His friendship with Pratt intensified after the antiques dealer opened his seasonal shop on Nantucket in 1991. Matthews pur-chased a house there two years later, and the two began spending big chunks of their summers together. Every Fourth of July they threw a bash at Matthews's estate. Wayne bought the lobsters, and Matthews bought the booze. Matthews chartered yachts to race in the Figawi and Opera House Cup races, and Pratt manned the sails. He wasn't a sailor per se, but his brawn made him a useful deck hand. "There was always some sort of interesting thing you could do with him," Pratt said. "When he did something, he did it fully."

A fraternity of two, they lit out for many adventures on Mat-thews's plane. When Leslie Hindman was dating Pratt, he and Bob once picked her up at New Jersey's Teterboro Airport in Matthews's plane. "It was a shitty little plane—not even a nice one," Hindman recalled. "I grew up around airplanes, so I know. So Bob starts fly-ing, and all of a sudden the instrument panel goes out, just goes black. And we're flying over New York, no contact with any tower, and I was just, 'Oh, my God, we're gonna cross into some other air-space, get hit by another plane. No one even knows we're up here.'

"They just said, 'Aw, who cares? We'll be fine, no problem.'" She shook her head, grinning. "They were crazy guys."

Pratt's move to Connecticut in 1993 meant close year-round prox-imity to Matthews. Woodbury is a short drive from both Middle-bury and Washington, another town in which Matthews had pur-chased a home. Bob hooked Wayne up with the real estate broker with whom Pratt bought the Main Street South store. "He's a good negotiator," Pratt said. "That was where I wanted to be."

Pratt, in turn, filled Matthews's houses with antiques. They never had a traditional dealer-customer relationship. When they first started doing business, Matthews acquired furniture from Pratt on promises to pay later. Sometimes he made good. Sometimes he showed up with a check when Pratt was going through a dry spell.

Other times, though, when Pratt requested payment, Matthews

reported that he was on the verge of a huge transaction, and that he would be able to pony up any day—but then the big payday would slip through his fingers. "He usually didn't have enough money to buy the things he wanted," Pratt said. "His tastes always exceeded his means. A lot of times the deal never came through."

When Matthews did pay, Pratt gave him significant discounts. They were good friends, and Pratt often just wanted to get the deal off the books. "It would end up being a fraction of what a normal customer would pay," Pratt said. "It got to the point of 'All right, give me X amount of money and let's be done with it' kind of thing."

Pratt's fondness for Matthews eclipsed these moments of exasperation. They talked long and often. They commiserated about their businesses, served as cheerleaders for the other's dreams. They talked about girlfriends. After a few years of extending Matthews lines of credit, Pratt decided to do business with him differently—to treat him more like family than a customer. Who wants to be constantly haggling over money with a buddy? "I thought, fuck it—I like him as a friend," Pratt said, "and I'm never going to make any money off this situation. I determined I'd do that with Bob because he was such a pain to deal with."

To Pratt, this was a clear line of demarcation. Matthews from then on could buy antiques at cost—with the proviso that he split the profit with Pratt if he sold an object later. Wayne even began loaning Bob antiques outright. The dealer justified it: Matthews had big houses near his stores; Pratt thought of the furniture in Matthews's homes as being in storage. Eventually Pratt returned the pieces to his showroom unless Matthews decided to pay.

As the years passed, the two began to buy together. This is a common practice among dealers, particularly as the market has spiked upward, the elite objects often eclipsing seven figures. Pratt began showing Matthews lists of antiques. One of the items might be a highboy priced at $100,000 that Pratt thought he could move for $150,000. They shared the cost. "He would resell it, because he was the expert," Matthews explained. "I don't know about highboys. And he would give me $25,000, and he would have $25,000."

One day Pratt brought up a different kind of deal: There was a document available, an original Bill of Rights. Pratt explained about the Indianapolis family, about the high asking price that he was trying to chip away at, about the profits they could reap if he found the right client. Pratt told him about the Declaration of Independence found in a $4 picture frame that sold for $2.42 million at Sotheby's.

Matthews was interested. But before he committed, he wanted to see the Bill of Rights with his own eyes.

Charlie Reeder led Pratt and Matthews into the bank vault where the Shotwell sisters were storing the parchment.

Reeder liked Pratt and found the fast-talking Matthews strangely mesmerizing. "He was clearly a big BS-er," Reeder said. "But he also seemed to be a very wealthy man." The airplane, in particular, made an impression.

Roughly two years had passed since Pratt's first visit. In that time, as a result of Pratt's persistent prodding, the asking price had dropped from $2 million to about $1 million. Now, Reeder hoped Matthews's appearance meant a deal might be consummated.

Pratt and Matthews had clawed their way upward partly by being unflinching negotiators. And good negotiators look for any reason to drive a price down—small flaws, perceived warts. On a house, Matthews might find loose paint or peeling shingles. In this case the two men assessed the Bill of Rights doubtfully.

Unlike the historians in Washington, they ignored the document's plain-stated elegance, its timelessness, its bedrock significance. What they saw was a poorly preserved sheepskin that was hard to read. That's what they told Reeder.

"Wayne looked at it," Matthews recalled. "He looked at the writing, and he commented that it was kind of faded, and it was kind of in a crappy little frame."

Matthews wasn't even sure the document he was looking at—encased in a "little skinny wood frame"—was real. "Bob did his dance around all over the place—'It isn't worth this, it isn't that,'" Pratt recounted.

When the two men were done with their evaluation, Reeder drove them back to the airport. Before Pratt disappeared into the plane, he pulled Reeder aside to ask whether the Shotwells might lower the price further. He reminded Reeder that the Bill of Rights had been looted from North Carolina. The state might try to get the document back—which was no small matter. A lower price would help attract potential buyers like Bob Matthews.

Reeder agreed to speak with the family and get back to Pratt soon.

6

The Document Hunter

THE FIRST TIME the mystery attorney called Ken Bowling, he offered photographs.

The year was 1997 or '98. The lawyer wanted to remain anonymous. He told Bowling, the preeminent historian from the First Federal Congress Project, that he had a client—also to remain nameless—who possessed and wanted to sell an original Bill of Rights. First, they needed to authenticate the document. Could Bowling do that?

Bowling said sure, he would take a look at the photos.

The anonymity didn't faze him. Just shy of sixty, Bowling had come to fully grasp the oddball Zeitgeist of the manuscript world. There was the secretive, paranoiac collector from Baltimore who in the 1950s specialized in early American papers. His interest wasn't patriotic; he'd been badly spooked by the Cold War and figured that when the Soviets invaded he could head down to Baltimore's docks and present the conquering admirals with the manuscripts. The Soviets were revolutionaries, too, right? When the collector's son sold the papers in 1972, the First Federal Congress Project obtained copies of some.

Collectors weren't the only ones capable of losing their senses around ancient, yellowed pages. There was something about old paper that made people act irrationally. Bowling often recounted the story of George Washington's undelivered inaugural address. In January 1789, working with aide David Humphreys, the first president drew up a strident speech about the new government. But his friend James Madison argued that it was both excessively verbose—at a whopping seventy-three pages—and threatened the rights of the states. Washington agreed and eventually delivered a shorter, softer speech. Years later, the original was eventually handed over to Jared Sparks, who began editing Washington's papers in 1829. Sparks figured that since the president never gave the speech, it wasn't part of the historical record—and thus could be used to placate the document collectors who frequently pestered him for Washingtonia. Sparks cut the speech into fragments—as many as eight per page— and mailed them far and wide. The manuscript has never been fully reconstructed.

"Sparks," Bowling said, his rubbery face creasing into a wry smile, "was a historian and documentary editor." Just like Bowling.

Other tales outline similar outrages: curators stealing from public collections they'd spent decades building, cataloging, and preserving; eccentric thieves who conceived and hatched elaborate plots to loot some of history's seminal sheaves; deranged profiteers who snipped signatures off great documents just to possess the autograph. Even the federal government was culpable. Bowling vividly recalled being a child in the 1950s and gazing at the original Declaration of Independence mounted in the Library of Congress, exposed to sunlight and coated in the residue of tobacco smoke. So much was lost or damaged. A person couldn't dwell on it, or he could go a little batty himself.

Bowling had a craggy face, deep-set eyes, a prominent nose, and gray hair he often wore in a buzz cut. His personality alternated between grandfatherly warmth and professorial imperiousness. While telling stories, he rapped his desk for emphasis, waved his arms, buried his face in his hands while searching for a detail, and then lurched suddenly backward from his desk. He swigged directly from a 1.5-liter bottle of water. The drywall behind his desk was a casualty of these conversational calisthenics: A horizontal line was chipped away at the point where his chair met the wall.

The feistiness appeared when he heard something he strongly disagreed with. Bowling was once told that Maryland's archivist had denied that the state was missing its copy of the Bill of Rights. "That's bullshit," Bowling barked, cutting off the elaborate explanation behind the claim. "Don't waste your time or mine."

Bowling grew up in Baltimore, close enough to the nation's capital city to foster a natural interest in the landmark edifices found there. During summers as a teenager, he hopped on twenty-five-cent commuter trains into D.C. to wander the Capitol and the memorials and think about all that led to their creation. At the Capitol, a guide recognized Bowling as a repeat customer and befriended him, eventually showing him sections not open to public tours.

His growing interest in history fully blossomed in college. After graduate school at the University of Wisconsin, Bowling found a mentor in Leonard Rapport, a documentary historian known as a relentless researcher with painfully exacting standards. Rapport couldn't countenance the idea of telling an incomplete story. In the 1960s he was editing documentary histories involving the Constitution and the First Congress when his boss announced plans to halt research, pronouncing the work done. Rapport knew better. "Leonard had been in repositories that were supposed to have been searched," Bowling said, "and found many, many manuscripts that were not in the collection." Rapport mutinied, steamrolling the boss to get the research extended.

He explained to Bowling that nothing brought the past alive like original documents, and that countless papers had been displaced— sold and scattered—throughout the nation's history. To find them, Rapport told his young protégé, you must leave the well-trod paths between academic libraries. Rapport showed him the catalogs of auction houses and manuscript dealers. "In graduate school," Bowling said, "I learned the importance of documents' contents. From Leonard I learned the importance of the documents themselves— what they could tell you, and where to find them."

Original documents often reveal unique bits of information. Sparks, for example, sometimes altered Washington's letters, fixing his grammar. Later biographers added layers of understanding by returning to the originals.

Bowling learned to examine underlined words; rather than reflecting the writer's emphasis, the markings were sometimes added by readers who came later. From originals he could take note of crossed-out words and margin notations. Address sheets, postmarks, docketing—they all brought the blur of history into sharper focus.

These details—long deemed insignificant, even intrusive—became Bowling's livelihood. He hoped to capture the history of early America. But first he had to get the story right.

As the 1990s drained away, Wayne Pratt proved to be prescient about the Shotwell sisters. The longer he stalled, the more he haggled over the Bill of Rights, the more the asking price dropped. In the spring of 1999 the older sister, Anne Shotwell Bosworth, was diagnosed with multiple sclerosis. The family was getting antsy. Nearly four years had passed since Pratt's first conversation with Charlie Reeder, and over that time the price had fallen to $500,000.

Pratt knew this game well. He knew the habits of people sitting on a treasure. The hard part was deciding to part with it. Once that obstacle is cleared, once such people see an object not for the thing itself but for the currency that it can be converted into, they can get impatient. They start thinking about the money. In their minds, they start spending it. Great antiques dealers wait for that itch to grow intolerable.

Sometimes it took persistence. In the 1970s an artist named David Wiggins took Pratt to look at a folk art sign at a New Hampshire country store. Pratt loved the piece; he thought it to be a one-of-a-kind classic. The proprietor, though, didn't care to part with it. Pratt, as was his wont, said he'd check back. Every year for thirty straight years, Pratt called to ask about the sign. Finally, in summer 2007, the seller relented. Pratt was electrified: "I just took [fellow dealer] David Schorsch up to see it. They took it out and he said, 'Oh, my God, it's a masterpiece.'"

Pratt, Schorsch, and Wiggins bought it for several hundred thousand dollars and sold it soon after for $675,000.

Pratt also had a knack for alighting in moments of high anxiety.

In 1988 Schorsch was involved in a horrendous car crash that shattered his right femur just as he became enmeshed in a messy legal battle over a folk art painting. Schorsch needed to unload parts of his private collection and business inventory to pay his expenses, but he wanted to keep the objects together as much as possible. Pratt happened to have several hundred thousand dollars on hand to buy the collection whole, at a huge discount.

"Because of his habit of appearing at scenes of distress, like the scene in which David Schorsch found himself," Thatcher Freund wrote in *Objects of Desire*, "Pratt was sometimes known in the world of American antiques as 'The Undertaker.'"

With the Bill of Rights, as the months passed, Pratt made it clear he had plenty else to occupy his time. He kept asking Reeder: What does the family want to do? Will they bring the price down enough to make something happen? "I worked them down over the years," he said. That was the way of his world.

As an antiques dealer, you had to be first. Pratt had recently paid $79,500 at Sotheby's for a folk art painting by the New England artist Sheldon Peck that dated to about 1830. Folk art at the time was surging in value. The seller, Wanda Bell, a collector from Nashville, had paid $25 for it only eight years before. Elite dealers make money by making discoveries, by bringing to market never-before-seen pieces that can immediately be identified as great.

Pratt wasn't only first with the Bill of Rights; he was the only one in line. Charlie Reeder didn't have any other options, and Pratt knew it. He would wait thirty years if he had to. Eventually they would come around.

Pratt's purported financier, Bob Matthews, was a plausible candidate for the philanthropic purchase. In recent years he'd learned the value of supporting important causes. The halo effect was good for business and provided ready access to other wealthy and powerful donors. He regularly purchased tables at fundraising events, the more glittery the better, and used these events to talk up his story: the buildings he owned, his sporting exploits. He recounted starring on his own polo team, which he created by offering the world's top players lavish salaries. He didn't just race sailboats; he competed on the *Weatherly*, the winner of the 1962 America's Cup.

This didn't always play well. Pratt's friend David Schorsch once attended a Christmas party at Matthews's home in Washington, Connecticut. Matthews greeted guests in a red fox-hunting outfit, complete with tails; his wife wore a tiara. Each guest had a snapshot taken with Bob, the way guests at the White House get a photograph with the president. "He wasn't somebody that I personally dug because he was a bit of a showoff," Schorsch said. "He just struck me as sort of obnoxious."

Yet Matthews had an uncanny knack for seeding his legend. In 1988, before he had met his wife, Mia, *Connecticut Magazine* named him one of the state's most eligible bachelors. A 1989 *Business Digest of Greater Waterbury* story reported, "Robert Viers Stephen Matthews is always hard at work. At 31, he appears at the top of his form, at the top of his field, at the top of the world."

The budget-conscious *Business Digest* normally didn't run interior color photos, but Matthews, loath to be rendered in black and white, wrote a check to cover the pricier production costs. The magazine also had a policy against lifestyle photos, but Matthews got around that one, too; there he was, pictured with his polo pony.

Boston Globe reporter Julie Hatfield, covering a 1997 Nantucket Film Festival bash at Matthews's mansion, noted that the man of the hour rolled in fashionably late: "When Matthews, who had been racing on the 12-meter yacht *Weatherly* with the New York Yacht Club, arrived at his own bash around midnight and saw the crowd, he exclaimed: 'Phew! I'm glad I reinforced the porches with steel beams,'" she wrote.

Because of the fog, he'd been forced onto the Nantucket ferry rather than fly—no dramatic arrival by helicopter this time. "Do you know how many years it's been," Matthews asked Hatfield, "since I had to take the ferry?"

What got surprisingly little attention was the way Matthews's real estate empire in Waterbury nearly became his Waterloo. When the Reagan renaissance crumbled in the late 1980s, the city's economy collapsed under the wreckage of the national savings-and-loan debacle and a corrupt mayor. Matthews had borrowed heavily on his properties, and in the wake of a market collapse, he owed far more on his buildings than they were worth. The banks and the FDIC foreclosed on at least five of his properties, absorbing enormous losses in the process.

But in what remains the abiding mystery of the Bob Matthews legend, the lenders never squeezed him for repayment. The story goes that Matthews walked into the banks, dropped the keys to his properties on the front desks, and left town forever. Matthews told the *Hartford Courant* that he benefited from "friendly foreclosures," in which banks accepted deeds as payoff for his debt. "I got lucky," he told the newspaper. "You know why? Because I wasn't arrogant . . . The guys who got in trouble, [they] said, 'I've got equity. I'm fighting for it.' . . . I cleaned up and took my hits."

But the damage to Waterbury lingered for years. Banks aren't viable property owners, and because Matthews's debt exceeded the property values, no one wanted to touch them. More than a decade later, Michael O'Connor, executive director of the quasi-public Waterbury Development Corporation, still rued the turn of events. "He set up deals . . . and walked away," O'Connor told the *Courant*. "In the Army, I think they call it slash and burn."

Not even the city's top officials could make sense of it. "I've always wondered about that," former mayor Edward D. Bergin Jr. said.

Matthews had once talked city planner Tony Mirto into teaching him a few magic tricks, and it began to seem as if Bob had a bit of Houdini in him: *Now you see him, now you don't.*

Part of the Matthews mythology was that he barreled through his fast-lane life at breakneck speed, repeatedly cheating his own mortality. As a boy he nearly died choking on food. He broke his neck falling off a horse during a polo match in the early 1990s. Matthews endured six visits to the emergency room while learning to ride, in fact. Each time he skated away unscathed. According to the *Business Digest* story, despite all those injuries, he was high-jumping six and a half feet on a horse only four months after taking up riding—a mere foot short of the world record.

Matthews resurrected his real estate business with equal aplomb. Before long he had started anew thirty miles away in New Haven.

Ken Bowling put Leonard Rapport's lessons to good use. In Washington he settled at the First Congress Project, and while his colleagues stuck to conventional research, Bowling devoured auction catalogs and began attending document shows. He was obsessed with one collection in particular: a set of 104 letters that had been auctioned off in the Biddle Sale, held in New York City in 1943 and '44.

The letters had been written to Benjamin Rush, an eminent physician and politician who represented Pennsylvania during the Continental Congress and whose frank correspondence during the Constitution's gestational period shed much light on the debates of the time. Rush received letters from more members of the First Congress than any other American—which made them hugely important to Bowling. But he was a controversial figure who often quarreled with George Washington—which led his family to close his papers to historians after his death. His son, James, left the papers to the Library Company of Philadelphia when he died. But before they reached their destination, someone culled four hundred pieces of correspondence from the collection. Those letters were handed down to Alexander Biddle after he married Benjamin Rush's granddaughter, in 1855. The letters eventually were liquidated with his estate.

The three-part Biddle Sale was a seminal event for collectors and dealers. There were dozens of letters written by signers of the Declaration of Independence; missives from the nation's first six presidents, including part of a renowned correspondence between Rush and Jefferson; and the First Congress letters. Many bidders dove in, and the letters fanned out across the collecting community. "Should an attempt now or later be made to assemble them," manuscripts dealer Mary Benjamin wrote of the pieces in 1946, "the task would be as impossible as the gathering of goose feathers scattered in a high wind. Collectors prize individual pieces too greatly to give them up lightly or altruistically."

Bowling, though, knew the documentary history he was editing would be incomplete without them. The letters "contain more of the

off-the-floor politics of [the First Congress] than any other group,"
he wrote in 1972, when he issued a plea in *Manuscripts* magazine to
anyone with information on the letters' whereabouts. Within a few
years he'd found sixty-four of the dispatches, in institutions such
as the Library of Congress, the American Philosophical Society, the
New York Public Library.

That was the easy part. Finding the rest required the sort of dog-
gedness his mentor had demonstrated. In 1970 Bowling discovered
two of the letters listed in a Carnegie Bookshop catalog, in New York
City. They were a gold mine: They detailed the arguments over the
location of the nation's capital. But the proprietor told him the letters had already been sold. Bowling wrote to ask whether the buyer
might provide copies for his research.

The reply was jarring: "You are exactly the kind of person my client does not want to be associated with." The implication was obvious. "I am a historian," Bowling said, "and the collector was of the
school that believed that if you show the content, the letter becomes
less valuable."

Oddly, the two Carnegie Bookshop letters turned up years later at
a Pennsylvania barn auction, in a sale alongside collections of *Play-
boy* and *Hustler*. Bowling chuckled at the memory. "Somebody sent
me the flyer, and there they were, listed with a bunch of skin maga-
zines," he said.

Bowling still occasionally locates a missing Biddle Sale piece
while scanning an auction catalog. Or he finds one while following
a hunch, a flash of intuition. In 2006 Bowling called the University
of Delaware. The graduate student assigned to comb the state's archives in the early 1970s on behalf of the First Congress Project had
found little, but Bowling suspected the search hadn't been terribly
rigorous. A librarian there referred him to the online archive. "They
told me, 'You can look for yourself,'" Bowling said. "And there it was.
The damn thing was listed."

Still, twenty-five letters eluded him.

Through it all Bowling maintained a delicate détente with the collecting community. They shared a passion. Sometimes they helped
each other. Bowling could provide historical context for letters—as

with antique furniture, backstory is paramount—and in return he got copies for his documentary history project.

His insistence on thorough, wide-ranging searches has inadvertently made him useful in several prominent cases involving document theft. In February 1987, for example, Eileen Dunlap, director of the Rosenbach Museum & Library in Philadelphia, received a call: A John Adams letter belonging to the museum was being advertised in a Massachusetts dealer's sales catalog.

The dealer told Dunlap that he'd bought the letter from Clive Driver, the retired former director and twenty-year veteran of the museum. Dunlap's staff checked inventory and found that the Adams letter—among numerous other items—was indeed missing. When Dunlap confronted Driver, he claimed to know nothing of the Adams letter's whereabouts and suggested the museum's records were inaccurate.

Fortunately, Bowling had taken the unusual step of stopping in at the Rosenbach library during the winter of 1970–71, where he'd made a list of all the materials relevant to the First Congress Project—including the Adams letter. His list proved the document was one of several Driver had stolen from the museum. Driver eventually was convicted on felony theft charges.

Because of the dark undercurrents that sometimes roil through the manuscript world, Bowling had low expectations when the anonymous lawyer called in the late 1990s to proffer photos of a Bill of Rights for authentication. Probably a fake.

But when Bowling took a close look, the document in the photos appeared to be an original. The thing looked like a holy relic.

A couple of photographs weren't enough to go on, of course. The pictures showed only the front of the broadsheet. Bowling needed to inspect the actual document, front and back, to be sure. He would ask the attorney for a look at the real thing during their follow-up conversation.

But Bowling never got the chance.

The attorney never called back.

• • •

By 1999 Bob Matthews had reached the height of his powers. A munificent donor and giver of epic parties, he caught the attention of the nation's political paterfamilias. And so, while laying plans for an American Ireland Fund benefit at his Nantucket estate, he got a call: Hillary Clinton, already raising money for a not-yet-official run for the Senate, wanted to come and give a short speech.

Less than a week before the August 20 event came even bigger news: President Clinton would make an appearance as well. That evening, about three hundred people paid $250 a head for the privilege of being shoehorned into Matthews's colonial revival shingle-style house, named Innishail, Gaelic for "haven of rest." Matthews had owned the residence, which had three levels of porches, for six years. The Matthewses described the property as "our little getaway" in a feature story in *Antiques & Fine Art* magazine.

The residence flaunted the Wayne Pratt imprimatur. After opening his island shop, Pratt began to aggressively market Nantucket baskets. Sailors first wove the containers in the 1850s to pass time aboard lightships, boats anchored offshore to alert mariners to treacherous shoals. Matthews's house was filled with the baskets. The *Antiques & Fine Art* layout included a photo of a nesting set of eight. "Wayne bought these right out of a house where they had been for decades," Matthews told the magazine. "They were covered with a thick layer of dust. What a great discovery—this is what collecting is all about!"

There were several Ralph Cahoon paintings—another Pratt specialty (though Matthews claimed, "I started collecting his work in the early 1990s, and in part drove up the market, which is still very strong"). A Massachusetts Federal inlaid maple card table reflected Pratt's predilection for New England furniture.

Wayne Pratt and his second wife, Sarah, attended the fundraiser that August night, the biggest of many big Bob Matthews nights at Innishail. President Clinton delivered a typically deft performance, playfully teasing the crowd with his wife's almost-but-not-quite candidacy.

The next day, a Saturday, the Pratts returned to Innishail for a dinner party. The place was still electric with post-Clinton buzz, but Wayne noticed that Matthews was missing.

He was told that Bob was not feeling well and was upstairs in bed. Pratt, puzzled, went to Matthews's room. "What's wrong with you?" Pratt asked. "You never get sick."

"Don't get too close to me," Matthews croaked. He said he felt horrible.

"Do you want to cancel?" Pratt asked.

Matthews demurred. It was too late. He asked Pratt to show the other guests around. Pratt walked downstairs, thinking, *That's not like Bob.*

Matthews had hired a caterer, so the dinner went off smoothly, much of the chatter involving Hillary's chances in the probable Senate race. After dinner Pratt asked Mia to have Bob call him the next day.

There was no word that Sunday. When Pratt called, Bob was still in bed. But Pratt's phone rang at 1:30 the next morning. It was Mia; Bob was in Nantucket Cottage Hospital. Pratt groaned, then hauled himself up to be with his friend. When he arrived, doctors had not yet diagnosed Matthews's malady; they were speculating about a flu.

When Pratt returned the next day, Matthews looked worse. He had a 104-degree fever and a yellowish complexion. Even the whites of his eyes were yellow. The doctors were now talking hepatitis but were awaiting lab tests. Pratt, anxious now, wrote a check for $900 to get the results expedited.

The results came back negative. No hepatitis. No one knew what was wrong, but Matthews was getting worse. His breathing was becoming labored. Pratt paced the room, wondering: What the hell? Had Matthews been poisoned with something—some kind of toxin, maybe—intended for the Clintons?

Sarah Pratt called a friend, a prominent California doctor, who urged that Matthews be moved immediately to Massachusetts General Hospital in Boston. The Pratts discussed the situation with Mia, and Wayne began asking the doctors to request a helicopter. They refused at first, saying Matthews wasn't yet a candidate for evacuation. Pratt nudged, then pushed, and when they continued to balk, he bellowed. He made a scene. He threatened to "sue the shit out of" the hospital and everyone involved.

The doctors relented. At Mass General the doctors told Mia that Bob appeared to have some sort of severe respiratory infection, and if they didn't operate it could kill him. Wayne remembers standing around Bob's hospital bed, holding hands with Matthews's brothers.

The doctors induced a coma and did the surgery.

Matthews eventually emerged from the coma and from the grips of the still-mysterious malady. He spent forty-five days in the hospital and recovered in a wheelchair, sucking on bottled oxygen. He dropped from 180 pounds to 130.

When he finally returned to Connecticut, Wayne Pratt took his emaciated friend for a celebratory meal at Carole Peck's Good News Café, a renowned Woodbury restaurant. Bob, still struggling with his appetite, nibbled on a ginger cookie and thanked his old friend for helping save his life. Chastened by the closest of his many close brushes with mortality, Matthews declared himself a changed man. He would no longer be a hard-driving capitalist. He would do yoga, and spend more time with family, and take nothing for granted.

Pratt always marveled at Matthews's recovery: *Houdini slips the handcuffs in the shark tank!* "I've never seen anybody that close to death," Pratt said. "I don't know what saved him; he was 99.7 percent gone. The thing about Bob, he always comes up on his feet."

Amid the hubbub of Matthews's mysterious affliction, Pratt managed to keep the Bill of Rights on his radar. By 1999 the asking price had dropped far enough that Pratt began to consider buying the document himself.

There would be obvious benefits. As a broker, Pratt stood to make only a small percentage of the sale price. If he bought the document for $500,000 and sold it for $2 million, the math looked very different.

Pratt also could possess the broadsheet, show it around. And he could share the expense with Bob Matthews, just like when they bought a highboy.

The deal finally came together in the spring of 1999, when Pratt, negotiating with attorney Charlie Reeder, managed to talk the price down to $300,000.

On June 2, 1999, before he fell ill, Matthews wrote Pratt a check for $150,000 for his half of the document. Once Matthews recovered, Pratt called Reeder and said he wanted to come to Indiana to finalize the deal.

For months Wayne Pratt had lobbied Matthews to partner with him on the purchase of a Pilatus airplane. Pratt had a weakness for aircraft and had become fixated on the Swiss single-engine turboprop planes. "Wayne was obsessed," Sarah Pratt said.

The plane cost more than $1 million, plus an hourly rate for the pilot and fuel. But Pratt figured he could get others to buy in to defray the expense. He planned to fly loads of antique furniture back and forth between Nantucket and the airfield in Oxford, Connecticut. The Pilatus could carry far more than Matthews's Piper Chief.

Pilatus offered prospective buyers a trial flight for a nominal fee. Pratt used this opportunity to return to Indianapolis.

Pratt and Matthews's second encounter with Charlie Reeder, the plainspoken Indiana lawyer, was much like the first. The two visitors did much of the talking. They described how Pratt had saved Matthews's life. They talked about President Clinton. Pratt again talked up John Richardson and his wife, though Peg Richardson had resigned as IRS commissioner more than two years earlier. "I think he kind of used the leverage," Matthews said, "that, you know, John Richardson's wife was Peg Richardson and, you know, he's a big lawyer and all that stuff, and that I was in the *New York Times* about three days before I went into my coma, with the president— President Clinton and his wife . . . you know, Bob is one of my investors, and . . . geez aren't we important and that kind of thing."

But after some discussion about the Bill of Rights, Matthews suddenly backed out. In light of his protracted illness, he said, he was no longer interested. His life-and-death struggle had changed everything. Matthews was considering retirement, or at least drastically downsizing his business interests.

This was a frustrating blow for the Shotwells. Roughly eight years had passed since they started shopping the parchment, and the fantasy of a multimillion-dollar windfall had fizzled. Now they couldn't unload it for $300,000.

What they didn't fully grasp was that Matthews's apparent disinterest was yet another negotiating tactic. Matthews and Pratt had orchestrated this feigned exit on the flight west.

Before boarding the airplane to head home, Pratt pulled Reeder aside and told him that he might still be able to swing some kind of deal—but with his moneyman out of the picture, the Shotwells were going to have to come down on the price one more time.

Soon after, Pratt called to say he was considering buying the document himself. But because the antiques dealer was now in on the deal alone, he wanted Reeder to take $200,000.

Pratt justified this bargain price another way. He pointed out—as he had many times before—that the Bill of Rights was a precarious purchase, the provenance issues with North Carolina still looming.

If the Shotwell sisters take $200,000, Pratt said, he would assume all risk for the cloudy title. If North Carolina sued for the manuscript's return, Pratt wouldn't ask the Shotwells for his money back.

Such refund policies were de rigueur in the industry. Say Dealer A buys a Thomas Jefferson letter from Dealer B, then sells it at Sotheby's to the highest bidder. Just after the auction, National Archives officials produce evidence that the document was stolen from their stacks. What happens then? Sotheby's would refund the winning bidder and hand the document to the National Archives. Dealer A, who just lost his auction income *and* his Jefferson letter, would in turn demand a refund from *his* source—Dealer B. Dealer B would then seek to recoup his investment, and so on down the line, until the chain of custody dead-ends.

Pratt offered to cut that chain short. In exchange for the lower purchase price, he would not ask for a refund, no matter what happened next.

Furthermore, Pratt promised to sell the Bill of Rights to a museum or a library, or to someone who would donate it to such an institution.

Reeder said he would check with the Shotwells. It didn't take long. So many years had passed. Maybe this was the sisters' only chance, with Anne now battling MS. The document was slowly fading with them. "We wanted to get a little something," Sylvia Shotwell Long remembered. "And we wanted to get it into the hands of someone who could preserve it."

The sisters had had more than enough. "It was terribly frustrating," Long recalled. "All the machinations, the dickering back and forth. It just went on and on, and I got so disgusted. I just said to my sister, 'Whatever you want to do.'"

So the deal was done. After 134 years in the Shotwell family, the Bill of Rights was leaving Indiana. Just one piece of business remained: the authentication. Pratt's lawyer, John Richardson, decided on the perfect expert.

He chose a man with an impeccable reputation as a peerless historian: Ken Bowling of the First Federal Congress Project.

7

The Leaves of the Sybil

WORD TRAVELED SLOWLY in 1897.
A full month after the *Indianapolis News* ran its story on Charles Shotwell and the historic parchment hanging on his office wall, the *News & Observer* of Raleigh, North Carolina, reprinted the piece. The story ran on June 10 under a different headline: "Stolen Historical Relic: Taken from the Capitol Here by a Yankee."

This obvious bit of journalistic provocation was not lost on Walter Clark. A distinguished man born into a prominent plantation family, Clark had served as a Confederate officer. In 1897 he was three years into a long tenure as a Populist justice on North Carolina's Supreme Court. He fostered an abiding interest in Carolina history and wrote about the state at great length.

On June 19, with the newspaper article rattling around in his head, Clark jotted a note to North Carolina's secretary of state, Cyrus Thompson, official custodian of the state archives. Referring Thompson to the story, Clark suggested that he contact his counterpart in Indiana—or someone in charge up there—to try to reclaim the pilfered parchment: "On its face it belongs to the State of N.C., and to your office"—Clark underlined those last three words—"and the State can reclaim it anywhere & at any time."

Thompson dashed off a letter to William D. Owen, Indiana's secretary of state, requesting help. But the summer passed with no reply, and Thompson might have let the whole thing drop if another letter hadn't arrived to jog his memory.

In September a resident sent him the original *Indianapolis News* story. Goaded anew, Thompson fired off another letter to Indiana, this one to the newspaper's editor. If the story was accurate, Thompson wrote, "the parchment is evidently the property of the State of North Carolina, and ought to be returned to this department."

He noted that he'd written to Secretary of State Owen but had gotten no reply. "I trust I may trespass so far upon your kindness," Thompson wrote, "as to ask you to write to me whether the facts set forth in the clipping are true, in order that I may, if possible, secure the return of the document to this department; and I shall be very much obliged."

Cyrus Thompson, who wore round wire-rimmed glasses and had a thick, rangy mustache and goatee, was renowned for his skills of persuasion. He was a gifted orator, known as the most enthralling speechmaker in his Populist Party. Josephus Daniels, the legendary newspaper editor and power broker, wrote that Thompson "had eloquence and vehemence . . . He didn't talk like anybody else, even in private conversation, and on the stump he had an original way, and my, how he could enthuse the Populists!"

Thompson set off a small cyclone of activity in the heartland. A chastened William Owen finally replied on September 29, apologizing for missing Thompson's earlier letter and promising to investigate the missing parchment. In a remarkable exhibition of bureaucratic chutzpah, the Indiana secretary of state then departed his office and headed for Charles Shotwell's home at the corner of Cherry and Lawn avenues in the suburb of Irvington.

The visit caught Shotwell by surprise, and he was none too happy about it. Owen had not been the first unexpected guest to arrive at his door. In response to Thompson's letter, a *News* reporter had just come to inquire whether Shotwell intended to return the parchment to North Carolina.

Shotwell by then no doubt realized the extent to which his *News* interview back in April was metastasizing into a major quandary. "I found him in a humor not the best in the world," Owen wrote, with Victorian-era delicacy, on September 30.

The *News* reporter "had made statements to which he took exception," Owen wrote. "He referred also to statements in a letter which you had written to the *News,* that seemed to displease him."

Shotwell, though, managed to regain his footing. The two men had a long conversation, and Shotwell showed the broadsheet to his guest, which, Owen reported, "gives every evidence in the world, upon casual observation, of being genuine." Shotwell repeated the story he told the *News,* layering on some additional detail: "He says that he was personally acquainted with the soldier from whom he bought the document before he went into the war and afterwards until his death," Owen wrote.

Though the soldier "took the document and other articles from the State House at Raleigh as souvenirs of that occasion," Owen reported, Shotwell defended him as "an honorable gentleman whose integrity could not be called into question."

But Shotwell also did some backpedaling, apparently hoping to head off any conflict with North Carolina. Owen wrote:

> Mr. Shotwell says to me that he has some reason to believe that the document is not the one containing the amendments which were finally adopted. His suspicion is, that a copy of the amendments were [*sic*] sent [to] North Carolina, which was discovered to be imperfect, and that another copy was substituted in its place. He says this inference is drawn from the fact that by comparison of the wording of the amendments in the document with the wording of the amendments as they now appear in the published Constitution, he finds some slight differences. He says that he has already set on foot investigation by which comparison will be made of the wording of the document which he has with wording of the documents in possession of other of the thirteen original states . . . He says that he is not ready to say just what his disposition will be to return the document, until that investigation is complete.

Owen didn't elaborate on the alleged discrepancies. "I would like very much to be of assistance to the State of North Carolina in procuring the return of the document," he concluded. "I cannot give any intimation, in the light of Mr. Shotwell's statements, as to what conditions he will impose for its return . . . Mr. Shotwell is a stranger to me, but my judgment is, that with genteel and courteous treatment, he will not be unreasonable in the matter.

"I shall see Mr. Shotwell occasionally for the purpose of having further talk with him, and will give you notification of any progress made."

Could an honorable gentleman also be a thief?

Charles Shotwell thought not. Throughout his life he asserted the document was a legitimate spoil of war. Since his friend was a soldier, Shotwell wrote later in life, "it was contraband of War and lawfully his possession."

Unfortunately, that interpretation doesn't jibe with law established during the Civil War. In 1863 the government adopted General Order 100, which criminalized individual gain among Union troops. These rules were later incorporated by the Hague Convention and served as the genesis for international conventions on the conduct of war. "Neither officers nor soldiers are allowed to make use of their position or power in the hostile country for private gain," Article 46 states, "not even for commercial transactions otherwise legitimate."

Perhaps recognizing that Sherman's troops had been flouting this doctrine for some time, the U.S. Army on June 12, 1865, added a layer of specificity to the no-looting directive. Special Order 88 mandated that all property that belonged in the custody of North Carolina's secretary of state—including archives—be turned over to that officeholder.

In modern times, experts on the rules of war found little wiggle room in these edicts. The United States' top expert on the rules of war, W. Hays Parks, the special assistant for law of war matters to the judge advocate general of the army, asserted that the Bill of Rights grab was "an unauthorized and illegal taking." Dr. Joseph Glatthaar, a nationally recognized Civil War historian and expert on Sherman's campaign through the Carolinas, agreed that legal title to North Carolina's public property could not pass to an individual.

Special Order 88 was a sort of legal dragnet, intended to round up the souvenirs collected by Sherman's troops during the first two months of their Raleigh occupation. On April 14 a soldier named John Metzgar wrote a four-page letter to his wife, using paper with the letterhead "Confederate States of America, Ordnance Office," in which he enclosed several North Carolina documents he'd taken from the Capitol. One of them was a 1792 bill proposing to improve the navigation of the New River. These, he wrote, were "the only trophies that I have from Raleigh."

Captain Samuel B. Wheelock of the adjutant general's office of the army snatched two of North Carolina's 1861 resolutions, including one calling for a state convention to consider secession. Wheelock even autographed them: "Taken from the Hall of Records, Raleigh, N.C. on the 15th day of April 1865," he wrote on the back, adding his name, rank, and unit.

After Special Order 88, these men—and all the rest of Sherman's bummers who grabbed pages from the state's coffers—were legally obligated to return the stolen papers. But some materials were long gone: Metzgar's river navigation bill has never been recovered. Wheelock's pilfered resolutions only recently returned to Raleigh through wildly circuitous channels. The University of Southern Illinois sent one of them back in 1968, when someone there recognized it as North Carolina property. How it had arrived in the university's holdings is unknown. The second turned up in 2006, when a person familiar with North Carolina's archives spotted it on a Beverly Hills auction firm's website and reported its presence to Raleigh. The state sent a demand letter, and the auction house acquiesced.

The thefts, though, were hardly isolated to a few rogue soldiers. All the state treasurer's reports were gone. Throughout the occupation of Raleigh, and for months afterward, treasurer Jonathan Worth chased after items "scattered from the mountains to the sea shore and every where smuggled."

In a September 1865 letter Worth vented his frustration at the federal government's complicity: "I failed at Washington to get the Govt. to give up the State property captured *after the proclamation by Sherman and Schofield to the army and people of N.C. that peace existed.* This capture was rapacious and illegal, as I think, and consequently impolitic. I succeeded however in getting an order forbidding further captures."

The sticky-fingered troops had plenty of civilian counterparts.

Take John Thomas Scharf, for example. Born in 1843 in Baltimore, Scharf was deeply sympathetic to the Confederate cause and made his way into Virginia as a teenager to enlist with the Southerners. He suffered wounds in three battles, then served a stint as a midshipman in the Confederate navy. He was heading off to Canada on a mission for the Confederate war department when he was captured and imprisoned; only the war's end spared him from standing trial as a spy.

A pardon from President Andrew Johnson opened the way for a remarkably varied career: Scharf was a journalist at three Baltimore newspapers, a lawyer, a member of the Maryland House of Delegates, and commissioner of Maryland's land office. In 1893 he was appointed special inspector of Chinese immigration at the port of New York.

But Scharf is perhaps best remembered as an indefatigable Maryland historian, writing what one biographer described as "many heavy books." He was also a voracious collector of historical papers. In 1891 Scharf donated a vast quantity of these documents to Johns Hopkins University, including "a mass of official Maryland records," according to one Scharf biography.

As a public official, Scharf had access to public records, thousands of which he took and never returned. By any modern definition he was a thief on a grand scale.

But in Scharf's time, rules were far looser. Long before he arrived, public officials had adopted the practice of taking records home at day's end, and Scharf was hardly alone in failing to secure their return.

In fact, a general lawlessness pervaded the presumably buttoned-down world of old records. Looting for scholarly purposes was commonplace. The first papyrus hunters who cracked open Egyptian tombs early in the nineteenth century, emerging with the enigmatic writings of millennia past, were glorified looters funded by the world's top museums. The work was so frenzied that teams of excavators sometimes faced off at gunpoint. Giovanni Belzoni, a legendary but amateurish archaeologist working for the British Museum, had no moral quandary about plucking rolls covered with hieroglyphics directly off the dead. "The purpose of my researches," he wrote, without the faintest hint of apology, "was to rob the Egyptians of their papyri of which I found a few hidden in their breasts, under their arms, in the space above the knees, or on the legs, and covered by the numerous folds of cloth that envelop the mummy."

E. A. Wallis Budge was knighted for his finds on behalf of the British Museum despite tactics that would get him arrested today. In Egypt in 1888, for example, he tracked down missing sections of an important early Aristotle work on a roll of papyrus. After finalizing his black-market acquisition, Budge had to smuggle the object out of the country; the Egyptian Service of Antiquities, working to stem the outgoing tide of treasures, would never allow the papyrus to be exported.

Budge had a novel solution: "At length I bought a set of Signor Beato's wonderful Egyptian photographs, which could be used for exhibition in the Egyptian galleries of the British Museum, and having cut the papyrus into sections, I placed these at intervals between the photographs, tied them up in some of Madame Beato's gaudy paper wrappers, and sent the parcel to London by registered post." In his book *Testaments of Time,* Leo Deuel described the items as "some of the most valued documents ever taken from Egypt."

The same anything-goes frontier sensibility held sway in America. The American Historical Association in the early 1900s reported that Pennsylvania's own official stewards were fleecing the archives. "Reports are current that . . . the manuscript archives of the State was systematically 'plundered' by certain State employees and others who had access to them, and there is considerable evidence to confirm these reports. The original manuscripts used in compiling the first series of printed archives, which . . . were to be bound and deposited in the State library, seem to have wholly disappeared."

Some papers were moved to Philadelphia for safekeeping in

1863, when Robert E. Lee's Confederate troops invaded Pennsylvania. Some of these were returned to the state library after the Civil War but later vanished. "It is well known," the report said, "that similar manuscript archives were sold at public auction sales in New York City."

On October 1, 1897, the *Indianapolis News* ran a second article on Charles Shotwell and his historic parchment. This story notably lacked the gee-whiz quality of the previous piece. "Mr. Shotwell was asked yesterday if he intended to return the document to the authorities of North Carolina," the article reported. "He seemed averse to committing himself to any definite statement as to his intentions, and said that it was his property, valuable to him as a relic and souvenir of the war, and that he certainly would not give it up on any 'demand,' no matter from whom such demand might come."

Interest in the broadsheet began to mushroom. Cyrus Thompson, North Carolina's records keeper, soon received a copy of the article from a Tar Heel transplant in Pecksburg, Indiana. If the parchment indeed was taken from North Carolina, wrote William B. Newlin, "it is property of the State and should be restored without any trouble. I believe steps should be taken to ascertain whether or not it can be secured. I was born and raised in the old 'North State' and take a great deal of interest in her still. Hence I write you."

In the ensuing days Thompson wrote to *News* managing editor Morris Ross, Indiana secretary of state William Owen, and Newlin, thanking them for their interest and assistance. "I am not making any comment," Thompson wrote to Newlin, "as to Mr. Shotwell's action and temper, apparent in this matter."

A final story on the affair appeared on October 5 in the *News & Observer*. "From the above it is evident that Mr. Shotwell does not like to part with the document," the article read, "and very naturally so; but it is clearly the property of North Carolina and should be in the State's archives. Dr. Thompson said he will make further efforts to recover it. He says in order to do this he is willing to indemnify Mr. Shotwell for the amount paid for the parchment."

• • •

Lost documents haunt North Carolina.

The state's institutional angst over missing records has roots in a declaration of independence. Not *the* Declaration of Independence, but a different one: one that probably never existed.

On May 19, 1775, a group of more than twenty-five prominent citizens in Mecklenburg County met to discuss the corrupt and heavy-handed British agents running the colonies. The list of grievances was long and growing: excessive taxes, dishonest sheriffs, illegal fees. In 1771 royal governor William Tryon had violently squelched the Regulators, a band of disgruntled farmers openly defying the Crown's rule. After dispersing the resistance, Tryon executed several prisoners; the rest were forced to swear allegiance to the Crown. Four years later, on that May morning in 1775, reports of the success of Massachusetts rebels in the Battle of Lexington reignited the colonists' grievances.

The next day, according to legend, the band of hardscrabble North Carolinians created and read aloud a formal decree of separation: the Mecklenburg Declaration of Independence. The document predated Thomas Jefferson's masterpiece by more than a year and included much of the same eloquent language.

Or so the story went. On April 30, 1819, amid a nationwide surge of interest in the American Revolution, the *Raleigh Register* tapped a wellspring of patriotic pride by publishing the text of what it claimed was the Mecklenburg Declaration. North Carolinians hungrily latched on to the document for obvious reasons. Neighboring Virginia had produced many key revolutionaries—Madison, Monroe, Jefferson, Patrick Henry—but the Tar Heels primarily played a supporting role.

The story of the Mecklenburg Declaration would be part of the bedrock of American history, if it were actually true. There were, however, some problems with the *Register*'s article. For one, no such declaration existed. John McKnitt Alexander, one of the men in attendance that day in 1775, reportedly possessed the document, only to have it vanish in the flames that consumed his house on April 6, 1800. The newspaper article, it later turned out, was constructed from Alexander's memory.

The record is clear that the Mecklenburg Committee passed a series of strongly worded anti-British "resolves" in May 1775. Historians who have examined the matter largely agree that locals later extrapolated a "declaration" from those turgid words of protest—especially after Alexander and others later tacked on passages from the real thing. Scholars have pointed out that sections of the alleged Mecklenburg document mirror, word for word, parts of the national Declaration—meaning that if the North Carolina version were real, Jefferson would have been plagiarizing a work from one of America's remotest colonies when he wrote the screed in 1776. Jefferson forcefully denied having heard of any Mecklenburg Declaration.

None of that mattered in the Tar Heel State. North Carolinians believed they'd kick-started the Revolution. Within six years of the *Register* article, the state had turned May 20 into a full-blown holiday. In 1825, on the purported document's fiftieth anniversary, the region held a huge celebration to mark the occasion, including a church service, a procession of veterans, and triumphant cannon fire.

In 1830 the state's legislature investigated and declared the story of the Mecklenburg Declaration to be genuine—shifting the tale from the realm of legend onto the official record. The date of May 20, 1775, remains on the state flag. Over the years, anniversary celebrations have featured parades, visits from U.S. presidents, dances, and reenactments.

The controversy has lived more lives than a franchise horror-movie villain. In 1905 Dr. S. Millington Miller of Philadelphia announced that he'd discovered a June 3, 1775, copy of the *Cape Fear Mercury* that contained the Mecklenburg Declaration, proving its existence. In an article he wrote for *Collier's*, Miller included a reproduction of part of the newspaper's front page. But experts on all sides of the debate quickly dismissed it as a fake, pointing out obvious incongruities and errors. Another fabrication, also quickly discredited, followed soon after. "To say that the ghost is laid, however, is foolhardy," Colton Storm and Howard Peckham wrote in their 1947 book, *Invitation to Book Collecting*. "Many North Carolinians still believe in the Declaration, the day is patriotically observed, and for natives it is at least political suicide to declare otherwise. Truth, crushed to earth, still lies in Carolina clay."

The failure to produce a Mecklenburg Declaration of Independence seemed to spur on North Carolina's institutional obsession with lost records.

After being elected in 1841, Governor John Motley Morehead made the preservation of the state's archives one of his personal crusades. Morehead was something of a renaissance man; he worked fiercely to upgrade education, communication, and transportation in what was still an isolated outpost. In 1844, cranking up his most heart-tugging rhetoric, the man known as the father of modern North Carolina evoked the Mecklenburg legend in a fiery speech. "As long as the American Union shall endure," he told the state's General Assembly, "so long will the History of the establishment of American Independence be a subject of deep interest to every Patriot . . . We are wholly unworthy of such illustrious descent, if we neglect to preserve by all means in our power, the history of gallant deeds by which they sustained that declaration."

Morehead meant it. He didn't want the state to spit the archival bit on his watch. State records keepers had, in fact, recently dodged a bullet. In June 1816 a fire on Fayetteville Street had come alarmingly close to the State House—close enough that Secretary of State William Hill convinced the legislature to fund construction of a fireproof building for public records. Because of Hill's foresight, the archives were unharmed when a fire razed the Capitol building in 1831.

Morehead wanted to expand those holdings by harvesting records of Carolina's early history on file in Britain. But someone pointed out to him that the state's existing Revolutionary-era records were in woeful condition, and funds would be better spent caring for those.

This commenced more high-octane speechifying. Morehead reminded his fellow statesmen that "it is our solemn and patriotic duty to preserve, by all means in our power, every memorial of that noble struggle. These memorials are now scattered over the State, and gradually disappearing, and like the leaves of the Sybil, they rise in value as their numbers decrease."

The legislature eventually funded the England document-gathering adventure in 1850. But the Civil War brought a drastic shift in priorities. In 1863 the General Assembly passed a secret resolution directing the governor to procure enough boxes for the removal of valuables, including all public papers.

The moving began in 1864, but it wasn't until the following March, as Sherman's troops threaded northward from Columbia, that Governor Zebulon Vance formally requested that state records be moved from the State House. On April 12, 1865, with Sherman poised on the city's fringes, a train left Raleigh carrying archives, funds of the treasury and banks, and officials. The Bill of Rights wasn't among them. The document was left behind in an allegedly secure place in the secretary of state's office.

Given the chance to reclaim the singular document twenty-eight years later, then, Cyrus Thompson might have sensed a mandate to pursue it to the far corners of the globe. And there is some indication he took up the chase. When his adversary Charles Shotwell was in his late seventies, Shotwell wrote:

> About the year 1886 or 1887 two gentlemen, The Secretary and Treasurer of the State of North Carolina, came to Indianapolis and demanded of me the parchment. They went so far as to enlist the help of the Treasurer of the State of Indiana to show me how they could take it from me, if I refused to give it up. I was able to convince them that it was contraband of War. After learning the history of my having it, they concluded that it was useless to try to take it from me, and so I have had peaceable possession of it ever since.

But this narrative was written almost three decades after the fact, and Shotwell's recall of events seemed to have gone soft. He was clearly referring to the 1897 affair. (There is no record in North Carolina of anyone knowing the document's whereabouts in 1887. And if a run-in with North Carolina officials had happened then, it's highly unlikely Shotwell would have so blithely repeated the story of buying the document to the *Indianapolis News* a decade later.)

Not even George Stevenson Jr. could produce any evidence of Cyrus Thompson traveling to Indiana. Stevenson was the modern-day doyen of North Carolina history, his career in the state archives spanning more than thirty-five years. He looked long and hard into the Bill of Rights story. In September 2007 he was battling acute emphysema and working limited hours. He sported a white mustache, gray hair parted on the side, and round glasses, and he exuded a bracing tobacco aroma. The mention of Shotwell—the bête noire of North Carolina's archives—so excited Stevenson he erupted into a coughing fit. Stevenson pronounced the name SHOT-*wull*, swallowing the final syllable like a tainted oyster.

Did Cyrus Thompson go to see Shotwell? "He did no such thing," Stevenson said, sucking on an unfiltered cigarette while sitting at a picnic table outside the archives building. "There's nothing in any of the records, and I went to some effort to look for it, because if it did happen, it would be important for us to know about."

Stevenson pointed out that such a lengthy trip in those days would have certainly garnered attention, given all that had already been said and written. (And Thompson wasn't a man to undertake such an epic journey quietly.)

Jeff Crow, the state's deputy secretary of archives and history, agreed. "It doesn't seem plausible," he said. "Thompson would have made the newspapers with it, or it would've shown up in his correspondence." Crow figured that Thompson considered the time and expense, and Shotwell's stated refusal to surrender the broadsheet, and simply let the matter drop.

Yet word of the supposed encounter endured in Shotwell family lore. The story goes that the southerners arrived, demanded the document's return, then got testy and cursed at Shotwell when he refused. Charles was a churchgoer, a member of the First Baptist Church in Indianapolis, and was duly offended. "The story my father told," recalled Sylvia Shotwell Long, "was that my grandfather said, 'If you had asked nicely, I would've given it to you. Now you'll get it over my dead body.'"

Why would Charles Shotwell invent this story? To recast his role as a kind of victim? To build sympathy for his claim to the parchment? The tale of boorish and vulgar southerners would have played well up North at that time.

Maybe Shotwell needed to believe the story. Maybe over time he even convinced himself that it really happened.

That way he wouldn't have to work out the vexing contradiction of being both a devout Baptist and the keeper of stolen booty.

8

Strangers

O N F E B R U A R Y 24, 2000, Wayne Pratt climbed aboard the eight-seat, twin-engine Piper Chief he'd recently acquired from Bob Matthews for a final trip to the Midwest. The plan was to pick up the Bill of Rights and a member of the Shotwell family and fly on to Washington to get the document authenticated.

Pratt was comfortable with these sorts of elaborate logistics—this was often the way he operated—but Sylvia Shotwell Long disliked this arrangement. After all of Pratt's machinations, she no longer trusted him. "I felt like we were going to be set up," she said. "To me, it was very risky." The family took out an insurance policy on the document just to be sure.

With the $200,000 deal now in place, the long-delayed sale began churning forward. Pratt sent $50,000 back to Matthews, who had originally paid $150,000 for his share of the parchment. Because the Shotwell sisters lived in different parts of the country—Sylvia had moved to suburban Atlanta after getting married—they signed the bill of sale separately: Sylvia on January 7, and Anne on February 15. The bill of sale stipulated they had obtained the document "through inheritance, and not by unlawful or improper means."

Richardson, Pratt, and Indianapolis lawyer Charlie Reeder had worked out a complex arrangement for the sale and authentication, all spelled out in an escrow agreement. On February 23 Pratt wired $150,000 from his Fleet Bank account into Reeder's trust account at

Fifth Third Bank in Indianapolis. (Pratt had sent the first $50,000 back in 1997, when he acquired an option on the document.)

The following day a Shotwell envoy would accompany Pratt and the Bill of Rights on a trip to Washington; this turned out to be David Bosworth, Anne's husband, because Charlie Reeder was afraid to fly. If the experts in D.C. pronounced the manuscript genuine, Pratt would then have three hours to make a final decision. He built in this last crevice of wiggle room in case the document was immediately identifiable as belonging to a particular state.

If Pratt still wanted to acquire the parchment, he would immediately send a fax instructing the Indiana bank's escrow agent to disburse the money to Reeder's trust account. And then Bosworth would officially hand the Bill of Rights over to Pratt.

If Pratt for some reason declined, Bosworth would bring the document back to Indiana—he planned to rent a car and drive home—and Reeder would wire the money back to Pratt within twenty-four hours.

Pratt's fondness for elaborate, even theatrical transactions was a source of eye rolling among his employees. "The more complicated the deal," said Marybeth Keene, Pratt's vice president, "the better. If he wound up with three people, five pieces of furniture, and some kind of payment plan, he would be thrilled."

He was also hands-on. He could have had Richardson handle the authentication, but Pratt enjoyed that part of the job. As Keene put it, he was "always, always on the prowl."

David Bosworth was in his seventies, bald and overweight, and had a congenital heart condition, which made Pratt uneasy about bringing him on his airplane. But once the men were onboard and relaxed, and it was just the two of them and the Bill of Rights on a two-hour flight, Bosworth settled in and chatted easily. Bosworth was as midwestern as *Prairie Home Companion*. Born and raised in Indianapolis, he'd been the owner and operator of Bosworth & Bosworth Sign Company from 1985 to 1997. He was a member of the Second Presbyterian Church in Indianapolis and was deeply involved in community life, from the Masons to the Gyro Club to the Exhausted Roosters, the name given to retired Jaycees.

"They were very down-to-earth," Pratt said. "Not a wealthy family, just nice midwestern people."

Eventually Pratt turned to the question of the Bill of Rights. The antiques dealer said, "I wanna hear everything you know about this."

As Pratt later recalled it, Bosworth did not like the South. Some midwesterners maintained family grudges dating back to the Civil War, that region having absorbed the harshest losses among Union forces. Bosworth would have loved for the manuscript to be a real-life vestige of the North's victory, Pratt said. But Bosworth didn't think it was so. Pratt claimed Boswell told a story embedded in Shotwell family lore about Charles Shotwell traveling around as a wagon-wheel salesman and buying the document off the wall of a hardware store in Vermont or upstate New York. Bosworth found that story to be more plausible than the one involving the Civil War theft, Pratt asserted. "He said, 'I honestly feel that way,' and I kind of believed the guy," Pratt said.

When the two men landed in Washington, John Richardson and a female colleague from his law firm met them for the trip to Foggy Bottom. At 2120 L Street they took the stairs to the second floor. Pratt carried the framed document in a cardboard carton typically used to transport framed art.

This was the party of four that First Federal Congress Project staffers later described as the shadowy, possibly armed guests who arrived bearing a Bill of Rights.

Charlene Bickford later told the story of the enigmatic strangers' visit repeatedly to various media, and it soon became a staple of the labyrinthine tale of the parchment's odyssey. This clearly irritated Pratt, who remembered the First Congress Project encounter differently. Once he and his party got inside the door, the antiques dealer recalled sticking out his hand and saying, "Hi, I'm Wayne." No one asked for his last name—and he figured that these were people interested in old things, so they probably recognized him as an *Antiques Roadshow* regular, Pratt claimed.

Bickford, however, didn't watch the show, and no one made the connection. Either by design or because no one asked, Pratt and Richardson didn't make their identities known. Pratt said he lifted the Bill of Rights from the box, laid it on the conference table, and said, "What can you tell me about it?"

Bickford then brought out facsimiles of documents of similar vintage—including other Bills of Rights—and laid them out next to each other, according to Pratt's version of events. She studied each in turn under a magnifying glass and speculated that the parchment might be Pennsylvania's lost copy, based on similarities to that state's other documents.

Maryland was also part of the speculation; in fact, Bickford suspected the document may have once hung in Annapolis. But the discussion never rose above the level of supposition, since Bickford made it clear that removing the parchment's backing was the key to learning anything conclusive. Pratt said the dialogue was affable and lasted more than thirty minutes. He offered to pay the historians for their trouble, and they declined.

Pratt was particularly aggrieved at the suggestion that he'd walked in with armed guards. "Guns? I was dressed like this," he said, raising his hands in a "Who, me?" gesture. He wore a sports coat, green turtleneck, and chinos.

"That kind of really pissed me off," he said. "I couldn't say anything [on his lawyer's advice], and every time you read about it in the paper your hair goes up on end. If it was wrong, they should've called the police, and they had time. We didn't run in and run out."

The two versions of that meeting converge only in the end: There is consensus that the visitors left convinced the Bill of Rights was authentic. Back outside, Pratt called Charlie Reeder in Indianapolis and said that, based on what he'd just heard, he needed to hire a conservator to remove the document's cardboard backing. Pratt didn't want to complete the sale until he was able to do that.

Given the terms of the sale, this step was imperative. Pratt was gambling on the provenance issue by assuming all the risk. If there was docketing on the back that clearly identified the parchment as North Carolina's, Pratt's risk would be exponentially greater. The state could claim it, and Pratt could lose his $200,000 investment. Bickford's speculation about the document's possible connection to a handful of other states gave Pratt hope. Maybe there would be no docketing on the back, and no one would be able to definitively link the parchment to any of the states missing their copies—including North Carolina.

Pratt offered to pay for the conservation work but told Reeder he would have to take the document home to Connecticut. "If you don't want to do it, it's OK," Pratt said. "I'll send David back with it."

But the midwesterners consented. No one wanted the deal to fall apart that far in. And Bosworth, who'd become friendly with Pratt on the flight to Washington, felt comfortable with the arrangement.

Richardson and Reeder agreed to suspend the escrow agreement until a paper conservator could peel away the backing.

Back up in Woodbury, Pratt's friend David Schorsch recommended Alan Firkser, president of Paper Conservation Studio, headquartered on Broadway in midtown Manhattan. Since opening in 1983, Firkser had built an international client base. He conserved and restored various works of art on paper, including drawings, watercolors, prints, and documents. He'd handled Picassos and Hoppers, among many others.

Pratt left the process up to the expert. Firkser used a scalpel to scrape away the cardboard but not water, which aids the removal process but can cause buckling on parchment of that vintage. In removing the backing and glue residue, Firkser would take care to disturb as little of the document's backside as possible, so that any docketing would remain intact.

Pratt, ever anxious, called every three or four days for a status report. But more than a month passed before Firkser finished the job. He completed the work on April 20, 2000, and charged Pratt $2,500.

When the document arrived at his Woodbury shop, Pratt eagerly examined the back. Sure enough, Bickford was right: There was a notation there, clearly written long ago. But Pratt had to lean in close to read the passage, which was so badly cracked and faded it was barely legible:

1789
PROPOSED AMENDMENTS TO
THE CONSTITUTION OF THE
UNITED STATES——

Pratt didn't know the story behind this note or its author—but on its face, the docketing appeared to be a positive development. The notation offered no clear evidence of the document's origins. It didn't mention Raleigh or North Carolina. This Bill of Rights, Pratt thought, could have come from anywhere.

He kept the artifact in his attic office, a small, secluded room with a slanted ceiling atop a narrow, vertiginous staircase in his shop, which outdated even the Bill of Rights. In the days after the document returned from New York, Pratt went up there, slipped it out of the Mylar sleeve he kept it in—to filter ultraviolet light—and spent hours pondering exactly what he had in the faded broadsheet with its inscrutable marking.

The document looked more impressive now. "It looked much better," he said, "once I took it out of the shit frame they had it in."

He could feel the whole thing coming together.

At any time during the past few years, for any number of reasons, Pratt could have let the Bill of Rights go. He was traveling a lot for *Antiques Roadshow* and had a thriving business. The parchment was far outside his field of expertise, and the road to resale was potentially pocked with land mines.

Still, he couldn't let go. Pratt liked great things and appreciated the parchment's significance. The furniture and the Bill of Rights were set pieces; together they represented a triumphal bridging of the same fascinating era.

But on a more prosaic, bottom-line level—always a factor for

Pratt—the parchment was exactly what he sought in an antique. Pratt constantly hunted for "the $20,000 difference"—a reference to the profit he hoped to net with any given object.

Antiques dealers are often ruled by emotion. But because of the way Pratt operated—he built a kind of extended family of clients who sold stuff back to him—he could be reptilian in his ability to analyze an antique only in terms of its ledger-book significance.

He once bought a Windsor chair he had coveted for years—one of the best he'd seen. This one, he announced, he was going to keep. But then a client came along and swooned over it, and the chair was gone within a week. His sister, Cindy Pratt-Stokes, owns a small Persian rug business in Kansas City, but compared to her brother she thinks of herself as a collector. "I have trouble letting things go," she said. "Wayne didn't have trouble selling anything."

Still, Pratt was discerning. He didn't like volatile investments. He avoided Shaker rocking chairs and painted furniture, for example, because he believed they were collectibles. "The thing with collectibles, they might increase in value for years and years, and then the floor drops out," he said. "They can suddenly drop in price. Antiques will steadily rise in value. They'll actually go up 2 percent higher per year than the return on a good stock."

Pratt pursued his antiques of choice with great vigor. "Wayne created many markets—Windsor chairs, block-front chests, Nantucket baskets," said Ron Bourgeault, the antiques dealer who became owner of Northeast Auctions. "One could compare him to a Wall Street trader creating markets."

The way this works is simple. Say you owned a Windsor chair when they were relatively unfashionable, and it was appraised at $1,000. Then Wayne Pratt began appearing at auctions, bidding aggressively on Windsor chairs, buying them for twice what anyone had paid before. He began lecturing about their historical merits, displaying them prominently in his stores, talking them up to customers who trusted his tastes. Before long that same chair might be worth $5,000.

The Bill of Rights? That would never decrease in value. The market for historic manuscripts had climbed steadily upward—and, as with great furniture, there had been a marked spike in prices for iconic pieces. The parchment had the $20,000 difference. Maybe even the $2 million difference.

So the entrepreneur in Pratt couldn't let go. Neither could the thrill seeker. "When you're in the antiques world, your life is about a treasure hunt," said David Schorsch, Pratt's friend and neighbor. "And there is a physiological reaction that happens when I encounter something great. I describe it as something that people experience at casinos. I think runners experience it. There's a sexual feeling that you can equate to it. You get butterflies in your stomach, and your heart goes faster, and that's what we go for, it's what we want.

"The items that have that mojo, that magic quality, sell the fastest. We want that piece that's so exciting and wonderful that a client walks up and says, 'Oh, I've *gotta* have that.' Obviously, that Bill of Rights was an object like that."

For Pratt, the prize was too great to ignore. "As a dealer, you want to sell it, or you want to own it," Pratt said. "That's just the way I am. I can't see something like that and not want to get involved."

After consulting Richardson, Pratt finally decided after a few weeks to go ahead with the purchase. In early June the lawyers consummated the transaction. Reeder signed on June 6. Richardson scribbled his signature on Pratt's behalf six days later.

More than five years after Wayne Pratt had first heard of the Bill of Rights, the deal was finally done.

Just a couple of weeks after Pratt finalized the purchase, something huge happened: The $4 Dunlap Declaration of Independence re-emerged. The prize hidden behind a junk picture frame in Adamstown, Pennsylvania, had electrified the antiquities community in 1991. Its owners, Visual Equities of Atlanta, had tried to sell in 1993 but had failed.

Much had changed by the year 2000. The Internet had come into widespread use, sparking a dot-com gold rush that had not yet gone bust. More importantly, Sotheby's latest auction had attracted two very wealthy and very determined bidders. New York–area dealer Seth Kaller was still trying to land a Declaration of Independence for his biggest clients, Richard Gilder and Lewis Lehrman, co-owners of what was becoming a landmark collection of historic documents.

Kaller's adversaries were Norman Lear, the creator of classic TV shows such as *All in the Family* and *Maude,* and his business partner, Internet entrepreneur David Hayden, the founder of a messaging service called Critical Path and cofounder of the company that created a search engine called Magellan.

The teams of heavyweights came out slugging. Lear and Hayden placed an initial bid of $4 million—an astounding opening salvo, given that the last time the Declaration had appeared on the auction block it failed to hit the reserve of $1.8 million. If there had been witnesses on hand, there likely would have been a gasp or two.

But there was no audience. Sotheby's had tried to drum up extra interest by holding the sale on the Internet—which in theory sounded like a hip, savvy bit of marketing gimmickry by the stodgy auction house. In practice, the concept proved to be a dud. Bidders had all day—until 5:00 p.m.—to up the ante. Kaller waited what seemed an ice age, two and a half hours, to answer with a $4.1 million bid. The two bidders, leery of connection problems, had posted agents at computers inside the auction house, further eroding the virtual-auction conceit. Lear and Hayden waited another two hours to bump their offer up by $100,000.

Each side held out for a last big push. At 4:57 p.m., three minutes before the auction's scheduled finish, Lear and Hayden raised their bid to $4.6 million. With fifty-two seconds left, Kaller jumped to $5.1 million.

The hammer would have dropped there, with Kaller the winner, had Sotheby's not created a set of Internet-only rules. The new policy specified the sale would end only after ten minutes passed without a bid, as a hedge against technological glitches. For the next forty-seven minutes, the two sides volleyed furiously, entering twenty-two more bids, until Lear and Hayden finally prevailed with a winning bid of $7.4 million. With Sotheby's 10 percent commission, the price tag grew to $8.14 million—by far an all-time high for any historical document.

"We had thought we would stop at six because we saw no possibility of its going past six," Lear told the *New York Times*. "How to explain it? There is no price on liberty. You've got to take a pill on this, but nonetheless that's the way we were feeling."

For Wayne Pratt, the auction's implications were staggering. He did the math: Twenty-four existing copies of the Dunlap Declaration, four in private hands, and one of them sells for $8.14 million. By contrast, only fourteen originals of the Bill of Rights ever existed, and probably twelve remained. Only one was privately owned: the copy in the New York Public Library. The last publicized sale of a Bill of Rights took place in the 1940s—and the buyer donated it to the Library of Congress.

There's no price on liberty? In Pratt's world, everything had a price. That's what Pratt was about—assigning value to greatness. Given the Bill of Rights' significance and scarcity, it didn't seem unreasonable to think the parchment might be the greatest single investment Pratt had ever made.

Never mind that the Dunlap Declaration had no provenance issues attached, or that it happened to attract two motivated buyers at once, or that Pratt—because of his artifact's title issues—might be unable to stage such a bidding war. To him, the sale possibilities were boundless.

Fifteen million dollars?

Twenty?

He thought that was not unreasonable, not unreasonable at all.

Wayne Pratt's style was folksy and informal. In a culture loaded with gossipy high-society mavens, nouveau-riche showoffs, and snooty dealers, Pratt was earthy—a beer-and-barbecue barbarian in the land of canapés and Château Pétrus. Even after seven years in Connecticut, he was more blue-collar Boston than fancy Litchfield County weekender. His idea of a fine evening was to invite a clutch of friends and clients to hang out through closing time so that he could author various scenes of blue-collar bohemia. Pratt opened wine, passed around glasses, and cut loose with uproarious, NC-17-rated stories, a Boston Red Sox game playing in the background.

Pratt was fanatical about the Red Sox and the New England Patriots, and he loved to talk sports. A decent high school athlete—he played football and ran track—he waged weekly racquetball battles with Jerry Conway, a building contractor turned client and friend. The two men also kayaked together on the nearby Shepaug River.

Pratt built a brand on this Everyman precept—to the point that he eventually added decorative services and period reproductions to his stores. Customers priced out of a $75,000 Windsor chair could buy a replica Wayne Pratt Antiques chair for $1,500.

To the antiques world's froufrou purists, this was not only unforgivably déclassé—it was heresy. "People were outraged," David Schorsch said. "They thought he was blurring the lines. There's a real snobbishness out there that says you should buy your reproductions at a reproduction store and your antiques at an antiques store, and heaven forbid they're under the same roof. But you're only blurring the lines if you're misrepresenting things. To me, Wayne saw a trend and fulfilled a need."

Antiques dealers can be stodgy. "People don't think outside the box, and then someone comes along and changes the model," Schorsch said. "No one likes change, but it's good business. And now he's got a thicker slice of the cake. Folks come by the busload, and they always come out carrying a bag. Maybe they only spent $50, but next time they come back they're comfortable because they bought something."

Schorsch was first struck by Pratt's average-guy élan thirty years ago, when he was a boy buying and selling antiques with his mother. The Schorsches met Pratt at a show in New Haven in the mid-1970s, when Pratt had Windsor chairs that David loved.

"We were initially drawn to the material, because we're first and foremost object people," said Schorsch, a smallish man with short blond hair and a broad smile. He sat in his store's front room with his tiny dog, Spotty, curled up next to him. "But Wayne is entertaining and warm and personable, and he and I and my mother just clicked. He's a likable guy. There are people in the business who are uptight assholes, and people in the business who you want to have a drink with and hang out with. Wayne's a guy people like to hang out with. And you can't overestimate the power of personality in sales."

During the second half of 2000, Pratt got clients and friends feeling comfortable and then led them up to his attic office to show off the Bill of Rights, which he kept laid out on a Regency desk. He pointed to the signatures at the bottom—John Adams and Frederick Augustus Muhlenberg—and explained how the first two amendments didn't fly, but the others were as you see them in the history books. Pratt watched his friends' reactions—the low whistles and smiles, the questions: *This thing is real? And it's an original?*

Eventually Pratt asked his clients if they knew anyone who knew anyone. As the months passed, he showed the parchment to about a hundred of his best customers. But no one offered any hot leads, and Pratt whiffed with all the big names he'd thought up. He now fully grasped that the manuscript was not the kind of low-overhead, quick-flip deal that he and Richardson had contemplated early on.

One limiting factor was the promise to the Shotwells to land the document in a museum or library. One client made noises about buying it for his own collection, but Pratt said he told all prospective buyers that the broadsheet couldn't just end up inside a safe. "I've made a lot of money in this business by keeping verbal agreements with people," Pratt said, "and it's always come back to benefit me. If you mess that up, somehow that's the one time it gets told to fifty people."

Despite this initial dry spell, Pratt avoided letting Bob Matthews get involved in selling the manuscript. Pratt was the expert; he did the buying and selling. Matthews was the investor. In fact, Matthews, after seeing the Bill of Rights twice in Indianapolis, had viewed the document only once more, after the conservation work had been done. Pratt had called him up to the attic to see their investment and show him the docketing.

Pratt once had a conversation about the manuscript with an executive in Matthews's firm. "Just never let him have it, because he'll run it down the road and sell it to anybody," the executive had told Pratt. The antiques dealer was fond of his friend, but he had no intention of letting him anywhere near the Bill of Rights.

The calendar turned to 2001, and a few months went by, and then a few more, the document still sitting on the Regency desk, drawing appreciative audiences but no buyers. As 2002 approached, Pratt decided the time had come to expand the pool of potential clients. It was time to recruit another dealer with an untapped pool of moneyed patrons.

And the North Carolina problem?

He and John Richardson had seen the docketing, and as far as they were concerned there was no North Carolina problem. The nothing document had become an anywhere artifact.

Plus, Pratt and Richardson had swept away the trail of bread crumbs when they finalized the deal with the Indiana family. Both the antiques dealer and the Shotwell sisters had signed a confidentiality agreement. The pact forbade the family from revealing their history with the Bill of Rights.

Pratt, in turn, was legally bound to keep the Shotwell family name a secret. And if no one knew the Shotwell name, there were no signposts pointing toward Raleigh.

Pratt had effectively sealed the document off from its history.

Or so he believed.

9

The Art Dealer

P ETER TILLOU WAS MANNING his booth at the 2002 Winter Antiques Show in New York City when Wayne Pratt emerged from the swirling crowd. Tillou knew Pratt. As a renowned dealer of antiquities and art up in Litchfield, Connecticut, he and Pratt worked in overlapping fields.

Still, it was unusual for Pratt to seek Tillou out—particularly with something that seemed urgent. Did Tillou have a minute to talk privately about something important? Pratt wanted to know.

Tillou did. When they found a private spot, Pratt leaned in. We have the greatest find ever, he said: an original manuscript of the Bill of Rights.

Tillou stared back, incredulous.

Pratt nodded.

Did Tillou know that a copy of the Declaration of Independence just sold at Sotheby's for $8 million? He did. Everyone knew that. This Bill of Rights had a remarkably similar background, Pratt told him. The people running a shop in upstate New York—some kind of hybrid hardware and antiques store—had found it on a back wall, hanging behind a painting, Pratt said. Fortunately, Pratt had learned of it first.

That Declaration, worth $8 million? This document was even rarer. The piece was easily worth $10 million, maybe $20 million, Pratt said.

Pratt already had things moving forward; he had a great attorney, a Washington lawyer named John Richardson, working on it. Did Tillou know that Richardson's wife was the former head of the IRS under Clinton? Tillou did not.

They just needed one more team member—someone with great connections to major buyers. Someone just like Peter Tillou. Any chance, Pratt wondered, you'd be interested in getting in on this? For the standard 20 percent commission, of course.

The Winter Antiques Show was the ideal setting for Pratt to make his pitch. Dealers spend the entire year accumulating objects to roll out every January in Manhattan. Only the top North American and European dealers are invited to exhibit. Roughly the same seventy-five or so merchants occupy the same places on the floor, year in and year out, competing for customers and buzz. The 2002 show was no different—even though that particular installment could have been a major comedown. That show was held at the Hilton because the usual site, the Seventh Regiment Armory, had been mobilized after the September 11 terrorist attacks only four months earlier.

Despite the aura of vulnerability and the tighter, unfamiliar confines, the show was nearly as electric as ever. Martha Stewart was on hand, and Mayor Michael Bloomberg purchased a New York militia flag from 1820 for $45,000. Pratt sold a Boston inlaid serpentine-front chest; his friend David Schorsch, invited for the first time, moved a Jacob Maentel watercolor portrait for $465,000. The show's priciest item was a Hellenistic hollow-cast bronze male nude, perhaps Poseidon, about three-quarters human size, for which Rupert Wace Ancient Art asked $4 million.

Tillou was right at home there and had been for many years. Two years earlier he'd created a major stir when he displayed a colossal six-by-nine-foot oil painting titled *The Crows Attempting to Provoke an Attack from the Whites on the Big Horn River, East of the Rocky Mountains.* The piece had hung undisturbed, and mostly unseen, in a baronial Scottish castle since artist Alfred Jacob Miller finished it in 1841. It had never been published or photographed before Tillou staged "its debut in America." The price: $8.5 million. The rest of Tillou's booth that year was typically eclectic: a Flemish painting circa 1630, a Goa sea chest, a rosewood and ebony wed-

ding box inlaid with bone from Germany, African and pre-Columbian sculptures, a Connecticut table, and so on. Tillou again demonstrated that "objects of quality from any time or place can work
together," *Maine Antiques Digest* noted.

If ever a Bill of Rights were to seem in context, it was at the
Winter Antiques Show. And Tillou was intrigued. Pratt's pitch was
compelling enough, and anytime a colleague starts talking about
$20 million, people stop to listen.

Pratt soon brought John Richardson over to meet Tillou, and
the attorney reiterated how exciting it all was, how remarkable the
find. Tillou would have to keep all of this strictly confidential, Pratt
said—except, obviously, to prospective buyers.

As the show wrapped up, Tillou anticipated driving over to Pratt's
store in Woodbury to learn more. But as he headed back north, a
question kept bouncing through his head: *Why me?*

Like David Schorsch and many other elite dealers, Peter Tillou was
something of a child prodigy. Growing up in Buffalo, he began collecting old coins at the age of eight, and the more he roamed the
city's shops and alleys, haunting the Salvation Army and Goodwill,
the more his collections and interests ballooned. The thrift stores
were "absolute gold mines," Tillou said. His mother, a well-known
portrait artist, took him on trips to study art in the Albright-Knox
Museum and drove him around on his hunts for old things.

At age twelve Tillou grew fascinated with antique arms and armor. He coveted a sword in Sal Licata's downtown pawnshop. Rum-
maging around the family attic for something to trade, he found a
violin. Only after the transaction took place did he learn his mother
had played the instrument as a child. She dispatched him to Licata's
to retrieve the prized violin, but by that time someone had already
snapped it up.

That incident left Tillou chastened but no less enthused about
the trade. At age fourteen he began traveling to shows, selling out of
booths rented by his uncle, a paleontologist who also dealt in antiquities. By the time Tillou enrolled at Ohio Wesleyan University, he
was buzzing around the entire Northeast, exhibiting at shows and

peddling antiques out of the trunk of his car. He took breaks from college classes for buying expeditions in Europe.

He developed a vast array of specialties: European and American arms and armor, Native American art, American blown glass, classic cars from the 1930s, American and European furniture, Old Master and nineteenth-century paintings, European and American medals, African and pre-Columbian art, and silver, pottery, and porcelain. But his greatest passion was art. Beginning in the 1950s, Tillou championed American folk art long before such paintings were recognized as important and valuable, helping to discover many early artists whose works are now widely celebrated.

Tillou owned galleries at various points in New York City, Florida, and London. When the *Robb Report* compiled a "best of the best" list, Tillou was among the antiques dealers profiled. He served on the board of directors and vetting committee for the venerable European Fine Art Fair, one of the world's leading shows, in the Netherlands and collected on behalf of the National Gallery of Art. He sold to some of the world's top collectors and was a developmental force behind one of the world's great collections of seventeenth-century still lifes.

Tillou naturally tilted toward the iconic. He attributed his success to one basic principle: Get the best of everything. He purchased objects solely on merit. Quality of material, originality of condition, and historical significance—they were all more important than a prominent name or stout price tag. He instructed his clients: Figure out how much you have to spend. And then, instead of buying three good objects, buy one great one.

Tillou and Wayne Pratt could have been buddies. They were expert folk art dealers who lived less than a half-hour apart.

But they rarely socialized. Beyond antiques and art, they had vastly different styles. Tillou, small-boned and jug-eared in his sixties, wore clothes with argyle prints and cardigan sweaters and spoke in a cultured and crisply enunciated baritone. His large salt-and-pepper eyebrows dominated the craggy oval of his face.

Tillou's and Pratt's adopted hometowns reflected their divergent sensibilities. Tillou lived and worked in Litchfield, a rustic-chic Connecticut town where entrenched Yankee wealth mingled with weekenders from Manhattan and the occasional Hollywood or television star. Tourists strolled past historic million-dollar homes to patronize upscale shops lining the vast town green. Woodbury, for all its upscale antiquing, had more of a proletarian vibe. After the antiques shops, its most celebrated attraction was the doughnuts at Phillips Diner.

Pratt attracted earthy, self-made entrepreneurial types: people like him. Tillou's client list included Teresa Heinz Kerry, wife of Massachusetts Senator John Kerry and collector of seventeenth-century Dutch still life pictures. Heinz Kerry and Tillou were close. In the mid-1990s they split the $2 million asking price for a seventeenth-century Dutch masterpiece by Adam Willaerts. "She and I bought it in London about 10 years ago," Tillou later recounted to the *Boston Globe*. "We're very good friends, and she said, 'Peter, let's buy it together.' It was an investment for her."

Tillou showed the painting at exhibitions. When he sold it for $2.7 million almost a decade later, to a dealer he declined to identify, Tillou and Heinz Kerry shared the profit.

Secrecy is a common and widely accepted part of the business of old things. It is axiomatic that if you don't keep your sources to yourself, competitors will swoop in and engage them. In 1998 Pratt paid $308,000 for a Boston Queen Anne mahogany card table with turret-shaped corners. The auctioneer, Carl R. Nordblom, told the *Boston Herald* that the table was "to die for"—but wouldn't reveal where it came from, saying that he would take the secret to his grave.

So Pratt's decision to equivocate about the origins of the Bill of Rights—even with another dealer—was not entirely surprising. Pratt came up through a culture in which half-truths and tall tales were the norm. In *Objects of Desire*, Thatcher Freund vividly describes Pratt's mentor, John Walton, as an unscrupulous, intimidating, "cigar-chomping pit bull of a man" who reveled in cheating his friends. Pratt "dreamed of being like Walton," Freund wrote.

Indeed, the business of old and valuable objects is nowhere near as genteel and amiable as it looks on *Antiques Roadshow*. Wayne Mattox, a midlevel Woodbury dealer who writes a weekly online column called "Antique Talk," said that sleight of hand is fairly commonplace. Say, for example, that a highboy that has undergone a few minor repairs generates little interest in the marketplace. If that hypothetical highboy disappeared into a storehouse for a dozen years and then was brought out and introduced anew, complete with a fanciful tale about its discovery in some anonymous attic—that could increase its value.

"It's something that happens in the antiques business," Mattox said. "People tend to make up stories a little bit about where things came from. People tend to play lots of shell games with provenance."

Mattox attributed this culture of prevarication to the same market forces that have corrupted manuscript collecting: Everyone wants the best and greatest stuff. "The American field has gotten so stuffy, so uppity, about its quote-unquote standards," Mattox said. "It's gotten to the point now where, anything with the slightest blemish on it, people say, 'I wouldn't deal with that.' If a piece has a repaired foot, it's, 'Why would you deal with a repaired foot? I would never touch that.' They'd want to break it over your head.

"But you know what's happened? There are a lot of fakes now because it's so hard to find stuff in the condition people want it to be in."

In May 2008 Dennis Buggins accused John Hobbs, a London-based antiques dealer known for his ultra-exclusive American clientele and stunningly high prices, of selling bogus pieces. Buggins had compelling evidence: He had been restoring pieces for Hobbs for twenty-one years and had designed and fabricated some of the objects Hobbs was selling as six-figure antiques. If true, the *New York Times* asserted, Hobbs was guilty of "deception and audacity on an extraordinary scale."

People of Hobbs's standing are increasingly trying to live up to impossible standards, Mattox said. "The business Pratt is in is really a nasty business right now," Mattox said, "and it shouldn't be."

Others contend that the criticism Pratt and his peers sometimes faced was undeserved. David Schorsch, Pratt's friend and fellow dealer, said accusations of dishonesty in the antiques business have to be examined for subtext and motive.

"I'll tell you a story," he said, curled up one day on a sofa in his shop. "Wayne had a block-front chest at the New York show, nice little chest. And he had [a price of] $125,000 on it. These chests sell from $65,000 to $400,000, so at 125 it's not the Ferrari, it's the BMW. Guy comes in, looks at the chest. It's vetted, there's a report on it, what's been done to it. It had come from Israel Sack, and before that it had come from the Morris collection. Guy negotiates, Wayne sells it to him for something like $100,000. Sometime later, this guy is doing some research and he finds an auction catalog from two years before, when Wayne bought the chest, and Wayne had paid $55,000.

"Wayne didn't tell him he bought it at this auction. The guy didn't ask him where he bought it; [Pratt] didn't lie about it. But this guy was angry because he thought *he* could have gone to that auction and bought it for $55,000. Long story short, he called up Wayne and threatened him. Wayne said, 'I'll buy it back, I'm happy to have it back, no problem.' So he gave the guy his money back, but it was ultimately about nothing. Wayne's business is buying and selling, and he had intelligence to buy it, he knew the right conservator to take it to, to make sure it was done properly, and he put it in his inventory for two years, and sold it.

"There's people in every business who like you and people who hate you. There are people that think I'm great, and people who hate my guts. And I guarantee you there are people out there who don't like Wayne."

But with the Bill of Rights, Pratt demonstrated a talent for filleting the truth, removing the innards, and repackaging it as whole. He maintained that he hadn't been untruthful with Tillou. He explained that he was merely repeating a variation on the story he'd heard from a member of the Shotwell clan: Charles Shotwell bought the document in upstate New York while working as a traveling salesman. Pratt said he believed that tale and thus had no reason to put any stock in the North Carolina version.

• • •

Still, the potential historical link to North Carolina would have been part of any responsible sales pitch. Pratt's selective retelling of the parchment's backstory was at odds with the ethics code of the Manuscript Society, which in 1978 published *Autographs and Manuscripts: A Collector's Manual*. In a chapter on ethics, John F. Reed wrote: "In purchasing, although the age-old theory of caveat emptor may possibly hold true under certain remote circumstances (such as carelessness by the purchaser rather than his ignorance), the vendor should nevertheless exhibit at all times the honesty expected of him. If he does not, and a trespass on honesty is publicly exposed, the vendor risks perpetual ostracism by the trade; once a reputation is lost, it cannot easily, if ever, be recovered."

There was good reason to try to codify industry practices: Secrecy and obfuscation had long been commonplace in the document world. Even today, bidders at manuscript auctions often don't know whom they're buying from, much less a manuscript's provenance. Catalog copy often seems oddly evasive. Rather than name a seller, auction houses often reveal nothing more than "property of a gentleman."

This don't-ask, don't-tell ethic has endured for generations. A.S.W. Rosenbach, the nonpareil rare-books and manuscripts seller of the early 1900s, once wrote that during Oscar Wilde's renowned trial, someone burgled the author's London home and stole numerous documents and letters. Rosenbach's brother Philip, who was also his business partner, later entered a celebrated London bookshop looking for Wilde material. A staffer led him into a back room, closed the door, and showed him original drafts of three Wilde plays.

"The bookseller behaved as though the room contained contraband," Rosenbach wrote. "It was obvious that the sooner he got those manuscripts out of his shop, the better he would feel. So my brother bought them immediately, believing that a man's conduct has nothing to do with his genius."

The manuscripts undoubtedly hurtled through the marketplace with no explanation of how they'd become available for sale.

Pratt's explanation of the Bill of Rights' origins was a spinoff of what's known in the business as "dead man's provenance"—that is:

No one knows where a particular document came from, because all of its previous owners have expired. And dead men can't talk.

Peter Tillou wasn't considering any of these potential pitfalls when, one cold day not long after the Winter Antiques Show, he drove the seventeen miles south from Litchfield to Woodbury. Pratt had called not long after the show, wanting to get together. Tillou still felt odd about being recruited to broker the Bill of Rights. He wasn't a document dealer and had rarely collaborated with Pratt before, and now they were going to handle one of the three most important documents in United States history.

Tillou tried to push those niggling thoughts aside. He would see the document first and figure the rest out later. For now, the math was pretty simple: Twenty percent of $20 million was $4 million.

In Woodbury, Pratt brought Tillou up to his attic office and showed him the parchment. Tillou was stunned by the size of the broadsheet. And the handwriting was spectacular. Pratt explained that a number of copies had been missing from official custody for longer than they'd been alive, but there was no way to know where this particular parchment came from. The marking on the backside was an alluring clue that turned out to be a dead end.

Pratt wanted Tillou to sign an agreement that spelled out the terms of their partnership and set parameters for a sale, but Tillou preferred not to; he wanted to ask around first. Let's keep things at a handshake until I find out if anyone's interested, Tillou said.

Then Pratt asked about Teresa Heinz Kerry. *So,* Tillou thought, *I should've known.* He had many wealthy, philanthropy-minded clients, but Pratt's interest in the ketchup heiress made sense, given her wealth and intimate connection to American politics.

Elite buyers rarely walk into auction houses and start bidding. People such as Heinz Kerry use brokers, who serve several functions: They provide expertise and credibility. They negotiate. And they often learn about new objects in the pipeline before they show up on an auction block. If you wanted to sell something to Teresa Heinz Kerry, you wouldn't look up the number for the Kerry residence in Boston. You would call Peter Tillou.

Pratt reiterated that confidentiality was paramount. Tillou promised to remain mum even around his son, Jeffrey, also a Litchfield-based antiques dealer. Then he drove the Bill of Rights home. Among dealers at their level, there is an extraordinary amount of trust. Pratt knew how many treasures Tillou already had in his house, a stately, multimillion-dollar white colonial house within walking distance of the Litchfield Green. At any given time Tillou might have pottery from the Tang Dynasty, three-hundred-year-old European portraiture, folk art paintings worth six figures. Tillou saw clients by appointment, so it wasn't as if the general public trundled in and out of the place. Pratt knew the parchment would be protected.

Tillou not only needed to safeguard the document; he needed to keep it hidden. When he returned to Litchfield, he carried the document upstairs to his bedroom and slipped the prized parchment under his bed.

Part of what made Tillou such a talented dealer was his unselfconscious, boyish enthusiasm for old things. He tended to have emotional reactions to objects—so much so that he didn't care if certain pieces never found customers. "When it doesn't sell," he said, "it's our soul food."

These emotive tendencies caused him to do what some might judge irrational. He once doubled the highest price ever paid for a piece of folk art with which he'd become smitten. "Given my emotional reaction to this treasure," he recounted of that transaction, "I felt at that moment as if I would have paid any price."

Having great things around made him feel more alive. "We're all keepers of things in life," he said. "I am very conscious of the thrills I have, and I want them passed on. And yes, it's my business. I make money off it. That's all part and parcel of the joy of it."

That was how he felt about the Bill of Rights. The document struck people differently. David Schorsch, who like Tillou had physiological reactions to objects he loved, was underwhelmed. "I saw it when Wayne got it," Schorsch said, "and it was an unimpressive object—so faded you could hardly read it."

Not Tillou. He felt the same electric sensations with the Bill of

Rights that he felt around a great painting. During the months he possessed the parchment, he often fetched it from its hiding place. "I would get it out," he said, "and just love it." He studied the signatures and amendments at length, focusing on the faded sections, trying to fill in the lines in his head.

"Probably one of the biggest thrills of my whole career was being able to have that document next to me," Tillou said. "I wanted to know all about it. I wanted to learn all about the signers. The tactileness of the document in your hands—just being the keeper for a moment. That was part of the lure, was, 'Oh, my God, I'm going to be able to handle this thing.'"

Tillou knew that certain objects came saddled with provenance problems. People in the business gossiped incessantly about who was suing whom over which painting. As much as the document thrilled him, Tillou didn't really know what to make of the thing as a commodity. He was, as he put it, "in way over my head."

So he called someone he trusted—a friend with formidable expertise in antiquities. "Listen," Tillou said. "I think I've got a Bill of Rights."

"Peter, fantastic," the friend replied. "But be careful."

10

The Bookseller

WHEN PETER TILLOU LAID the parchment on his desk, Bill Reese knew immediately that it was real. As a long-time dealer in rare books and historic manuscripts, Reese had examined the handwriting of John Adams and his compatriots countless times, and the signatures looked dead-on. The fact that the Bill of Rights was on parchment—that was telling, too. Only on rare occasions, for something of great consequence, did a document of those dimensions wind up on parchment. Reese and Tillou were sitting in Reese's second-floor office in New Haven one February afternoon. "It looks awfully good to me, Peter," Reese said.

Reese wondered where in the world such a treasure could have come from. In thirty years in the business, Reese had never seen or heard of a Bill of Rights for sale—just the occasional rumor, quickly dismissed as spurious. Tillou repeated the story Wayne Pratt had told him, about the titillating discovery behind a painting in upstate New York—omitting Pratt's identity, as he'd promised to do. Tillou didn't know anything more, except that he was obligated to get the document into a museum or institution.

To Reese, the story sounded plausible. But he would need to learn more. "A lie can get halfway around the world," Mark Twain once observed, "before the truth can even get its boots on." Reese had heard plenty of hard-charging tall tales.

Reese was fairly sure that a handful of the original thirteen states were missing copies, so the provenance question was critical. "Before anything happens," Reese told him, "we have to find out whether this really doesn't belong anywhere else."

In Reese, the parchment had finally arrived in front of a dealer who could fully comprehend its magnitude and uncommonness. He had started selling Americana while a student at Yale. The William Reese Company, created not long after he graduated, dealt in preeminent printed and written early American material—rare books, manuscripts, pamphlets, broadsides—ranging in scope from the earliest expeditions of Columbus to the end of the exploration era in twentieth-century Alaska. Reese also bought and sold great works of natural history, color-plate books, maps, and American and English literature. Nicholas Basbanes, author of *A Gentle Madness* and other books about the book trade, described Reese as "the world's leading dealer in Americana." Lou Weinstein, owner of Heritage Books in Los Angeles, once called him "without question the American bookseller of his generation."

Reese's 250th catalog featured twenty-five of the most sublime items he owned. Among them were a copy of the first run of the Monroe Doctrine, in 1823; a book in Latin called *De Moluccis Insulis*—the first printed account of Magellan's circumnavigation of the planet, published in Cologne, Italy, in 1523; one of three remaining copies of an inaugural printing of the Gettysburg Address, issued three days after Lincoln's speech; and a Ptolemy atlas from 1513. At the 2007 Antiquarian Book Fair in New York City—the biggest event of its kind—Reese occupied booth A1. That assignment was no coincidence.

His business inhabited two adjacent townhouses on Temple Street in New Haven. Reese had a wall fourteen feet long and ten feet high of Americana reference books alone. He operated by appointment; there was no placard identifying his presence in the buildings. His inventory of forty thousand items took up two miles of shelving—eventually forcing an expansion into a nearby warehouse. Internet sales accounted for about half his invoices, but only about 7 percent of his revenue. The vast preponderance of his business, income-wise, came from working with clients who could afford to invest in his best finds.

Reese was in his late forties, though he looked younger. He had thick glasses and a tumble of McCartney-esque hair that dangled haphazardly over large ears. His deep, resonant, basso profundo voice accentuated his fluid storytelling skills. He would have been a shoo-in for an NPR gig if not for his other talents. His laughter exploded like a thunderclap.

Even as a young man, Reese seemed unusually focused. At Yale, Reese walked into the six-story-high rare-book library to introduce himself the first day of his freshman year. "The thing about him is that he has an astounding memory, and he just devours knowledge," his mentor, Archibald Hanna, curator of the school's collection of western Americana, recalled in Basbanes's book *Patience and Fortitude*.

Hanna put Reese in contact with booksellers, including Peter Decker, a respected authority on Americana who brought Reese along on scouting trips. During Reese's sophomore year one of Decker's most prodigious collectors died. The customer had left his books to a cousin, who had no interest in the material and who immediately put it up for sale for $40,000.

Reese accompanied Decker to look at the collection. Even a relative novice could see that the client had left behind an astoundingly valuable cache of George Armstrong Custer items, Civil War material, Native American stuff. "So what happened is this," Reese recalled. "Peter looked at me and said, 'This is an incredible deal, but I'm eighty-two years old, and I don't want to mess with it. You should buy it.'" Reese called his parents and asked to borrow the money. Soon after, he hauled away twenty tons of books. Selling the volumes out of his dorm room, he paid his parents back within six months and still had most of the collection left. And at age nineteen, Reese knew exactly what he would do with the rest of his life.

He had the hungry, absorbent mind of a born historian. Reese riffed spontaneously on the motives and agendas of the United States' first politicians—and not just the marquee names, but also men like Edmund Pendleton, a Virginia patriot who maintained for years what Reese described as "a wonderful series of correspondence" with James Madison. One of the aspects of the job that excited Reese most was finding heretofore unknown letters that expanded the breadth of historical knowledge.

Before Peter Tillou showed up with the Bill of Rights, Reese had heard fresh rumblings about an original entering the marketplace. He was highly dubious. "I was frankly pretty dismissive of it," he recalled. "I thought it was somebody thinking they had something they didn't have.

"People come to me all the time with things that are wrong," Reese said. ("Wrong" is bookseller-speak for an item that is counterfeit or otherwise not what it appears to be. With an authentic document, on the other hand, Reese might say, "I knew instantly that letter was right.") "The number of people I've gently informed their Declaration of Independence is not the real thing, it's probably in the hundreds—especially after real copies of the Declaration have come up"—particularly the $4 flea-market copy.

Poorly kept secrets—often involving objects that turned out to be wrong—are an inescapable element of the trade. "At one New York Book Fair years ago," Reese once wrote in his droll insider column for the *Rare Book Review,* "no less than four booksellers took me to one side and, after swearing me to secrecy, proposed we jointly buy a great bargain (I was to do all the work and sell it) which they knew to be on the floor of the fair hidden under a table. I had been shown the item in the first hour of the set-up and had turned it down, but it was nice to be so broadly confided in."

Reese lowered his guard, though, upon hearing about the Bill of Rights from Tillou, whom he deeply respected. The two men had met in the 1970s, when Tillou was frequently purchasing estates and often wound up in possession of old books he knew nothing about. He asked around and was told to call Bill Reese in New Haven.

"Usually," Tillou said, "what I thought was absolutely marvelous, Bill would say, 'Oh, yes, Peter, that's the second edition, so, $250.'

"I'd say, 'Oh, no, that's $1,000.' And he would say, 'Well, this isn't the right edition for that price.'" And then Reese would kindly but unassailably explain why the book was a $250 book. "That," Tillou said, chuckling, "is how I got to know him."

Tillou called Reese every time he wound up with old books or manuscripts, and eventually they invested in other projects together. Reese purchased a number of paintings and some furniture from Tillou. Reese was a generation younger, but over the course of all those deals they became close friends.

Twenty million dollars. That, Tillou said, was the asking price his source had been throwing around for the Bill of Rights. Reese scoffed. "That's crazy," he said. "No one's going to give you $20 million. Forget about it."

A more realistic price might be $5 million to $7 million, Reese said. But before they could talk money, they had to unravel the mystery of the document's history. More to the point: They had to divine whether the parchment could be linked to any of the states that were missing their copies—"in which case," Reese said, "we want nothing to do with it."

Reese had learned to be wary. Every significant dealer in historic documents and letters has at some point been fooled or burned or threatened with a lawsuit or actually sued, or all of the above. Hanging just inside the door of Reese's office was an original copy of the Texas Declaration of Independence, from 1836. Or that was what it appeared to be. Reese had purchased it in 1975, when he was twenty, and sold it to a collector, thinking it one of the great scores of his nascent career.

Thirteen years later he was in Texas having lunch with fellow dealer Tom Taylor when Taylor described uncovering a series of counterfeit Texas papers. It seemed that a prominent dealer had been printing remarkably authentic fakes—including knockoffs of the state's famed Declaration of Independence. "It was one of those moments of blinding horror," Reese recalled with a laugh. "Suddenly my enchilada didn't taste very good."

Reese instantly knew he'd handled one of the fakes. Reese told Taylor of his suspicions, and when he returned home he got in touch with his client. Once Taylor confirmed the document was indeed counterfeit, Reese took it back from his customer, who accepted store credit in return. The bogus declaration now serves as a

permanent *aide-mémoire* of the trapdoors and tripwires of his livelihood.

The reality, though, was that sometimes vigilance doesn't help.
On numerous occasions Reese had purchased materials at public
auctions, then listed the items in his catalogs—only to hear from,
say, an archivist in New Jersey that he was peddling state property,
and could he please immediately return it to Trenton? Reese tried
to avoid items of dubious provenance, but often there was little time
to do any sleuthing beforehand. Sometimes he bought boxes of papers en masse and only later realized what he had.

With the Bill of Rights there could be no such confusion. Reese
hoped that maybe the parchment was a previously unidentified extra—a version above and beyond the known fourteen that wasn't the
property of any sovereign. Reese thought it was possible a copy was
made for one of the signers: Adams, Frederick Augustus Muhlenberg, or John Beckley, clerk of the House. Reese knew that Congress had required the secretary of state to sign and certify each bill
it passed and send copies to each state—and that often there were
extras. "Those are not that uncommon," Reese said. "They're scarce,
but a couple show up every year."

He'd never seen conclusive evidence that there were *only* fourteen originals of the Bill of Rights. "I believed then—and believe
now—that there are more copies," he said. "This assertion that by its
very existence it has to belong to a state? There's absolutely no documentation of that. It's completely an assumption—and so if you
can assume that, why can't you also assume the other?

"There were a lot of anomalous things in the publications of the
First Congress that were not continued thereafter. It's not surprising: They were setting things up, they were establishing all these
new functions, and the government moved, from New York City to
Philadelphia."

So there was a spark of hope. When Reese and Tillou were done
talking, and Tillou headed home, Reese began to formulate a plan.

First, he alerted a colleague that he might have a Bill of Rights
for sale. Only a few top collectors would make that kind of philanthropic investment. One, in particular, leaped to mind: the Gilder

Lehrman Institute of American History. In the past decade Richard Gilder and Lewis Lehrman had collectively spent millions of dollars to create a massive collection of historic documents and letters—one of the largest ever compiled. They had narrowly missed out on the famous flea-market Dunlap Declaration of Independence back in 2000, finishing second to Norman Lear's $8.14 million. The Gilder-Lehrman team's motive was not to invest for profit. Their purchases went into a permanent, open-to-the-public collection kept at the New-York Historical Society.

Reese called Seth Kaller, the consortium's broker, asking if his clients might like to get involved in donating an original Bill of Rights. Absolutely, Kaller said.

Reese repeated Peter Tillou's story, then detailed his plan to tease out the document's enigmatic past. He would need some time. Reese's wife had recently died, and in his grief he wasn't getting much work done. But as a rule, he avoided rushing anything of this magnitude. Despite having eight employees, Reese still personally authorized all purchases and cataloged the most important items himself. Meticulous preparation was a hallmark.

Kaller wished Reese luck and told him to keep in touch.

Wayne Pratt called Peter Tillou occasionally to check in, see if the art dealer was making any progress. "What's going on at your end?" Pratt said. Had Tillou spoken to Teresa Heinz Kerry yet?

"Before we offer it," Tillou replied, "we need to know more about it." To that end, he had taken the document to *the* expert in the field, Bill Reese. "You'll *love* him," Tillou said excitedly. "He'll dig the story out."

Tillou naively thought that Pratt would be pleased to hear this. But the response from Woodbury was terse.

Pratt wondered why Tillou had involved another party. This was supposed to be between us, he said. Then Pratt reminded him of their confidentiality agreement and hung up.

Bill Reese appointed two of his employees to spearhead the research. Nick Aretakis and Joe Newman would piggyback Bill of Rights inquiries on top of their other work. Whenever one of them headed off on a business trip that took them close to one of the original thirteen states' archives, they built in time for parchment-related reconnaissance.

The researchers obtained facsimiles of the Bill of Rights from the seven states that still possessed their originals. They also examined those states' holdings, to learn how documents were filed in the late eighteenth century, what kinds of systems the clerks used.

In the five states missing copies—New York, Pennsylvania, Maryland, North Carolina, and Georgia—Aretakis and Newman located documents that had arrived at roughly the same time, in late 1789 and early 1790, and copied whatever docketing was on the back.

The concept was simple: Match the docketing on the wayward Bill of Rights with the docketing on a record of the same vintage, and you solve the mystery.

Reese also had to contend with what he called the two "loose" copies. The Library of Congress has a Bill of Rights of unknown origins. (The copy that belongs to the United States government is in the National Archives.) The library described the manuscript on its website as "John Beckley's copy"—referring to the clerk from the First Federal Congress. This label lent credence to Reese's theory that the scriveners may have created extras. The so-called Beckley copy had arrived in the Library of Congress in 1943. Hollywood producer Barney Balaban had purchased it from a rare-books dealer and donated it to the library.

The New York Public Library had an original Bill of Rights as well. So where did *that* copy come from? Reese wondered. And if the loose copies belonged to any of the states, why hadn't the states demanded them back?

If Reese was correct about the existence of a fifteenth original, everything would be easier. Reese and Tillou could sell the parchment without any provenance-related anxieties. The document would be a heretofore unknown treasure—the kind of find that sparks ferocious bidding wars in auction houses. Serious collectors always dig deeper for an icon.

Over nearly three decades, Reese had moved many seminal historical items into major collections. Now, he spent more time acquiring objects than selling them. "Nothing's easier to sell than great stuff," he said. "The problem is getting your hands on it."

Dig deeply enough into the history of the fourteen known Bill of Rights manuscripts, and you find that over most of the last two centuries they were treated like any other American document—which is to say, not well at all.

Take South Carolina's copy. During the Civil War alert state officials loaded up and shipped out important documents, including the Bill of Rights, ahead of Sherman's army, saving them from the conflagration that leveled Columbia on February 17, 1865. But the state-appointed caretakers who came later were nowhere near so farsighted. During Reconstruction—a dark time for public archives—the Bill of Rights simply vanished. It was missing for an entire lifetime, until the end of World War II, when someone rooting around in the State House basement came across a trove of records. "Many valuable documents that no one knew were in existence have been found," Alexander Salley Jr., the venerable secretary of South Carolina's Historical Commission, reported in 1946. "The most notable of these perhaps is South Carolina's copy of the Bill of Rights."

He added, "Our copy is dirty and damaged. I am endeavoring to find an expert cleaner." As someone who held his job for over forty years, Salley may have been savvier about preserving his livelihood than he was skilled at protecting historic papers, so he didn't elaborate on the damage.

The more detailed version was this: For decades, the state's Bill of Rights sat in the basement, sometimes under dripping steam pipes. There was no climate control, no buffer against the smothering dampness of the Deep South. Mold bloomed like rhododendron. Chunks of parchment rotted and fell away. "It was a very humid environment down there," said Rodger Stroup, the state's present-day archivist. "It's amazing what survived."

Georgia has a similar story, with a less fortuitous ending. As in South Carolina, a couple of conscientious state employees commandeered two wagons and whisked away historical papers ahead of Sherman's army, ensuring they escaped the flames that consumed Atlanta. Yet no one has seen Georgia's copy of the Bill of Rights since the war's end.

Archivist Greg Jarrell believes the parchment was misfiled long ago, possibly in the 1800s, and is still lost somewhere in Atlanta. Georgia's state archives are understaffed, and the agency has 250 million documents in its custody, Jarrell said. In other words, the odds of finding it were no worse than 250 million to one, but probably only marginally better.

And yet, in January 2007 Jarrell was digging around on behalf of a Louisiana woman who'd called with a genealogy request. Sifting through the microfilm catalog of a volume called *State Officers Appointments 1789–1827,* he saw an entry with a strange date: March 2, 1777. Odd, Jarrell thought. That document didn't belong in that book. Something had been misfiled.

Then something "went off like a cannon" in his brain. Jarrell scurried to the vault, pulled down the bound volume of originals, and there it was: "When in the Course of human events . . ."—the opening lines of the Declaration of Independence.

The find made national headlines; the state archives director, David Carmicheal, proclaimed the document "our copy of the Declaration."

Jarrell believes the Bill of Rights is down there somewhere, too. "My gut feeling," he said, "is that one day it will turn up."

New York's almost certainly burned in the Capitol Fire of 1911; it hasn't been seen since. In Maryland the Bill of Rights was apparently stolen, though details of its disappearance have been lost to history. Pennsylvania's copy vanished under equally dubious circumstances. Noted manuscript dealer Walter Benjamin once wrote that in the 1880s "a man in Harrisburg made frequent trips to New York carrying a large carpet bag bulging with old state papers. These he sold to C. D. Burns, Simon Gratz, Dr. T. A. Emmett, and other collectors." The New York Public Library obtained its Bill of Rights from Emmett's collection.

Someone stole New Jersey's parchment around the same time,

but that state was more fortunate—or maybe its employees were merely more alert. The document wound up in a New York art gallery's sale catalog, accompanied by a detailed description. State officials spotted it and demanded its return.

Fifty or so years later, New Jersey displayed its parchment during the 150th anniversary of the Constitution, and then mislaid the Bill of Rights a second time. About eight months passed before an employee found it in the public record files, prompting an announcement of its "discovery" by state librarian Sidney Goldmann. Thus New Jersey has the rare distinction of losing its Bill of Rights twice—once without the broadsheet leaving the grounds.

Delaware lost its copy because of a simple clerical blunder: State officials in 1789 approved the amendments and then—apparently caught up in their newfound esprit de corps—promptly sent the parchment back to the federal government. The feds, naturally, refused to return it for the next 213 years. In 2002 Delaware's congressional delegation finally convinced Washington to at least let the state display the document part-time. Delaware now may show its own Bill of Rights for up to 460 hours annually.

Fortunately, the Delaware copy got stashed away and as a result is in relatively pristine shape. The official United States copy wasn't so lucky. Much like the one and only original Declaration of Independence, the federal Bill of Rights was damaged by exposure to light, smoke, and other pollutants. Both icons are now barely legible in places.

Only a few copies skated across the centuries unscathed: Connecticut's, for example, survived in such pristine shape it was displayed at a world's fair in Spain in 1992. The copies belonging to Massachusetts and Rhode Island also remain in good form.

But those are the exceptions. And in many cases the ham-handedness and neglect beggar belief. In 1969 a graduate history student named John Kaminski visited New Hampshire while conducting research for both his dissertation and several documentary history projects relating to America's formative years. After searching the newly opened state archives, he asked around: Did anyone know where he might find any other eighteenth-century documents?

Someone suggested he check the secretary of state's office, where historical papers had been housed previously.

A receptionist there shrugged at his request—"She didn't know what I was talking about," Kaminski said—and waved him in. While poking around a large back office, he noticed a bunch of rolled-up papers sitting atop a six-foot-high steel supply cabinet tucked in a corner. He began unrolling them. Most were unremarkable, but among the leaves he noticed a parchment.

Kaminski unrolled the broadsheet and stared in astonishment. He was holding New Hampshire's original Bill of Rights. "You can imagine how flabbergasted I was," he said. "My goodness, what a shocking thing." Also in the pile was an important record from 1788.

Kaminski told the first person he could find that he'd come upon some very valuable documents that should be locked away. He also requested a copy of the Bill of Rights, and within a couple of months state officials sent him a glossy ten-by-fifteen-inch print and negative.

But the story doesn't end there. In 1988 Kaminski returned to Concord for the Constitution's bicentennial festivities. The Granite State had a bigger celebration than most; as the ninth state to ratify the document, New Hampshire had the distinction of closing the deal for the new nation. Supreme Court Chief Justice Warren Burger joined in the merriment.

As part of the celebration, event staffers handed out reproductions of the state's original Bill of Rights. Kaminski examined the facsimile; something seemed off. Maybe, he thought, it was just a bad copy. But the actual document was also on display, so Kaminski worked his way over for a look.

When he got up close, he was chagrined to see that it wasn't just the facsimile that didn't look right. The document looked markedly worse than when he'd found it on top of the filing cabinet nearly two decades earlier. The parchment had been exposed to sunlight—or something—that had caused the ink to fade. Kaminski saw letters lifting away, especially around the edges. "Somehow or other," he said, "the document was safer where it was, on top of that filing cabinet."

When Kaminski returned home, he reexamined the glossy print he'd purchased. It was surreal but true: His photographic reproduction now looked better than the real thing.

Bill Reese's quest to determine the mystery Bill of Rights' origins unfolded over several months. His top Americana experts gradually filled a binder with materials from thirteen state archives. On June 21, 2002, Reese sent everything to Seth Kaller.

The dossier included photocopies of all eleven known originals. Library of Congress officials had denied Reese's request to examine their Bill of Rights but sent a scanned image of the front. The New York Public Library was similarly standoffish. Reese had to settle for the likeness on the library's website.

The condition of the archives in the five states missing their Bill of Rights varied wildly. New York's archives, Reese wrote to Kaller, were "the poorest in terms of preservation and scope" because of the 1911 Capitol Fire. State officials had thrown documents out windows in a desperate bid to save them from the flames. Bystanders probably walked off with some of them—manuscript dealers suspect this occurred because old New York papers with singe marks occasionally turn up for sale. The docketing samples Reese's researchers found in Albany showed that the state had used a simple numbering system: The first document received was marked "number 1," and so on down the line. Pennsylvania had the largest number of surviving federal documents of any of the five states, Reese reported. His researchers had returned from Harrisburg with five docketing samples. Reese recognized the hand of Thomas Mifflin, Pennsylvania's first governor, a familiar figure to scholars of early America. Reese's staff collected six docketing samples from Maryland, which also conformed to a predictable, recognizable system.

By contrast, the Civil War had clearly disrupted the archives of North Carolina and Georgia. Though Reese's team had obtained five docketing samples from Raleigh, they found only a "scattershot collection of material from the early Federal period" in North Carolina's capital. There was no evident pattern to the docketing; notes were made in different hands and lacked any coherent system. One couldn't look at the docketing of the various pages and say that they clearly belonged together. The docketing had faded significantly in many cases, making comparisons even thornier.

Reese enclosed seven examples of docketing from Georgia but noted that the state "had a paucity of material from the Federal government from the period around 1789."

Reese began to form suspicions about where this Bill of Rights probably *didn't* come from; in particular, New York and Pennsylvania seemed like long shots. But given the lack of conclusive evidence, he decided to keep such speculation to himself.

The bottom line was clear enough: There was no smoking gun. None of the docketing samples appeared to match the writing on the back of the Bill of Rights.

As Reese's research wound down, Peter Tillou brought the parchment back to New Haven. Reese wanted it photographed, front and back, for his dossier. He hired Joe Szaszfai, who had done extensive reproduction photography for the Yale University Art Gallery and the Yale Center for British Art, for the job. Szaszfai had impressed Reese by perfecting the delicate art of capturing reproductions of daguerreotypes. Having studied the document under magnification, Reese knew he would need an expert.

The ink had lifted away badly in places. Half the word *Proposed* was gone. The capital *S* in *States* was largely missing, as was the crossed *t* in the word *to*.

It wasn't just the faded ink. Parchment is naturally blotchy, and in this case the mottled surface rendered the faded ink even more difficult to decipher. Even by eighteenth-century standards, the notation was badly eroded.

So for Szaszfai, photographing the Bill of Rights' docketing was a stiff challenge. "He worked at it very, very hard," Reese said, "and got it about as good as you can."

Reese noticed some glue residue on the back—a clear sign some-one had done some conservation work on the parchment, had re-moved it from some kind of backing. Reese figured that was the rea-son for the faintness of the docketing: The parchment was probably mounted to a bad piece of acid board. The scraping required to get the backing off could have removed some of the ink.

The fact that it was on parchment was a disadvantage in another sense: Parchment is animal skin, and ink can't penetrate the surface in the same way it soaks into the fibers of paper. Ink on old parch-ment can flake away if it's not carefully conserved. The ink would have been particularly vulnerable to flaking during the conservation work.

Reese asked Tillou to ask his source for a conservation report. When conservators restore a document, they typically generate a de-tailed account of their work, complete with before and after photos.

Back up in Woodbury, Pratt didn't look on this request favorably. He wanted to discourage Reese's explorations without openly ob-structing them. He told Tillou that an expert had removed an old cardboard backing, and that he would see if he could find the re-port. He would have to get back to him.

Reese found this answer—the latest of a trickle of opaque and unhelpful responses—utterly maddening. His research had run its course, only to deliver him to the same cul-de-sac in which he started. Reese pressed Tillou for more information on the parchment's prov-enance. Could his source tell him more about this hardware and an-tiques store in upstate New York? What was the proprietor's name? Couldn't that person assist in their search for answers?

Tillou circled back to Pratt, but the furniture dealer declined to say anything else. But he dangled one very large carrot: He prom-ised to furnish all relevant information about the Bill of Rights when Tillou and Reese had a buyer lined up. When there was money on the table, Pratt said, he would tell them everything they wanted to know.

11

The Buyer

B Y LATE 2002, almost a year after he had first eyeballed the
Bill of Rights, Bill Reese still hadn't solved the riddle of the
parchment's provenance. Seth Kaller, the dealer of upper-tier
historic documents, had waited patiently on the sidelines. Kaller
had only one additional insight into the mystery: He believed the
document *hadn't* come from North Carolina.

When Reese first approached him about the manuscript, Kaller
had immediately flashed back to a previous brush with a Bill of
Rights. The year was 1994 or '95. Kaller received a call from someone offering North Carolina's copy of the Bill of Rights. The caller
swore Kaller to secrecy, a vow that he always took seriously. "Over
twenty years we've had a reputation for paying huge finder's fees," he
said, "and for protecting our sources, which is why we keep getting
offered new things."

The caller sent a several-page description: the document's dimensions, its history, its identifying features. The broker claimed
North Carolina had declined an opportunity to buy it back. When
Kaller heard that, his interest grew. The folks in Raleigh would no
doubt still welcome a chance to display the document; Kaller's idea
was to create an exhibit that revolved between North Carolina and
New York. The Gilder Lehrman Institute, Kaller's top client, was
the likely buyer, and the two men driving that collection weren't
interested in locking stuff away. They were building a public col-

lection. "Can we talk to North Carolina and arrange it with them?" Kaller asked.

The broker said no, Kaller could not contact North Carolina. And it ended there, without Kaller getting a look at the original. But one part of the description stuck in his head: It said there was no docketing on the back.

So when Kaller heard about the manuscript Bill Reese was handling, with its faded docketing, he figured: *So, whichever one it is, it's not North Carolina's.*

Not until later did he realize the broker couldn't have known whether there was any docketing on the reverse of the Bill of Rights. At that point the parchment was still glued to its cardboard backing.

For an extraordinary artifact, the Bill of Rights had lived a remarkably itinerant life. The document had spent more than a century with the same family, in the same city—but once the Shotwells decided to sell, the parchment became a sort of inanimate Gulliver, roaming from city to city, town to town. There was the jaunt from Indianapolis to Washington, then the trip up to Woodbury, Connecticut. The parchment traveled to New York City for conservation work, then back to Woodbury before making the short trip north to Litchfield, where it spent time under Peter Tillou's bed. From there the Bill of Rights bounced down to New Haven. Jaded, veteran antiquities dealers felt awe in its presence. But they were equally befuddled. Everyone who saw it hungered to get involved—to intertwine their lives with the parchment's—but there were so many questions, so much unknown. Wayne Pratt's obfuscation only amplified the doubts.

And so the document bounced from dealer to dealer: from Leslie Hindman to Wayne Pratt to Peter Tillou to Bill Reese. The document had become a multimillion-dollar baton.

Next in line was Seth Kaller.

Kaller was born into the antiquities-collecting trade. His father, Myron, dealt in stamps; his mother, Judith, had a coin business.

Seth and his two younger sisters spent large chunks of their formative years traveling to shows. Dinner-table conversation revolved around what this old stamp or that rare nickel was worth.

Young Seth pursued stamps but didn't feel the same covetous burn that his father exhibited. He loved studying the letters that came in old envelopes that stamp collectors sought for their frank markings. The missives plunged Kaller into a different time, bringing long-gone characters to life. He began forming a collection and inevitably began selling letters and documents as well. "For me," Kaller said, "it became all about the content. I'd buy a letter from Warren Harding, who is the least popular president among autograph collectors, if it had great content."

In 1988, just after graduating from the University of Pennsylvania, he began advising museums and private clients looking to buy notable old papers. Once he recognized the field was undervalued, he talked his family into helping him launch a historic-documents business in Asbury Park, New Jersey.

A moment of supreme gumption launched the family to stratospheric success. In 1988 Myron Kaller read a newspaper interview with Barton Biggs, the global investment strategist for Morgan Stanley, in which Biggs advised that investors put a percentage of their money into collectibles. Myron wrote Biggs a letter: Perhaps Morgan Stanley should practice what it preached and start a collection of historic documents—a collecting field on the verge of taking off. Biggs brought the letter to Lewis Lehrman, a managing director.

Lehrman happened to be a historian; he once won a Carnegie teaching fellowship as an instructor of history at Yale. He invited the Kallers in to talk. Seth brought the best stuff he had: letters from Jefferson, Lincoln, Sherman, Robert E. Lee. "Lew was intrigued," Kaller recalled. "He knew these things existed, but he didn't know they weren't already in a museum."

Lehrman had recently begun working on philanthropic projects with a good friend and fellow stockbroker extraordinaire, Richard Gilder—two minds and checkbooks collectively being more influential than one. Gilder, one of Wall Street's most renowned money managers, was the kind of restless genius who could make and give away several fortunes in his lifetime. In 1979, celebrating his twenty-fifth Yale reunion, Gilder listened to his classmates bemoan the university's poor financial management. He proposed an idea: They could pool their donations and hand them over to a professional money manager. At their fiftieth reunion they would give the school the original contribution, plus the earnings. By 2004 the $75,000 in seed money would turn into more than $110 million.

Lehrman was equally ambitious. He won the Republican nomination for governor of New York in 1982, narrowly losing in the general election to Mario Cuomo. Lehrman and Gilder both bought into the idea of historic documents—but they wanted to do things differently from other collectors. At the time Malcolm Forbes was America's top buyer of historic papers. He loaned out his documents for exhibitions, but his was clearly a private collection; scholars couldn't hunker down in Forbes's offices for research. Lehrman and Gilder envisioned a world-class compilation of documents and letters that would forever be open to the public, a tool for teaching American history. The collection would be their enduring legacy.

In 1989 the Kallers became their official brokers. Seth instantly became a kind of boy wonder in the manuscripts world. Youthful, round-faced, and soft-spoken, his hair combed straight back, Kaller resembled a leaner version of the comedian Jon Lovitz. No one knew what to make of him when, a little more than a year out of Penn, he began bidding knee-buckling sums of money at auctions, shattering records. In October 1989 Kaller purchased a copy of the Emancipation Proclamation signed by Lincoln for $115,000 at Sotheby's—the first of a string of electrifying buys. "That acquisition," he said, "really spurred the collection."

Even when he fell short, he made a splash. In February 1990 he was the underbidder for George Washington's copy of *The Federalist*, which went for $1.43 million. The pre-auction estimate was $250,000 to $400,000, and Kaller's participation drove up the price. "Nobody really expected us to be there, bidding $1.25 million," Kaller recalled. "That was early enough on that people were surprised."

The shock wore off quickly. By December 1992 Kaller was winning the bidding for a handwritten section of Lincoln's celebrated "house divided" speech opposing slavery. The fragment sold for $1.54 million—more than three times Sotheby's high estimate—and made the 1995 *Guinness Book of World Records* as the highest price ever paid for a manuscript.

In 1992 Gilder and Lehrman placed their collection on deposit at the Morgan Library and Museum. Two years later they created the Gilder Lehrman Institute of American History and continued their spending spree with Kaller as the point man.

The Gilder-Lehrman collection, Kaller said, is now "the greatest American history collection that's ever been assembled. It's probably not the largest, but I'll put our top hundred things against anyone else's top hundred." Thanks in no small part to his two deep-pocketed patrons, Kaller's business multiplied. In 1997 Seth moved the operation, Kaller's America Gallery (slogan: "History you can own!"), into Macy's Herald Square in Manhattan.

The First Federal Congress Project eventually benefited from Gilder and Lehrman's largess. On numerous occasions, when Ken Bowling came across a First Congress document for sale, he called Kaller and asked him to buy it. The document would become part of the Gilder-Lehrman collection, but Bowling would get a copy. "It's phenomenal," Bowling said, "what they've done with their money on behalf of the study of American history."

On January 9, 2003, Bill Reese brought the Bill of Rights to New York City for a meeting with Richard Gilder, Lewis Lehrman, and Seth Kaller. Reese had stored the document in his safe while he and Kaller prepared their presentation. Together they had decided on a price: $5 million.

The idea was to ask Gilder and Lehrman to buy the document for a museum. The parchment's totemic value was off the charts: It connected onlookers to the United States' greatest strengths—to the fundamental freedoms so easily taken for granted.

Reese and Kaller had carefully selected the document's proposed destination. Two important libraries—the New York Public and the

Library of Congress—already had copies that they rarely displayed, so the two brokers had hunted for an institution that not only had the means to store and protect such a document, but also would exhibit it.

Reese and Kaller had considered the Montpelier Foundation, the 2,650-acre estate in Orange County, Virginia, that preserves James Madison's home and legacy. That would have been fitting, but the foundation's facilities and security capabilities were not equal to a document of that magnitude.

The dealers had eventually hit on the perfect destination: the National Constitution Center, a museum that was currently under construction in Philadelphia. Set to open on the Fourth of July that year, the Constitution Center would be situated on Independence Mall near the Liberty Bell. The fact that the museum was in Pennsylvania, one of the states missing its Bill of Rights, was an added bonus. Perhaps the state might even go in on the purchase.

The pitch hit all the right notes. Gilder and Lehrman were big on icons. In 1993 Gilder had pledged $17 million to the Central Park Conservancy. The money didn't just spruce up America's most famous urban park—it also accelerated a plan to wrest responsibility for its management away from the city. When the conservancy took over in 1997, the park flourished. Gilder also gave about $20 million to the Rose Center for Earth and Space at the American Museum of Natural History.

Money was no deterrent. Gilder and Lehrman had already spent close to $100 million on historic documents and artifacts. They were on the verge of relocating their collection to the long-struggling New-York Historical Society, where they would spend another $1 million on a basement vault with a public reading room.

Both men loved the idea of the Bill of Rights. In characteristic fashion, they were keen that the document not be locked away. They offered seed money, and Gilder even volunteered to act as a liaison. He knew Ed Rendell, the former Philadelphia mayor who two months earlier had been elected governor of Pennsylvania. The Constitution Center was one of Rendell's pet projects, and Gilder offered to send Rendell a note about it.

Bill Reese's mind swirled as he headed home to New Haven. Now, with a prospective buyer in place, he could finally get more answers—the conservation report and provenance information—out of Peter Tillou's source and finally crack the story of the document's past, or at least puzzle over a few new clues.

Reese called Tillou to update him and to send him back to his source for the promised materials. "I have a serious buyer," Reese told Tillou, "and it's time to come across with that stuff."

Tillou was in an awkward spot. He had promised to keep Wayne Pratt's identity secret, so he was stuck serving as go-between in a mounting power struggle between his friend and his Bill of Rights business partner.

Pratt didn't help any. His strategy remained the same: Stall as long as possible in the hope that a deal would get done before anyone unraveled the document's secrets. So when Tillou called with good news about a possible buyer, Pratt was pleased. But as for the conservation report: Sorry, he told Tillou. He couldn't find it.

"OK, then, let me talk to the conservator and find out what was done myself," Reese fired back when he heard this news.

The cat-and-mouse game continued. Pratt first professed to have forgotten the conservator's name, and then couldn't recall the business's location, either—first it was Washington, D.C.; next it was New York City.

As for the provenance question? Instead of more specifics on the now-legendary upstate New York hardware store, Reese heard a second story: The document had actually come from an old couple in Ohio, neither of whom was still alive.

Reese hadn't been particularly concerned with the hardware store tale; most dealers are cagey about their sources. Reese assumed that whoever owned the Bill of Rights had scored a great bargain and didn't want word of a $5 million deal going across the transom.

But this new tale, of an expired Ohio couple—this was classic dead man's provenance. "That story was different enough," Reese said, "that it really bothered me."

• • •

Forty-two bronze figures stand amid a key exhibit at the National Constitution Center. The eerily lifelike re-creations of the men who came to Philadelphia to debate the creation of the Constitution are among the museum's most popular attractions. The statues serve as a pointed reminder that sometimes it takes a collection of great minds to do big things.

The museum, located two blocks north of the Liberty Bell on Independence Mall, is a prime example. The Constitution Center was forever a great idea that seemed to have no chance of becoming reality. Its origins date to 1987, when two civic leaders proposed a somber, erudite environment in which to ponder and debate the sovereign document. When that idea flopped, museum officials reimagined the center as a sort of political amusement park, complete with Disney-esque moving seats. Abandoning the think-tank ghetto seemed more promising, but the museum's nascent board still lacked support from Philadelphia's power base.

In December 1996 the museum's board scored a coup. The board sold Ed Rendell, then the city's mayor, on the idea that the museum could realign Philadelphia's tourism landscape. For visitors who'd come to learn about the nation's birth, the Constitution museum was a logical bookend, explaining how the newly freed nation managed to glue its disparate parts together. The museum would demonstrate how the Constitution shifts and flexes with changing times. "Williamsburg, Boston—we'll blow everyone else away," Rendell told the *Philadelphia Inquirer.*

The mayor signed on as chairman and tapped into his old network of deputies to bring the Constitution Center to life. In particular, he called a former aide-de-camp named Joe Torsella. A few years earlier Torsella had been the whiz kid of Philadelphia politics. Rendell had met him in 1986, when Torsella was a bright Penn student who had volunteered to work on Rendell's unsuccessful run for governor. In 1991 Rendell made him issues director of his mayoral campaign, and after winning the election he tapped Torsella to run his policy unit. At age twenty-seven, Torsella was believed to be the youngest deputy mayor in Philadelphia's history. But he spent the next twenty-one months successfully scaling back the troubled disability system to help Philadelphia close a record $1.4 billion deficit. In his book *A Prayer for the City,* about Rendell's bare-knuckles first term, Buzz Bissinger described Torsella as "a true and earnest believer in the midst of crotchety wolves and coyotes."

Torsella, compact, animated, and youthful, his black hair stylishly swept back, left the mayor's office in autumn 1993 to begin a career as an entrepreneur. When Rendell called in late 1996, Torsella asked how long the museum project would take. "A day or two a week for three months," Rendell said.

Torsella quickly became president and CEO. "There was a sense," he recalled, "that this was an incredible idea, but no one could quite figure out what the Constitution Center could be, or that it was really possible to make it happen."

Over the course of several years, Torsella and his staff untangled bureaucratic thickets, recruited U.S. Supreme Court justices as advisers, and hired world-class architect Henry Cobb.

Philadelphia money began rolling in. John Bogle, architect of the Vanguard Group mutual funds empire, became board chairman. Rich DeVos, the billionaire cofounder of Amway, joined as a trustee.

The museum's perennial budget deficits turned into a surplus in eighteen months. Torsella began to feel confident the Constitution Center could raise $185 million in public and private funds and open as planned on Independence Day, 2003.

Ultimately, the edifice would be neither a glorified think tank nor a sociopolitical Six Flags. There would be a Signers Hall, where visitors could append their names to the Constitution. There would be high-tech exhibits that brought to life the humanity behind the document. The splashy glass-and-granite structure would be smart and literate but still relevant to a wide audience. Torsella hoped to draw a million people a year.

The key was to get visitors involved. "The way I've always thought of the National Constitution Center," Torsella said, "is a place where you go and enter as a visitor, but leave as a citizen."

At best, the museum would be a tipping point for Philadelphia's revival. It wouldn't just enhance the three hundred thousand square feet it occupied on Independence Mall. The Constitution Center would transform everything around it.

On January 13, 2003, Richard Gilder e-mailed Ed Rendell, Pennsylvania's governor-elect. Gilder wrote that he'd been offered a chance to help purchase an original Bill of Rights for the National Constitution Center. The document couldn't be traced to any of the five states missing their copies—but, fortuitously, Pennsylvania was one of those states.

Gilder offered to pay $1 million toward the $5 million purchase price and to help raise another $1 million. From there, given the museum's fundraising chops, the other $3 million should be well within reach. Was Rendell interested?

Rendell was eight days from his inauguration. The scene in Harrisburg was chaotic. "We were getting set up, doing transition work, trying to figure out where the men's room was," recalled John Estey, then Rendell's chief of staff. "There were so many things going on."

Still. This was Dick Gilder and the Bill of Rights. Rendell could find time for that.

As a rule, Joe Torsella wasn't interested in documents. The museum had acquired a copy of the first printing of the Constitution, but beyond that, he and his deputies weren't keen on artifacts. Torsella didn't believe they attracted people. He favored interactive exhibits. Plus, if you buy expensive old things, you have to conserve and secure them.

And then on January 14, 2003, a fax arrived at the National Constitution Center from Ed Rendell. Torsella's old boss had printed Richard Gilder's e-mail and sent it over.

Call me, Rendell wrote.

Torsella was floored. An original Bill of Rights? For that Torsella could make an exception to the no-artifacts rule. "That immediately struck me as one of a few things that absolutely belongs here, that people should connect with," Torsella said.

The only thing was, the museum would open in less than six months. If this was going to happen, they would have to move fast.

12

A Revelation

WAYNE PRATT WAS PREPARING for opening night of the Winter Antiques Show on January 16, 2003, when Peter Tillou stopped by. Pratt knew instantly what he wanted to talk about. Coincidentally, almost exactly a year earlier, at the same show, Pratt had been the one seeking out Tillou about the Bill of Rights.

The show was back in the Seventh Regiment Armory, on Manhattan's Upper East Side, after a one-year hiatus. Pratt was preparing a booth that industry reporter Laura Beach later described as "an ingenious replica of a 16-foot Maine interior with painted plaster walls by Rufus Porter." Pratt planned to display what he called "the best sideboard in America"—an inlaid serpentine number by Nathan Lombard.

Tillou would exhibit a large painting of a floral wreath by seventeenth-century Italian artist Giovanni Stanchi. But the parchment was the subject at hand. Bill Reese has a customer and wants something in writing, Tillou said. Many dealers settle for verbal agreements, as Pratt did with Bob Matthews. But given the intrigue that had swirled around the parchment to that point—Tillou had not yet revealed the identity of his source—Reese requested a written contract.

We're close, Tillou said. But we need the formal authority to make this transaction.

Pratt drew up the paperwork on the spot. On one sheet of paper he wrote, "Peter Tillou and Bill Reese have a two-month option to sell the Bill of Rights, at a price agreed to by me, Wayne E. Pratt, at five million dollars."

On a second he scrawled, "Peter Tillou and William Reese will receive a net commission of $1 million from the sale of the Bill of Rights when sold for $5 million."

Then he signed his name at the bottom.

The next day, January 17, Reese took the Bill of Rights to Philadelphia for a viewing at the National Constitution Center offices. Along the way he pondered what he'd just learned from his friend Peter Tillou. Wayne Pratt, by signing the option agreement, had finally dropped his cloak of anonymity. Reese found this bit of news disquieting. "When I found out it was Pratt," Reese said, "that disconcerted me somewhat, because I didn't like his reputation." He'd heard rumblings about fast and loose ethics—the kind of talk that wends its way through insular communities. Pratt's evasive tactics on the questions of the document's provenance did nothing to reassure Reese.

For the moment, though, Reese saw no reason to derail the proposed sale. Constitution Center officials clearly were enthused about the document; Joe Torsella had spoken with Richard Gilder about financing the purchase. The museum seemed to be the ideal destination for the Bill of Rights.

In Philadelphia, Reese and Seth Kaller met Torsella and his top deputy for exhibits, Steve Frank, in the museum's temporary offices in the Bourse, an office complex near Independence Mall. Built in 1895 and renovated just shy of a century later, the building nonetheless felt trampled under the heels of time. Torsella held the meeting in a grim fifth-floor conference room.

The setting notwithstanding, the museum officials were dazzled. To Torsella, the parchment was an extraordinary specimen. Frank stared at the looping, sturdy scrawl of John Adams's signature. The excitement was partly due to their intense focus on that period of history. But there was more: The document had a presence, and the room felt more alive. Both men immediately sensed the parchment should be the museum's centerpiece.

Torsella and Frank had already started hashing out the remarkable problem of possessing two holy relics. Because such documents are so fragile and prone to fading, they would have to keep their Constitution in dark storage for six months of every year. Maybe the Bill of Rights could rotate into the exhibit that was vacated when the Constitution went into the vault.

The sale would have to happen quickly. The museum was scheduled to open on the Fourth of July. Much as Torsella wanted to drop everything for this, he had to spearhead the construction of a huge building and the installation of all of its exhibits. As with any major project of this kind, there were constant niggling issues: contractor delays, budget overruns, permit issues.

Torsella suspected that a Bill of Rights purchase would be complex. He talked with Reese about the five states missing their originals, and Reese's inability to link the parchment to any of them. Both men agreed that the hardware store tale sounded odd and wondered what more there was to the story. Reese floated his theory that it might have been a scrivener's copy.

Despite these lingering questions, Torsella felt convinced they had to pursue the parchment. He'd spoken to the museum's key players, and the unanimous reaction was "Let's go for it if we can." There was a lot of excitement.

Now, Torsella felt the buzz of staring at the Bill of Rights up close and reminded himself to slow down. It was too early to worry about shoehorning the manuscript into the museum's blueprints. At this point Torsella didn't need an architect. What he needed was a good lawyer.

The way the market for historic manuscripts was spiking, no one at the museum blinked at the parchment's $5 million price tag.

The previous spring Sotheby's had auctioned off the late Malcolm Forbes's collection in the most celebrated historic-manuscript sale in more than a decade. Forbes was a legend in that world. Few buyers actually show up in the auction room anymore, preferring to act through a broker or call in their bids, lest anyone know what they're buying and for how much. Forbes was the opposite: He relished the attention. His competitors labeled him a profligate spender and deemed his bidding outrageous—which he loved. "The whole Forbes persona was, here's this cheerful mogul buying big stuff," Bill Reese said. "He was the last of the great Daddy Warbucks kind of characters—a diamond in his stickpin—and he had this 'I'm having a great time' kind of attitude. People of great wealth now, by and large, are trying to conceal who they are."

The manuscripts market had cooled during the dot-com boom because so many buyers were dumping capital into the stock market. But things picked up again after Norman Lear paid $8.14 million for the Dunlap Declaration of Independence in June 2000. With the economy sputtering in 2002 and investors looking for stable investments, the Forbes auction brought a tense, electric atmosphere. The sale bagged $20 million on its first day. Reese saw far more competition for high-end documents than usual. At least four people bid more than $400,000 on a Robert E. Lee letter that Seth Kaller finally snapped up for $650,000. Kaller, often buying on behalf of Richard Gilder and Lewis Lehrman, spent more than $4.5 million.

The bidding proved that Forbes's supposedly decadent spending was in fact prescient investing. In 1979 Forbes spent $4,000 on a fragment of George Washington's undelivered inaugural address; that piece sold for $358,000. A Lincoln letter on his campaign strategy cost Forbes $16,000 in 1983; that went for $501,000. A "decent" Jefferson letter, as Reese described it, increased in value from $1,800 to $94,000.

Some buyers of historic documents simply want a conversation piece for their wall. They're often not concerned so much with a document's content as with what owning the document says about who they are. A lawyer looking to convey a certain level of gravitas might display a Thomas Jefferson letter. Investors may not even care much about the content; they may view a two-hundred-year-old letter simply as a commodity that can be flipped for profit.

Then there are collectors—the people driven by passion for the material. Many of those aficionados lack the money to get anywhere near the best stuff anymore and were largely shut out of the Forbes sale.

There are few statistics on the size of today's historic-documents industry. Even pinning down the number of dealers is a tricky proposition, said Edward Bomsey, a Virginia-based dealer who in 2008 became president of the Manuscript Society. "No one, I believe, has statistics on autograph/document sales," he noted in an e-mail. "Impossible to even imagine such a number because anyone can be a 'dealer.' And professional dealers, well, some of them at least, lie like hell as to their sales to puff themselves up!"

Steve Harmelin was sitting in a board of trustees meeting at the Barnes Foundation when a secretary interrupted. Joe Torsella was calling with an urgent matter; could he step away?

Harmelin was the first person Torsella had thought of as the Bill of Rights viewing wrapped up on January 17. Harmelin was an early supporter of the National Constitution Center and now served as the museum's general counsel. He brought serious credentials: Harmelin was managing partner of the prominent law firm Dilworth Paxson. During the course of his forty-year career, his talent for negotiation had earned him a corner office in the firm's skyscraper offices.

Torsella brought Harmelin up to speed on the Bill of Rights. "This would be a great thing," Torsella said, "and I think we can get the financing for it." But he needed Harmelin's guidance for everything else.

Harmelin was instantly enthralled. A balding man in his sixties, Harmelin had a prominent nose, paper-thin lips, and a sandpapery voice. In conversation he had a habit of pressing his fingers together to form the shape of a tent—a timeless bit of lawyerly body language. Harmelin knew something about rare, historic objects. He was a trustee at the Barnes Foundation, which houses the most important collection of French Impressionist paintings outside of France. Harmelin founded the Philadelphia Constitution Foundation, an organization that had exhibited an original of the Magna Carta.

American history was one of his abiding passions, his grandfather having engineered an elaborate escape from Eastern Europe a century earlier. Harmelin still remembers his grandfather's stories of living under the repressive Hapsburg monarchy. "The deal in Eastern Europe in those days was that you knew what city you woke up in," he said, "but you were never quite sure what country it was." Harmelin thus felt a deep sense of fealty toward America's guarantees of liberty—many of them enumerated in the Bill of Rights.

When Harmelin reentered the foundation meeting, he found it hard to concentrate. A *Bill of Rights?* Harmelin at that point had no concept of the peripatetic history of the fourteen originals; he found it inconceivable that all the existing copies weren't sealed away in government vaults. But if there *was* one legitimately available— well, then. That could represent the highlight of his philanthropic career.

On January 28, eleven days after first laying eyes on the document, Joe Torsella presented the idea of purchasing the Bill of Rights to the museum's thirteen-member executive board, including Governor Ed Rendell. It was an easy sell. The group instantly shared Torsella's enthusiasm and unanimously authorized pursuing the parchment's purchase as a special project. One board member offered to kick in money.

There was precedent for obtaining a great document under unusual circumstances.

Steve Frank had had plans to pick up the first printing of the Constitution on September 11, 2001. When airplanes slammed into buildings in New York City and Washington that morning, Frank assumed the donors would want to postpone—but they asked him to fetch the document anyway. He got lost several times en route, and when he stopped for directions people instead asked him what he knew about the attacks. By the time he finally retrieved the document, the museum's offices had closed. The Constitution spent the night in his living room before going into a secure repository at the University of Pennsylvania.

"I didn't realize it then," Frank said, "but the feeling we experienced after that tragedy, the real base of that unity, was in that document. In retrospect, that was a very appropriate thing to do on that day." The Constitution forever linked New Yorkers to Californians to Kansans. It was right there, on paper.

Like everyone else who had heard Wayne Pratt's story about the Bill of Rights' origins, Joe Torsella and Steve Harmelin were puzzled. How had the document wound up in upstate New York—or was it Ohio? Was it legitimately for sale? Was the document even genuine?

The museum officials worried that someone else might claim to be the rightful owner after the deal was done. But what could they do? They already had the nation's preeminent rare-books expert and a top dealer of historic documents working on their behalf. If Bill Reese and Seth Kaller couldn't untangle the parchment's back-story, who could? Torsella took solace in Pratt's standing in the antiques world. He was clearly an established authority, and a television personality to boot. Pratt was no fly-by-night type.

Kaller encouraged Torsella to independently authenticate the Bill of Rights. For Kaller, this was routine; he recommended that all of his clients autonomously verify all their purchases. This was a vestige of his family's stamp-collecting background.

In early February, Steve Frank sent the Bill of Rights dossier that Reese had compiled to Jim Green, an official at the Library Company of Philadelphia, a research institute that specializes in early American history. Frank asked whether Green might authenticate the parchment. Green demurred; he sometimes purchased documents from Reese and Kaller and felt his involvement would create a conflict of interest. Green recommended that Frank instead send the notebook to the reigning expert in documents of that era: Ken Bowling, of the First Federal Congress Project.

• • •

Wayne Pratt had much more on his mind than the Bill of Rights. His personal life in recent years had undergone radical changes. Pratt had lived as a bachelor for twenty-three years, dating on and off. This suited him. He considered his staff and friends to be an adequate proxy for a full-time family. When he opened his Nantucket shop in 1991, he bought a sprawling house on the island with six bedrooms. Affordable summer housing is scarce on Nantucket, so much of his seasonal staff stayed there, eating like an extended family from a communal kitchen.

Then, in 1994, Pratt met an auctioneer named Sarah Shinn. A tall, slender divorcée with straight blond hair and a toothy smile, she was more than a decade younger but had already forged an impressive resumé. She'd earned an MBA from UCLA and in 1981 latched on at Sotheby's, where she'd learned the art of auctioneering from the esteemed John Marion. After a dozen years she had become a vice president and director of the firm's arcade department. But in 1994 she left Sotheby's to launch her own business, LeBaron Antiques Trading (LeBaron is her middle name), and work as a freelance auctioneer. One of her gigs was at Northeast Auctions, the New Hampshire firm owned by longtime antiques dealer Ron Bourgeault. After one of her auctions, Pratt asked her out to dinner.

"Wayne was sort of hitting on me," Sarah recalled, "which I thought was kind of disgusting because he was standing next to a woman who looked very proprietary"—Marybeth Keene, Pratt's longtime business partner. Sarah brushed him off, assuming they were a couple (in fact, Keene's husband, Rory Killeen, worked for Pratt). Wayne asked Sarah out again several times over the next few months, and she declined each time. She didn't know his story and didn't want to ask; a few innocuous questions could trigger an avalanche of rumors in the gossipy circles they moved in.

Finally, when Shinn happened to be working alone with Bourgeault, she casually inquired about Pratt. Bourgeault encouraged her to accept the dinner invitation, so she relented. "I thought it might be good for business," she said. "He was a pretty big bidder, so I thought I probably shouldn't be so rude to this guy."

Once word got out that they were dating, in autumn 1995, she had to drop her auctioneering jobs to avoid accusations of bias. That winter Sarah accompanied Wayne on a ski trip to Canada's Lake Louise. Both were avid skiers; she, in particular, loved black-diamond runs. But Lake Louise is mostly renowned for its romantic, storybook setting: cozy resorts sprinkled across a landscape of spectacularly serrated, glacier-scoured peaks and neon-blue lakes. Lake Louise is the kind of place where storybook things happen. And sure enough, soon after their return, Sarah called Wayne with some news: She was pregnant. Pratt was flabbergasted. Sarah had tried unsuccessfully to have children before. "Oh," he said. "I know a doctor who can fix that."

Sarah replied that she'd always wanted a baby and wanted to go through with the pregnancy. She absolved him of all responsibility. She didn't need his financial support; she had a successful career and family money, too. Her father, George, had recently retired as chairman and chief executive of the First Boston Corporation, the New York investment bank.

Once Wayne heard Sarah's intentions, he switched tracks. They were having so much fun together, he said, why not get married? Who cared if they'd only been dating for five months? They were an unlikely couple—she refined and privileged, he a rough-edged, ursine fellow from south of Boston. Pratt joked later that it took two months to talk Sarah into accepting.

They were married on July 27, 1996, at the Spurwink Church in Cape Elizabeth, Maine, a nearly two-hundred-year-old edifice that overlooks a classic New England tableau of coastal salt marshes.

James Pratt was born two months later. Wayne, who first became a parent in his twenties, was a father again at age fifty-three. James's godfather was Wayne Pratt's best friend, Bob Matthews.

Matthews had been thriving for years, his puzzling illness notwithstanding. Now in New Haven, Matthews had the same uncanny knack for scooping up distressed, bargain-priced properties, and he was still the hyperactive speed talker, stalking a room in conversation. But he was savvier for his Waterbury collapse. The brash and naive developer who once burst into the mayor's office and demanded subsidies was gone.

The resurrected Matthews was all honey, no vinegar. Though nominally a Republican, Matthews began making big donations to elected officials in both parties. He quickly learned the advantages of checkbook friendships: They launched him into the orbits of the powerful. His office soon was festooned with photos of Matthews at a Clinton "White House coffee"—his inclusion in the big-donors-only fundraising event serving as a precursor to Matthews hosting the Clintons in Nantucket. There was Matthews with John McCain, and with Ted Kennedy and the Shriver clan on Bob's yacht, the *Bon Vivant*.

Though he appreciated this proximity to America's political patresfamilias, Matthews also lavished pecuniary attention on the locals. He gave generously to campaigns and charity events, ingratiating himself to the local power base.

"He's a politician buyer," said Paul Bass, editor of the alternative *New Haven Independent* and a veteran reporter who wrote about Matthews often. "He cultivated the power brokers the moment he got here."

Bass, best known for his caustic, antiestablishment columns, experienced this firsthand. Matthews once took Bass out on the *Bon Vivant,* and the reporter found him to be enormously fun—a dexterous raconteur and gracious host. But Bass had no illusions about what was happening. "Matthews thought he could get better press doing that than if he didn't talk," Bass said. "And he did. The stories were negative, but they were gentler than they would have been."

Compared to the journalistic valentines Matthews was used to, though, the rougher coverage must have been jarring. "Matthews' method: Buy, at low prices, buildings and/or companies pounded by the early-'90s recession," Bass wrote in 1998. "Call on government pals for public money or guarantees. Leverage that for private investment. Then, through tireless networking (some on his yacht or at his $12 million Nantucket mansion), find new tenants and customers."

Among Matthews's government pals was a "City Hall deal-maker,"

Sal Brancati, Bass wrote in another piece. Brancati personally interceded with the New Haven tax assessor in 1996 to win Matthews an unusually high tax break: The city dropped the assessment of one property by more than $4 million, roughly slicing it in half.

Matthews also received a 50 percent cut in the assessment of a building he purchased at 300 George Street. Southern New England Telephone Company had offered the property as part of a downsizing initiative; the edifice was one of New Haven's biggest and best situated, located near major highways and the Yale School of Medicine. Matthews paid $500,000 for it in 1996. "Then, thanks to these 'friends,'" like Brancati, Bass wrote, "Matthews boosted the value of [the] George Street building not by improving it, but by getting its tax assessment lowered and nearby public parking spaces discounted."

Around that same time Brancati's office issued Matthews a $250,000 loan to purchase New Haven Manufacturing. The news reports were glowing. Matthews "has provided what little excitement there was to be had in the New Haven commercial real estate market," *Business New Haven* reported. "Now the flamboyant 39-year-old has stepped in to rescue a venerable New Haven manufacturer from Chapter 11 limbo and what he characterizes as near-certain doom."

Pratt didn't mix with the political crowd, but he had one thing in common with New Haven's power brokers: They all looked out for Bob. Waterbury wasn't the only skeleton dangling in Matthews's well-appointed closet. There was also the executive from Fabricated Metal Products, the metal-stamping firm in nearby Naugatuck that Matthews had purchased in 1989. The acquisition had created some hopeful buzz: The Donald Trump of Waterbury was expanding into manufacturing. But in 1993 the company's former president, Robert L. Hughes, sued Matthews, claiming he was forced to quit after refusing to sign company documents containing false information.

Pratt commiserated. He always took his buddy's side. Running a business was a minefield. Hughes was envious of Matthews's successes because *he* wanted to buy the company, Matthews said. Hughes deserved to be fired for paying himself bonuses, and now *he* was filing suit? Can you *believe* the guy? Bob countersued.

Then there was Jennifer Naegele. Matthews had had a lot of girl-friends, and Naegele was one of the most serious; in 1995 she was briefly his fiancée. The Minnesota native's family had earned a for-tune on billboards; her father was also a Rollerblade founder. Bob and Jennifer were the perfect corporate merger.

But somewhere on the way to wealthily ever after, the relation-ship disintegrated. Naegele broke off the engagement and wrote a letter to wedding invitees in which she alleged Matthews had si-phoned off large amounts of her money by convincing her to endow one of his associates with power of attorney.

Bob was outraged. His associate had actually *saved* Naegele mil-lions of dollars by investing her money wisely and eliminating out-rageous trustee fees, he said. The ingrate. He'd even bought her a Mercedes as a gift. She was clearly unstable, Bob contended.

Pratt commiserated. Women. They could be difficult, no ques-tion.

Pratt was loyal. Bob, after all, was the godfather of Wayne's son. Isn't that what great friends do? Look out for each other?

The notebook containing information about the mystery Bill of Rights arrived in the Washington offices of the First Federal Con-gress Project on February 12, 2003. Steve Frank had two requests. First, he wanted Ken Bowling to authenticate the document. And then, if Bowling deemed the manuscript to be genuine, could he confirm that it was impossible to determine its origins?

Bowling's memory played back over the odd incident three years earlier, when the furtive visitors had appeared with a Bill of Rights glued inside a picture frame. Could this be the same manuscript? If so, the visitors had taken Charlene Bickford's advice and hired a conservator to remove the backing. Bowling flipped through the pages, stopping on the image of the docketing on the parchment's verso:

1789

PROPOSED AMENDMENTS TO
THE CONSTITUTION OF THE
UNITED STATES——

Bowling scanned the other docketing samples in the dossier. Clearly, these held the key to the mystery: He would need to match the docketing on the Bill of Rights with docketing on another document from the same era. Bill Reese had already tried to do that, but to Bowling, this approach—gather together whatever was available from the early Federal period—seemed too random, too much like a needle in a haystack.

Bowling had a better idea. He stood up and walked into the room he and his colleagues had ironically nicknamed the Vault—a roomy storage closet where, among supplies and empty boxes and haphazardly scattered office detritus, they kept files of documents peripherally related to the First Congress. These broom-closet cabinets held what Bowling was after: copies of six or seven of the transmittal letters George Washington sent to the governors of the thirteen states along with the Bill of Rights. These facsimiles were of little material significance to the project. Once documents left the congressional realm, as the Bill of Rights had at that point, they were outside the scope of the staff's work—which explained their storage in the Vault. When the room got too cluttered to move around in, the staffers waded in and threw a bunch of stuff out.

Bowling fished out the Washington letters and returned to his seat. His plan hinged on one elementary fact: In 1789, when the Bill of Rights arrived in each of the states, it was accompanied by the Washington letter. That meant that the clerks had almost certainly signed them in simultaneously. So the docketing on one of those letters should be in the same hand as the faded notation on the mystery Bill of Rights.

Bowling settled down with the notebook and the photocopies from the Vault on the big central table in the conference room.

His first step was to authenticate the document. He studied the handwriting. He knew these clerks' hands well from his thirty-plus years of research, and the writing perfectly matched their formal script. The signatures of John Adams and Frederick Augustus Muhlenberg were flawless. Bowling felt certain this manuscript was the real thing.

The docketing was a different matter. The notation was in an unfamiliar hand. Bowling was masterful at deconstructing the arguments of that First Congress, of divining various motives and agendas. He was not a handwriting expert. Helen Veit, the staff's specialist in that area, sometimes teased him for suggesting that the scriveners' scripts all looked the same. Veit could instantly identify the different clerks' hands and could spot subtleties no one else noticed. She was a fan of Benjamin Bankson, the First Congress clerk who possessed an extraordinary calligraphic flair. "It's gorgeous," she said. "It looks like he was writing wedding invitations."

Veit had a talent for scanning entire lines of handwriting for similarities. "She looks at these things holistically," Bowling said, "whereas I'm comparing the *C* on this one versus the *C* on that one, painstakingly, one letter at a time."

As Bowling methodically plugged away, Veit walked in and peered over his shoulder. Bowling explained. The brokers handling this document contend that it's impossible to determine where it came from, Bowling said. Veit looked down at the pages spread around the table and knew almost instantly.

She said, "You can too tell where it came from. It came from North Carolina."

She pointed to the notation on the back of a document dated October 2, 1789—the transmittal letter that Washington had sent to North Carolina Governor Samuel Johnston.

Bowling looked from the docketing on the Bill of Rights to the docketing on the letter she was pointing to and back again. After scrutinizing both, he could see it.

The pattern of the writing was the same. But it wasn't just that. The more they looked, the more they were able to match up tiny details.

The jaunty bend of the *7* in *1789*. The distinct flow of the word *of.* On both documents the clerk had written *The* with a tall, thin *T* and *h*, no loop on the *h*, and crossed both letters.

Bowling and Veit spent their days immersed in events that took place more than two centuries ago. Their work mostly went unnoticed by the larger world. They didn't make headlines.

Yet they had just unraveled something very big. For good measure they examined another letter, from Washington to North Carolina Governor Johnston, dated June 19, 1789. That docketing matched, too: same hand.

Bowling excitedly called in Charlene Bickford, and she agreed: The same person had docketed those three documents in Raleigh more than 213 years before.

"It was totally obvious that it was the same clerk, the same pen," Bowling said. "I can't understand how anybody could ever think otherwise."

13

Time Runneth Not Against the King

KEN BOWLING IMMEDIATELY CALLED Steve Frank at the National Constitution Center with the news. Frank was astonished. "It was just stunning," he said, "that the evidence was hiding there in plain sight the whole time."

Bowling's two-paragraph letter to Seth Kaller dated February 12, 2003, under the letterhead "Documentary History of the 1st Federal Congress," was terse. Bowling directed Kaller's attention to the docketing on the two Washington missives, and then to the notation on the Bill of Rights. "As you will see, the docketing on the two letters noted above is the same handwriting (and format) as the docketing on the verso of the Bill of Rights manuscript."

He concluded, "Consequently the document you are researching is without question the North Carolina copy of the Bill of Rights."

Kaller called soon after to ask how Bowling had solved the puzzle so quickly. "His professional reputation was on the line," Bowling said, "and it was very embarrassing."

Bowling's letter described the Bill of Rights as "priceless." Kaller asked him to delete that term. He had a buyer willing to pay $5 million, so the document didn't fit that description.

One of Kaller's first thoughts was that he'd been duped a decade earlier. The caller who had offered North Carolina's Bill of Rights in the 1990s had said the parchment lacked docketing. Now that

Kaller knew that wasn't true, it all made sense. "The second I heard Ken's conclusion," he said, "I just knew that it was right."

When Kaller flipped through Bill Reese's notebook again, he had a stunning realization: Reese's researchers had copied the very same docketing sample that Bowling and his colleagues had used to crack the mystery.

But Reese's team had copied only the backside. What Reese and Kaller didn't have was the *front* of that sample: the George Washington letter itself.

If the two men had known what that correspondence was—if they'd known it had arrived together with the Bill of Rights—they might have examined it more closely and might have made the connection on their own.

Ken Bowling's letter rocked the National Constitution Center offices. Joe Torsella and Steve Frank immediately huddled to try to figure out what this meant. In one sense it was good news: Now, at least, the museum officials knew the document was real. They were relieved they hadn't wasted their time on a forgery.

But Torsella and Frank were also hoping for an easy path to an acquisition—which would have been the case if the manuscript were Pennsylvania's, or an unknown extra. The implications of the North Carolina link were unclear. Would the state be willing to cooperate on the document's purchase, as Pennsylvania would have been? They would have to find out.

Bowling's letter bounced through the network of brokers handling the Bill of Rights, all the way back to Peter Tillou. It thus fell to Tillou to call Pratt on the morning of February 17. Without bringing up Bowling's finding, the museum officials wanted to try one more time to find out what Pratt knew—and ask whether there were any lingering title issues. Once again Pratt had little to add.

"Regarding our phone conversation this morning," he wrote in a follow-up letter, "I can guarantee that I purchased the document several years ago, but signed a confidentiality agreement regarding it's [*sic*] history and who I purchased it from. There are no existing challenges to ownership of the item that I am aware of.

". . . If I can be of further assistance," he concluded, "please do not hesitate to call."

Once museum officials got over their initial shock at Bowling's news, they dove into action.

Attorney Steve Harmelin began wrestling with the question of whether the museum could legitimately buy it. He tasked an associate, Rubin Weiner, to plunge into the law books in pursuit of answers. Meanwhile, Torsella began tossing around ideas with Seth Kaller, who had signed on to represent the museum in a potential Bill of Rights purchase. Torsella was clear on one issue: He didn't want to pit the museum against the state of North Carolina in an ownership squabble. He planned to let North Carolina officials know what was going on. It was just a question of when, and how.

What if, for example, the Constitution Center acquired the document and then approached North Carolina for its blessing? Torsella could simply call the governor's office and say, "Good news—we just bought your missing Bill of Rights; let's share custody of it."

But no one knew how the southerners would react. Torsella knew nothing of the document's Civil War–era disappearance from Raleigh, or of Charles Shotwell's misbegotten claim to ownership. He didn't know that North Carolina had been nursing an institutional grudge for the past century.

The museum officials decided the first step was to find out what Wayne Pratt really knew. The antiques dealer had promised full disclosure when Reese had a buyer; now it was time to meet, make an offer, and force Pratt to ante up. The parties agreed to a February 26 meeting in New York City.

In the run-up to the big meeting, Kaller and attorney Steve Harmelin held a conference call to coordinate their plans. They talked mostly about the asking price. They were willing to pay $5 million for a Bill of Rights with a clear title. But given the latest twist—North Carolina's apparent claim—the museum officials thought it was fair to ask for a substantial discount. They had leverage.

In other words, they would do exactly what Pratt had done when he negotiated with the Shotwells.

Rubin Weiner often drew oddball assignments at Dilworth Paxson, the prominent Philadelphia law firm where Steve Harmelin was a partner. The young lawyer was, in a sense, the oddball associate at Dilworth. Rather than zeroing in on corporate law, Weiner had focused on public-sector issues at Harvard. After graduating, he'd headed for California, where he represented the cities of West Hollywood and Santa Monica in cases involving cat ordinances and homeless people. He'd eventually circled back East for family reasons, but his new employer didn't typically handle municipal cases. As a result, Weiner tended to land out-of-left-field tasks like the Bill of Rights research.

Weiner found the investigation fascinating. He had grown up in the South, where William T. Sherman was considered the devil incarnate, so Weiner was surprised to find how generous the Civil War general had been in negotiating peace. The Union in general had been fair with North Carolina—passing the special order mandating the return of all state archives.

Weiner looked for any window of legitimacy for the Bill of Rights purchase. He investigated basic "finders-keepers" rules. He looked at cases involving salvage operations—shipwrecks, for example—that turned up stolen property. He explored statutes of repose to determine whether the state's ownership might have expired at some point. None of it led anywhere promising.

Unlike private citizens, governments enjoy a legal protection known as *replevin*—a common-law concept that dates to British rule. Replevin's underlying principle was that the king was too busy running an empire to be aware of how well his various agents were running his affairs—and so he shouldn't be held responsible if a governor gave away half the palace vault after guzzling too many tankards of mead. Thus, a government retains ownership of its property forever, unless it officially authorizes the sale or disposal thereof. The principle in Latin translates to "time runneth not against the king."

North Carolina, like other states, enjoys an overwhelming advantage in property disputes—much to the consternation of document dealers such as B. C. West Jr.

In 1974 West, who was based in Elizabeth City, North Carolina, published a catalog that included two court indictments from the 1760s signed by William Hooper, a state prosecutor who later inked his name on the Declaration of Independence. There was nothing singularly spectacular about the indictments. Manuscript collectors gravitated to them because of Hooper's signature. Aficionados have long sought to collect the signatures of each of the Declaration's fifty-four signers. West sought $850 for the indictments.

Most times his catalog never would have blipped on the state's radar. But just as West published the catalog, two things happened. In May of 1974 an assistant archivist in North Carolina named Paul Hoffman was flipping through a catalog from Sotheby Parke Bernet, a New York City auction house that later became Sotheby's, when he noticed for sale a 1790 letter from George Washington to North Carolina's governor offering congratulations on the ratification of the Constitution. Hoffman believed the letter was clearly state property and showed it to state archivist Thornton Mitchell. Mitchell agreed and began looking into recovering the correspondence.

Then, a month later, thieves struck in Raleigh, swiping a number of historic papers from the state archives. Figuring the items would soon turn up for sale, the office staff began scouring auction catalogs. Soon enough, they came across West's William Hooper offerings.

Though West's items were not part of the theft, the staff nonetheless determined that they were bona fide public records. The North Carolina attorney general's office asked West to return the documents. He declined. In February 1975 the state filed a temporary restraining order preventing West from selling the documents until the dispute was resolved.

By pursuing West, Thornton Mitchell was gambling his legacy as state archivist. A jowled, solemn-looking man who wore thick, black-framed glasses, Mitchell had planned to retire in 1981. He knew that if West prevailed, the state's quest to reclaim the Washington letter would be seriously undermined. Mitchell would depart as the state archivist who crippled future efforts at recovering missing records. Mitchell, though, focused on the opposite perspective: A win against West would create a legal precedent that the state could leverage for the return of the Washington letter. Mitchell felt that "someone had to have the guts to try to slow or to stop the flow of public records into the manuscript market that had so impressed us as we read catalogs after the 1974 theft," he later wrote.

Archives staffers conducting background research for the West case found precedent in England (which still ruled the colonies during Hooper's time) for permanent ownership of public documents. "Any record touching on the affairs of the realm was potentially a record of the sovereign government," concluded William S. Price Jr., the editor of the state's colonial records project. In England, Robert J. Cain, North Carolina's contract researcher, found copies of judgments that labeled various records as "the King's treasure."

The West trial took place in October 1975. A number of expert witnesses from the manuscript world—noted dealers Charles Hamilton and Mary Benjamin among them—flew in to testify on West's behalf. Judge John Webb found that although the law was in the state's favor, it was unclear how long the Hooper documents had been missing from North Carolina's custody, or how they had disappeared from the archives. As a result, he ruled in favor of West.

The state appealed, and a higher court reversed Webb's ruling. By a two-to-one vote, the appeals panel agreed with state lawyers who argued that a public record cannot be legally separated from state custody unless the legislature votes to discard it. Title to public records cannot be forfeited by carelessness, negligence, or even the intentional conduct of a government agent. The court also ruled that mere possession is not evidence of ownership.

West appealed to the North Carolina Supreme Court. But in a five-to-two decision the justices upheld the appeals court. "These documents," Justice I. Beverly Lake wrote, "being bills of indictment, bear upon their face notice to all the world that they were part of the court records of the Colony of North Carolina and, therefore, property of the State." Victorious state officials got the Hooper documents back and then engineered the return of the George Washington letter.

The Manuscript Society, which had rushed to West's defense, condemned the ruling. P. William Philby, the society's president, called the decision a "travesty." The organization subsequently warned in its 1978 book *Autographs and Manuscripts:* "A purchaser should be particularly cautious about buying any letter or document that may have been held in a public archives unless the manuscript is accompanied by a release from that archives."

What did all this mean to the National Constitution Center's plan for acquiring the Bill of Rights? The bottom line, Rubin Weiner reported to Steve Harmelin, was that if North Carolina dragged them into court, the museum's chances were virtually nil.

February 2003 was an old-school winter month: harsh cold, ice, and snow. The intemperate weather subsided just enough on February 26 for five men to converge on midtown Manhattan to discuss a 213-year-old parchment. Seth Kaller, who by then had moved his shop to White Plains, New York, had the shortest trip, from suburban Westchester County. Bill Reese traveled from New Haven; Wayne Pratt, from Woodbury, Connecticut. The two lawyers headed north: Steve Harmelin from Philadelphia; John Richardson, from Washington.

The meeting took place at the Yale Club, located on Vanderbilt Avenue near Grand Central Station. Reese had booked the Thornton Wilder Conference Room, a meeting space in the club's finely appointed library.

Harmelin, Reese, and Kaller were all intensely curious. None of them had met Pratt before. The dealer's standing in the antiques world was still a source of optimism—at least for Harmelin and museum CEO Joe Torsella. They inferred from Pratt's regular appearances on *Antiques Roadshow* that he bore PBS's imprimatur. Pratt also participated in the Winter Antiques Show and Philadelphia Antiques Show, among other top trade events.

Reese was not so sanguine. He'd heard unsavory things about Pratt's dealings and had serious misgivings about the shell games

Pratt had been playing with the document's provenance and the still-AWOL conservation report. Reese had asked for that report two or three times, and Pratt had responded affirmatively: "Oh, yeah, that's right, I'll send it right over." But it never showed.

Pratt and Richardson, meanwhile, only that day learned the National Constitution Center was the proposed buyer. As he settled in at the meeting, Pratt initially felt good. The museum sounded ideal.

Pratt kept this to himself; Richardson had insisted on doing the talking. After the pleasantries were over, the attorney repeated the now-familiar story: The document had come from a shop in upstate New York and lacked an identifiable link to any state. Pratt had signed a confidentiality agreement, so Richardson couldn't provide further details.

That was when Harmelin pulled his trump card: Based on his expert's findings, he had strong reason to believe the document had come from North Carolina.

Pratt looked stricken. He started to speak, but Richardson cut him off. Both men appeared agitated. Richardson huffily denied the North Carolina connection and claimed he had experts who had found otherwise.

OK, then, Reese said. Who are they, and what did they conclude?

We can't share that information, Richardson said.

For Reese, who had endured months of dodgy answers, this reply triggered more exasperation. "If there was one moment I was utterly convinced it was just all bullshit, it was then," he said. "What earthly reason could there be for not answering? I mean, we're sitting there with a potential buyer. It was a very, very concrete thing at this point."

Richardson then took a different tack: North Carolina had had a chance to buy back the parchment and declined. "The state abandoned it," he said.

Harmelin countered that that didn't sound like abandonment; maybe North Carolina just didn't want to pay for its own property. He and Richardson butted heads for a while, parsing issues of legal ownership.

When they reached a stalemate, Harmelin tried to preempt the dickering. I'm prepared to offer $2 million, he said. I know you're asking $5 million, Harmelin said, but the museum deserves a discount because of the cloudy title. Furthermore, the offer would be contingent on North Carolina's approving the deal.

That last issue was nonnegotiable. "We're not going to do this without North Carolina's consent," Harmelin said. They couldn't spend $2 million of the museum's money and then get sued by the state.

A gauzy layer of tension settled over the room. For Pratt and Richardson, this was a serious comedown. Two million? That was ten times more than Pratt had paid for it, but he owed so many commissions and fees, he'd barely make back his investment.

He had done the math in advance of the meeting, and the numbers didn't look nearly as robust as he'd expected. Pratt had sunk a decent amount of cash into the Bill of Rights in the nearly three years he'd owned it, but the biggest expense by far was John Richardson. Three weeks earlier, in anticipation of a sale, the Washington lawyer had sent Pratt a letter summarizing his stake in the manuscript.

From June 15 to December 31, 1995, Pratt owed $38,541.50 in legal fees. For the rest of the time Richardson had been working on the Bill of Rights—from 1996 through January 2003—his hourly charges totaled another $112,034.50. Multiplied times three—the terms to which Pratt had agreed—the fees added up to $451,728.

Richardson also was due a 30 percent cut on the profit. On a $5 million sale, that number totaled almost $1.44 million. All told, the attorney stood to make $1.89 million.

Pratt would owe another $1 million to brokers Tillou and Bill Reese. And he'd promised a $200,000 finder's fee to Leslie Hindman. After Pratt's and Matthews's own investments, a little over $1.7 million was left. He and Matthews would get about $850,000 each.

That number wasn't bad, but it was hardly the windfall Pratt had envisioned. "I was pissed at John," he said, "because he was getting so much money."

If he sold the document for $2 million, he would hardly see any profit. And on top of that, he would have to deal with the North Carolina problem as well?

That would not do.

Pratt squirmed. He started to argue with Harmelin, but Richardson cut him off. Pratt sat, fuming.

Harmelin could sense both men's distress. He tried another approach: "You know, a charitable contribution of the document could have some major tax benefits for you. Why don't you think about that?"

Recounting the meeting later, Pratt scoffed. He remembered Harmelin offering just $1 million. "I was pissed," Pratt said. "You bring me here and tell me you're only going to pay $1 million because it's North Carolina's? Fuck you."

This wasn't the way his world worked. With old furniture, no one cared where an object came from, or who had owned it. All that mattered was authenticity. Americana people were known to get on the floor, blast antiques with high-wattage flashlights to examine every detail. They were sometimes referred to as "termites." But if the termites agreed an object was right, virtually nothing else mattered.

Pratt was frustrated. He was frustrated that the First Congress Project had suggested the document could be Pennsylvania's, only to change tracks later. He was frustrated that his story hadn't held up. He was frustrated to be subjected to the same bargaining tactic he'd used on the Shotwells.

"I guess they don't want it," Pratt said to Richardson after the meeting. "I'll take it and sell it to another museum. What they're trying to do is steal it."

Wayne Pratt was not accustomed to being challenged. In the past few years he had solidified his standing as a leading authority in his field.

He was accepting a growing number of speaking engagements. Pratt covered early American furniture in the Smithsonian's annual walking tour, an educational event for docents and staff. He took part in a panel discussion on antiques at the Minneapolis Institute of Arts that was later published in the *Maine Antiques Digest*. He participated in forums on Windsor chairs and Boston furniture at the Winter Antiques Show.

The ultimate bully pulpit, though, was *Antiques Roadshow*. Pratt began making appearances on the PBS program not long after his marriage to Sarah Shinn, joining the cast of appraisers in 1997, during the show's second season. During that cycle, at a stop in Secaucus, New Jersey, Leigh and Leslie Keno—the program's identical-twin stars—looked at a card table someone had bought for $25 and recognized it as a rare eighteenth-century piece. The Kenos placed its value at $200,000 to $250,000—at that point the *Roadshow's* highest-appraised item. The table later sold at auction for more than a half-million dollars. That year the *Roadshow* became the most-watched prime-time show on PBS; at its peak it drew more than fifteen million viewers every week.

The program was a boon for both public television and the antiques industry. Viewers scurried into attics and garages, looking for old treasures, which flushed more old things into the marketplace. In a striking example of entertainment industry symbiosis, the television exposure helped elevate the prices of antiques, which in turn made the show still more popular. There was drama in the way each appraisal built toward a climax: the disclosure of an object's value. It was antiques porn. Asked to explain the show's popularity, host Dan Elias once said, "For one thing, there is the whole money aspect, which people really like. It's like the lottery. You watch somebody win the lottery or something like that. And it is similar to a lot of game shows, like 'The Price Is Right.'" As any Bob Barker fan knows, popular game shows never go off the air.

The program always emphasizes backstory. In Denver for one show, Pratt examined a set of cigar-box dominoes made from whale bones. Inside the box, he noted, was the word *Minerva*. "That was a whaling ship that went to San Francisco, and then they had a mutiny," Pratt said. "They decided they wanted to be in the Gold Rush. They sold the boat in San Francisco; it was a very famous boat, and I believe these pieces were on that boat."

Pratt estimated the whale bones were circa 1830 or 1840, and "in great condition—the best I've seen in *yeeahs*." He appraised them at $4,500 to $5,000.

This was interesting TV. But how did Pratt know the dominoes were on the *Minerva*? And the dating of the pieces—did that hinge on their presence on that particular ship? There was no time for any such sourcing; it was on to the next piece. Pratt was an expert, and viewers had to take him at face value.

Pratt himself was struck by the power of that stage. "TV is an amazing thing," he said. "It's almost scary—people believe everything they see on television."

An eager participant, Pratt was surprisingly mediagenic. He cut a formidable figure with his imposing bulk and his dancing eyes and his south-of-Boston accent. Other appraisers came to him for advice, fellow dealer David Schorsch said. His appearances helped his business.

Every year after the Winter Antiques Show, Wayne and Sarah Pratt headed off to vacation on St. Barts, where they mingled with the antiques glitterati. They clinked glasses there regularly with R. Scudder Smith, editor of *Antiques and The Arts Weekly*.

Pratt was the industry lodestar in Woodbury, which had grown into one of New England's top antiques destinations. Pratt's presence was a factor in Schorsch's decision to move to the town, in 1997, from wealthier Greenwich, Connecticut. Pratt employed fourteen or so people, plus seasonal help, and spread his money around, hiring local furniture and paint restorers and buying from area dealers. He donated the $8,000 to $10,000 he earned annually from speaking gigs to local Woodbury charities: the Lions Club, the choral society, youth baseball. He gave a scholarship to a Woodbury high school senior and hosted a benefit golf tournament for older players, cheekily titled the Wayne Pratt Antique Shoot-Out.

There were headaches, to be sure, but Pratt was living the dream. "Everybody wants to be an antiques dealer," Wayne Mattox said. Mattox was a Woodbury-based dealer who wrote an online column but had yet to get a whiff of a Winter Antiques Show invitation. "It's the closest thing to buying a lottery ticket that you can do legally. You buy things for a couple thousand dollars, and sell them for $20,000 to $50,000. It's like the stock market, only everybody who works hard at it has insider information."

Pratt was the ultimate insider. Now he was on the outside looking in, and in his mind, the historic-documents world was conspiring against him.

The meeting at the Yale Club was over within thirty minutes and left Pratt bristling with anger. Who were these people to try to lowball him—and question his word? Harmelin, for one, struck him as a "flamboyant asshole."

"It was insulting," Pratt said. "It was the document they were insulting."

The tension that smothered the room didn't relent until Pratt and Richardson got up and left.

Reese, Kaller, and Harmelin sat looking at each other for a moment. And then Reese said, "They're lying." He felt certain about that. Having met Richardson and Pratt, Reese now believed their stories of the antiques-hardware store and the deceased Ohio couple were fiction.

Kaller was inclined to agree. "I trust Bill explicitly," he said. "I never knew Peter Tillou before this, but Bill trusts Peter explicitly. We'd all heard of Wayne Pratt and would never have expected this kind of thing.

"Bill realized that they knew all along about North Carolina, and they weren't going to be apologetic about it."

Less than twenty-four hours passed before the phone rang in Bill Reese's New Haven office. It was John Richardson, calling to inform Reese that Wayne Pratt wanted the Bill of Rights back. A courier was coming that day to fetch it.

Not long after that a Pratt employee named Joe Constantino arrived at Reese's Temple Street building. Reese had him sign for the manuscript. The bookseller wasn't at all surprised that Pratt was reclaiming the parchment.

Reese called Seth Kaller to let him know the Bill of Rights was gone—presumably headed to Woodbury. Kaller, in turn, called the National Constitution Center.

Museum officials took the news hard. What were Pratt's intentions now? Was that the last they would hear of him—or of the document? Had Harmelin played his hand too aggressively?

They knew one thing: They weren't ready to give up. Bill Reese's option didn't expire until March 16. Until that date passed, they would exhaust all of their options.

They decided to do two things. First, Torsella wrote a memo to his executive committee informing them that the Bill of Rights—originally of undetermined origin—could now definitively be traced to North Carolina.

Second, Torsella began making plans to contact someone down in Raleigh.

14

The Joy of Illegitimate Possession

W
HEN THE LETTER FROM the stranger up in Pennsylvania arrived at his office on the campus of the University of North Carolina, J. G. de Roulhac Hamilton was not at all pleased. Somehow, a man from up North had gotten his hands on North Carolina's copy of the Bill of Rights. This was particularly unwelcome news. Hamilton was one of the South's leading historians and authors, a man who valued such documents more than most.

The date was February 1925. The two-page missive was typed beneath the letterhead "Reid Editorial Service, Harrisburg, Pennsylvania." The writer, a man named Charles Reid, explained that he'd been scouring Hamilton's history books for "detailed information about the incidents connected with the entrance of the Union Army into the city of Raleigh, the sacking of the city and the state house."

Reid went on: "I have recently come into possession of the original copy of the first thirteen [sic] amendments to the Constitution of the United States given to the state of North Carolina . . . This document was taken from the state house at Raleigh by one of the Union soldiers who came from Ohio. I am greatly interested in obtaining any details of the events surrounding the incident. Any suggestion would be greatly appreciated."

The manuscript "was taken from a vault in the office of the Secretary of State of North Carolina by a soldier of Sherman's Army on the march from Georgia to the sea," Reid continued. "This soldier was one of a company who went through the state house, helping themselves to whatever they found. The soldier took the document home with him to Tippecanoe, Ohio."

A final addendum notes: "This document has been kept with very little exposure to the light and is still in splendid condition. It is a remarkable piece of penmanship and every line of it is almost as legible as when it was first written."

Hamilton no doubt seethed at reading this. A professor in Chapel Hill for the past nineteen years, chairman of the history department for the past seventeen, Hamilton was also a prolific author, having written numerous books on North Carolina, the Civil War, and Reconstruction. He counted on primary sources—letters, records, proclamations—remaining in official custody. These documents were the lifeblood of his profession—whose cause he would soon take up as his personal crusade, by spearheading the creation of the university's Southern Historical Collection. To amass materials for the repository, which opened in January 1930, Hamilton trundled across the South in a relentless search for documents, his bulldoggish zeal earning him the nickname "Ransack." By the time he retired in 1948, the collection contained more than two million manuscripts. He now has a building named after him on the Chapel Hill campus.

Even at this early stage, Hamilton already seemed to intuitively know how to deal with collectors. Threaten them, and they disappeared as abruptly as they had turned up. So instead of writing the sort of intemperate reply he no doubt craved to, Hamilton engaged the Pennsylvanian. He dashed off a cordial note on February 9, informing "My dear Mr. Reid" that Cornelia Phillips Spencer's *The Last Ninety Days of the War in North Carolina* contained the best account of Union troops entering the city—but that book was out of print and difficult to find. Hamilton noted that Reid could find a "much briefer account in my 'Reconstruction in North Carolina.'"

Hamilton went on: "You are mistaken as to the sacking of the city. The State House was pretty thoroughly rummaged over and looted to some extent, but there was a notable absence of that sort of thing in the case of the city."

And then Hamilton, having softened his correspondent with

southern gentility, tried tweaking Reid's sense of civic duty. "Might I suggest," he wrote, "that since the document in your possession is the property of the State of North Carolina . . . that it would be a very graceful and appreciated act on your part to follow the example of numerous other persons in the North, into whose possession documents with a similar history have come, and restore it to the State of North Carolina? . . . I can assure you that such action will be highly appreciated in the State."

Hamilton mailed the letter—and then he vented. He addressed a separate note to R. B. House, secretary-treasurer of the North Carolina Historical Commission. The commission was created in 1903, becoming only the third official state archive in the United States. Hamilton enclosed a copy of Reid's letter and his reply. Then he attached a note. "It would not be worth suing the man," Hamilton wrote, "and there are some objections to making an official claim to it, but at the same time, I hate for these damned rascals to get away with it. You can take such action as you think wise."

Until Reid's letter arrived in 1925, no one in North Carolina had heard a whisper of the lost Bill of Rights for almost thirty years. The last contact regarding the missing document had been with Charles Shotwell back in 1897—and the way that incident had ended, with Shotwell adamantly refusing to surrender the parchment, state officials suspected they'd heard the last of it. And now? Harrisburg, Pennsylvania, was hundreds of miles from Indianapolis. The relic seemed to have changed hands.

On February 13 R. B. House sent a quick reply to Professor Hamilton. "I think you have made clear to him what he ought to do in the matter of returning the manuscripts [*sic*] to the State of North Carolina," he told the historian, "and I think it would be wise to give him a little time to do the right thing, if he wants to."

But Reid wasn't interested in making a donation. A month later, on March 16, he wrote to Julian Carr of Durham, North Carolina, with a sales pitch. In the seven weeks that had passed since Reid's letter to Hamilton, Reid Editorial Service of Harrisburg had morphed into Charles I. Reid Lectures and Concert Tours of

767 St. Nicholas Avenue, New York City. And his job as fact seeker —harvester of information about the historic manuscript—had morphed into work as a broker. He announced that the document's owner "has commissioned the writer to find a purchaser for it."

Reid didn't identify the purported title holder. But he wrote, "This parchment has, as far as I know, never before been available for purchase, and has been in the possession of the present owner since 1866.

"It is thought that you might be interested in a first opportunity to obtain this most important of historical documents, for your private collection or for presentation to the state of North Carolina," Reid wrote. "I am prepared to obtain prompt consideration of your offer."

Carr was an obvious choice for such an acquisition. He was one of the state's great business magnates, a certifiable Tar Heel icon, the creator of the advertising blitz that had turned Bull Durham Tobacco into the world's top-selling cigarette brand. Carr organized the first textile mill in the city of Durham, opened the First National Bank of Durham, and built a railroad and several hotels. He also coaxed Trinity College to move to Durham. The school has since changed its name to Duke University.

But there were two problems with Reid's plan. The first was that Julian Carr had died the previous April at the age of seventy-eight. The second? Carr, not surprisingly, had had friends in high places.

Word of Reid's letter to Carr quickly leaked back to the official keepers of North Carolina's records. Thomas Gorman, Carr's private secretary and the executor of his estate, sent a copy of the correspondence to Fred Olds, founder of a museum called the Hall of History, which featured a collection of historical documents. "[I]f you see fit, you can write to the party," Gorman wrote. "It appears to me that the document referred to ought to be, by rights, returned to the State Archives, at this time, without any reward . . ." Gorman also forwarded Reid's letter to R. B. House of the North Carolina Historical Commission.

A reader with any knowledge of the parchment's history could have quickly surmised that Reid represented Charles Shotwell, the Indianapolis man who had refused to surrender the Bill of Rights twenty-eight years earlier. Shotwell, though, had decided to take his chances. In February 1925 he was approaching eighty and plotting a move to Southern California to live near his two sons from his first marriage. His motive was simple enough: He needed funds for his convalescence. And as the document's caretaker for fifty-nine years, he didn't want to give it away.

The Shotwells sensed that the document was growing in value and significance. In the spring of 1907, Charles's wife, Clara, put the Bill of Rights on deposit at the Indiana State Library, which had recently advertised its services as the only fireproof repository in Indianapolis. The library's newsletter included a one-sentence notice about the parchment under the heading "Interesting deposit."

Fortunately for the Shotwells, their son, Grier, was there to help. The child who had arrived so late in Charles and Clara's life was an achiever right from the start: He had been a top student at Shortridge High School, where he was captain of the football team, editor of the school newspaper, and member of the debate team. Grier had attended Lafayette College, in Pennsylvania, until World War I interrupted his studies. But instead of heading for the trenches, Grier went to Columbia University's School of Military Cinematography in February 1918 for training as a master signal electrician. Grier shipped out to Russia in July—only four months before the war's end.

A surviving photograph shows the young Shotwell, dressed crisply in a military uniform, looking through a camera in front of Russia's Monastery Church of Archangel, onion-shaped domes rising in the background. Standing next to him, also looking snappy and operating a movie camera on a tripod, is Lieutenant Charles I. "Chip" Reid.

When Grier returned home in August 1919, he was commissioned into the Officers' Reserve Corps and headed back to Lafayette. He graduated with a degree in philosophy in 1920 and immediately pursued a law degree at Northwestern University. He returned home and passed the bar in Marion County, Indiana, in February 1925.

Charles Shotwell was no documents expert. And the 1897 encounter had been jarring enough that he wanted to avoid dealing directly with North Carolina. And anyway, his son was a lawyer now with a smart and ambitious war buddy. By deputizing Chip Reid, the Shotwells gained a layer of separation.

Grier Shotwell sent Reid a photograph of the Bill of Rights in 1924. Soon after, the elder Shotwell mailed Reid a letter detailing the document's journey from the waning days of the Civil War.

Reid had some inkling of what he was up against, but there was no way to predict the mindset of the people running the state archives. Maybe they were more pliable than their predecessors. Or maybe Reid could appeal to their vanity. The parchment's return would make for sunny headlines down in Raleigh. It would be a feel-good story. There was no way to know until you asked.

Inevitably, however, Reid's letters sent the same ripples of displeasure through the capital that the *Indianapolis News* article about Charles Shotwell had twenty-eight years earlier.

R. B. House, an ambitious, baby-faced, bald-headed bureaucrat, had risen to his lofty post before his thirtieth birthday. He had recently launched a scholarly magazine on North Carolina history and was keenly aware of the state's long-standing interest in reclaiming its lost property. He wasn't about to let Reid's attempts to flog the important relic pass without comment. On March 24 House fired off a letter to Reid. "It appears," House wrote, "that you are seeking a purchaser of the original of the bill of rights as submitted to the State of North Carolina.

> I, of course, do not know the history of this document since its disappearance from North Carolina, but it was stolen from the State Capital in 1865 and therefore the title to it has never passed from the State of North Carolina to any individual. I rely upon your interpretation of these circumstances to take what action you think right in the matter. I am sure, however, that no person in the State

of North Carolina would be willing to purchase the documents under such conditions, and thus give commercial standing to such an act as its being taken under the circumstance attending to its disappearance. The document, of course, is entirely of sentimental value, as part of the original records of the State.

Reid responded immediately. The secret was out, and House didn't seem as hostile as Reid might have expected. Perhaps Reid saw a flicker of hope in House's lack of overt antagonism.

Whatever he read into House's correspondence, Reid decided to embrace the state's involvement. In his return letter Reid again summarized the story of the Union soldier who took the parchment and "carried it home with him to Tippecanoe, Ohio and there sold it to the present possessor in 1866.

"I do not know, after the opinion you have given, whether any private title could exist," Reid wrote. "The old gentleman who bought it of [*sic*] the soldier did so in the belief that it was contraband of war, which may have been the case at that time."

Reid recounted Shotwell's story—probably apocryphal—that North Carolina officials had journeyed to Indiana to claim the document in 1897, only to have Shotwell turn them away.

The possessor is a very old man and has treasured this manuscript for the past 59 years. I believe a need of money has prompted him to offer it for sale. In view of the fact that, as you say, it has a sentimental value, aside from any personal value he may attach to it, only in the state of North Carolina and is a public document, I believe he would be disposed to consider and accept any reasonable honorarium for any equity, real or imaginary, he may have in it, and I would so recommend to him. He has certainly preserved the document well and it would return home in about the same condition in which it left.

House was unmoved. His first letter to Reid had only hinted at his growing irritation. After reading Reid's reply, House apparently concluded that he and Reid had reached an unbridgeable divide:

Reid's client would never return the document for nothing, and North Carolina would never pay to get it back. "I acknowledge your letter of March 25th," House wrote two weeks later.

> The document you are attempting to sell, though clearly the property of the State of North Carolina, is not important enough to engage in controversy over. So long as it remains away from the official custody of North Carolina, it will serve as a memorial of individual theft. Since this fact must be clear to anyone acquainted with history and law, not to mention honor, it is interesting to note the present whereabouts of the document and to speculate on how long the joy of illegitimate possession can hold out against scruples arising from intelligent consideration of facts involved.

He signed off, "Very truly yours, Secretary."
And with that, the correspondence abruptly ended.

Charles Reid went on to find modest success as a promoter of lectures and concerts. He signed several notable clients, including Princess Alexis Obolensky. Then, one November day in 1929, Reid rented a biplane from New York City's Roosevelt Field. He'd recently completed a course in flying, earned a pilot's license, and was taking a client, Robert Bailie, a twenty-three-year-old lion tamer and adventurer, for a jaunt above the Manhattan skyline.

As the plane swooped over Long Island Sound, heading toward the East River, the engine began sputtering. Reid continued on over Manhattan, but the plane continued to knock and cough and eventually began to lose altitude over Central Park. While Reid worked frantically to keep it from diving, Bailie crawled out on a wing and parachuted to safety, landing with only a few bruises. Reid courageously hung in even when the engine conked out, preventing the plane from crashing onto a crowded street. The guttering, yawing craft slammed into the upper reaches of a still-under-construction, twelve-story YMCA building on West Sixty-fourth Street, then fell to a lower roof—the first airplane to strike a New York City building. Reid, who died instantly, left a wife and two young daughters. He was thirty-four.

Charles and Clara Shotwell moved to Long Beach, California, in 1927. The couple rented a home on Mira Mar Street for $40 a month and lived there until Charles's death in May 1937, at the age of ninety. His son Grier journeyed to California to bring home his mother, who lived with him until she passed on a year later. The Bill of Rights returned to Indiana as well.

R. B. House left his post at the historical commission at the end of 1925. No one in North Carolina heard anything more of the document for a full lifetime. Instead, there were only questions. Was North Carolina's righteous approach the wise choice? Is it always prudent to stand on principle? Or should the state have simply acknowledged that many things happen during wars that wouldn't take place in a perfectly principled world, and paid a nominal fee to reclaim its relic?

And what of Charles Shotwell and Charles Reid? In the end they didn't make a value judgment so much as a strategic blunder. They believed that only someone connected to the Tar Heel State would be interested in acquiring that particular Bill of Rights: "It has sentimental value," Reid wrote, "only in the state of North Carolina."

The two men couldn't have been more wrong.

Charles Shotwell was a man who loved history and who lucked into one of America's great manuscripts—but he was not a collector. A collector would have known better. A collector would have known about the currency being spent on that sort of document, and the euphoria that devotees felt as a result of being in the same room with such a numinous artifact, and the madness that sometimes resulted when you mixed all that money and passion together.

15

Nowhere Fast

E D RENDELL'S PHONE CALL went through on Friday afternoon, February 28, 2003. This was one of the more unusual tasks Rendell had undertaken in the few weeks he'd been governor of Pennsylvania. He was about to talk to Mike Easley, his counterpart in North Carolina, about an original Bill of Rights.

Joe Torsella, the CEO of the National Constitution Center, had asked Rendell to make the call two days after the Yale Club confrontation with Wayne Pratt. Torsella wasn't ready to give up and wanted to make a good impression with the folks in North Carolina the first time the museum approached them with the idea of acquiring the parchment. The situation was delicate, and Torsella wasn't about to just barge into the Capitol and announce plans to purchase the state's missing multimillion-dollar relic.

Torsella knew little of the document's quarrelsome history, so he thought if he could separate the document from Pratt's chicanery, North Carolina might just go for some kind of sharing arrangement. But he was fully aware of the need for a diplomat's hat-in-hand deference, lest the whole thing sound ludicrous: *I'm from a Philadelphia museum that hasn't opened yet, and I want to buy your copy of the Bill of Rights. That sound good to you?*

So Torsella had called his old boss, Rendell, the museum's most prominent booster—and the guy who'd gotten the museum involved with the parchment in the first place. A phone call from a governor carried cachet and would instantly demonstrate the museum was legitimate.

Better yet, Easley was also a Democrat. They were natural allies.

When Rendell called, Easley was working in the southwest bedroom of the governor's mansion in Raleigh, where he often holed up to avoid the racket of daily public tours.

Listen, Rendell said after they'd chatted for a few minutes. We've been offered a Bill of Rights, and our experts have determined that it's your copy. What would you like us to do?

Easley, a lawyer, had served as a district attorney before being elected the state's chief executive in 2000. It was a busy time in Raleigh. In a couple of days he was scheduled to deliver his second State of the State address—one that pundits expected would unofficially launch his reelection campaign. Soon after that he would unveil a new $15 billion state budget aimed at tackling the state's fiscal crisis.

So Easley thanked Rendell for the phone call and told him he would need a little time to look into the matter. Then he did what most busy elected officials would do: He delegated the matter, in this case to a staff lawyer named Hampton Dellinger.

The following Monday, Joe Torsella and Laura Linton, the museum's executive vice president, called North Carolina to follow up and wound up on the phone with Dellinger, son of renowned constitutional expert Walter Dellinger. Linton suggested three possible approaches: One, the Constitution Center could buy the document with North Carolina's approval. The museum would hold a press conference at which the governors could jointly announce a plan to permanently house the parchment in Philadelphia but regularly exhibit it in North Carolina. Two, the museum could collaborate with North Carolina on a purchase and arrange to share ownership. Or three, the museum could stand down and let Carolina officials pursue the document on their own.

Dellinger told Linton he would circulate those ideas and get back to her.

• • •

One key figure was absent from this new round of discussions: Bill Reese. A year earlier he had felt palpable excitement about handling the Bill of Rights. Moving a relic of such immense value would have solidified his standing as the nation's top seller of rare, historic books and manuscripts. More than that, he loved being around such objects.

But after Wayne Pratt's courier repossessed the parchment, Reese soured on the whole thing. From the beginning he'd felt that if the Bill of Rights belonged to a state, he didn't want to be involved. He'd been down that road before.

He was also annoyed. Reese had deployed his staff all across the Eastern Seaboard to track down the parchment's history—a history Pratt apparently already knew. Reese regretted not divining the North Carolina link on his own. "I was just kicking myself for not putting two and two together earlier," he said. "I felt like I'd been duped."

If the museum wanted to continue its pursuit of the parchment, Reese figured, Seth Kaller was more than capable of shepherding the deal along. "If the Constitution Center can muster a political settlement where everybody's happy, then God bless them," Reese said. "I'm happy to see it done, and if I didn't make any money on it, fine."

Reese understood the museum's fixation. Torsella wanted to make the museum as great as possible—and a document of such immense totemic value would clearly bring the entire enterprise up a notch.

Down in Raleigh, no one could exactly get a fix on what to do. Easley was busy with his speeches, and few people outside North Carolina's archives had any clue as to the peculiar history of the state's rare parchment. The whole thing sounded sort of surreal: some guys up in Pennsylvania calling about a Bill of Rights that's supposedly ours. Who knew North Carolina even had one?

Hampton Dellinger turned the matter over to Reuben Young, Easley's chief legal counsel. But then something fortuitous happened: In the first of a series of unlikely coincidences, Young's wife,

Pam, was a deputy secretary in the Department of Cultural Resources, which houses the state archives.

Pam Young went and asked Jeff Crow, "Have you ever heard of
anything about North Carolina's copy of the Bill of Rights?" Crow,
the deputy secretary of archives and history, knew the lore. He dug
out a file containing the decades-old correspondence related to
Charles Shotwell. Pam Young passed the file to her husband. "Of
course this was all very hush-hush," Crow said. "I didn't know exactly what was going on."

On Friday, March 7, Reuben Young sat down with Governor Easley. Given all that had happened over the past 138 years, Young was
disinclined to buy the document or transfer title to the National
Constitution Center. Buying it meant paying for stolen property and
breaking ranks with all previous officials who had resisted that option. Letting the museum buy it meant losing out altogether.

But no one knew what to do. Phone lines between Raleigh and
Philadelphia kept buzzing, but the conversations had a tentative,
searching quality: strangers feeling their way around a dark room.

Governor Rendell's chief of staff, John Estey, tried to get on the
phone and help from Harrisburg. The Carolinians seemed to want
reassurances—"to make sure they weren't dealing with some crazy
crackpots from Pennsylvania," Estey said.

Estey could relate. The situation wasn't much more settled
in Harrisburg. Rendell had been in office for a little more than a
month, and his staff was still finding its footing. "There were so
many things going on," Estey said, "that we didn't know what each
other was doing. The nature of government is that it doesn't move
as fast as people in the private sector might. There are a lot of layers
to move through." If the tables were turned, Estey said, and someone had called wanting to buy Pennsylvania's copy, he would have
needed a week or more to figure out the backstory and decide what
to do.

In this case there wasn't much Estey could do. He encouraged
his North Carolina counterparts to talk to the museum and reas-
sured them that the Constitution Center folks were good, responsible people.

The situation seemed locked in suspended animation—as if all the players involved were cartoon characters madly pinwheeling their legs but going nowhere. Down in North Carolina, Reuben Young called Laura Linton on March 9 to say he would talk to Governor Easley again and get back to her the following week. As Linton and Torsella discussed this latest development in the museum's offices, they began to feel edgy. The days kept rolling past with no resolution in sight.

Nine days. That was how much time they had left, Torsella thought. The only way for them to get their hands on the document was through Bill Reese's sale option, which expired on March 16. (Reese had told the museum that his option to engineer a sale remained viable even if he wasn't directly involved.)

Nine days. Sit tight, Reuben Young had said the last time they'd talked. We'll figure this out soon.

Wayne Pratt was unaware of all of these behind-the-scenes machinations. But he couldn't have been terribly surprised: He had known all along that the Bill of Rights was a gamble. The thing was, he liked risk. He liked adventure. You couldn't be best friends with Bob Matthews and play life safe.

Take the time in May 1997, for example, when Matthews came looking for a favor. Matthews always bragged about his highly placed connections, but none of them rivaled his bond with Connecticut Governor John Rowland. The two had met back in the early eighties, when they were both young and hot in pursuit of outsized ambitions. Rowland, a Waterbury native who had just graduated from Villanova, decided at the age of twenty-three to run for Connecticut's House of Representatives. Bob's brother David Matthews gave Rowland office space in a downtown building and campaign materials from his unsuccessful run for a House seat two years earlier.

Rowland and Bob Matthews eventually became good friends; they shared a sense that the world didn't see them coming. Rowland and Matthews spent hours kibitzing, hanging out at Waterbury haunts, playing golf, and talking politics and business.

Rowland's meteoric political ascent is legendary in Connecticut.

He won the House seat, served a couple of terms, and got elected to the U.S. Congress at twenty-seven. A master of regular-guy appeal, the dark-haired, round-faced Rowland projected a wisecracking, elbow-jabbing, wink-wink persona that beguiled voters and media. In 1991 Rowland moved to Middlebury, becoming Matthews's neighbor. They were so tight that Rowland briefly lived in the carriage house on his friend's estate a year later after a difficult divorce.

Rowland was unflinchingly loyal to his old Waterbury buddies. After Rowland was elected governor in 1994, Matthews received state-funded grants through the Connecticut Development Authority, a state agency whose members the governor appointed. Matthews, meanwhile, opened his yacht to Rowland in July 1995, during the Special Olympics World Games in New Haven.

Rowland's divorce added a layer of urgency to their relationship. He had three children with his former wife and later became the stepfather of two more. His 1996 tax return showed he'd paid $47,207 in alimony; his gubernatorial salary was $78,000. And in 1997 he purchased a cottage on Bantam Lake, in upmarket Litchfield County, for $110,000, stretching his finances further.

Around that time Matthews approached Wayne Pratt, looking for a favor. Matthews wanted to buy Rowland's Washington, D.C., condominium—a tiny, 278-square-foot place that the governor owned from his years as a congressman. Matthews didn't care to extend his empire inside the Beltway—but he did want to help Rowland out with the condo. But since Matthews did business with the state, it wouldn't do for him to buy the condo himself. That wouldn't look good.

Bob explained. He would write Pratt a check for the condo's purchase price. Pratt would then write a check to the governor. Matthews would reimburse Pratt for any related expenses.

Matthews had already turned the condo into Rowland's personal ATM machine. The previous year the governor had begun renting the place to Kelly Deal, Matthews's niece, for $1,750 a month—at least three times the going rate. The rent checks came from Uncle Bob.

Pratt mulled over the request. The whole thing sounded like typical Bob. It sounded iffy. But this was Pratt's best friend, and how many best friends do you have in life? The two men were so close that if Sarah Pratt couldn't find her husband, she called the Matthews house first. "It was," she said, "almost an abnormal relationship." Just a few months earlier Matthews had taken the Pratts— Wayne, Sarah, and six-month-old James—on a tour of the Virgin Islands in his yacht. How do you say no to someone like that?

Plus, Matthews reminded Pratt, they were talking about the *governor* here. Rowland was immensely popular in Connecticut and was tight with the Bush family; there were rumors that if Texas Governor George W. Bush ran for the White House, Rowland would be on the short list of potential running mates.

Pratt mentioned the proposed deal to his lawyer. "Why not?" the attorney told him. "The guy's probably gonna be vice president someday."

There was yet one more motivation: Pratt wanted to crack the inner circle. Pratt didn't know Rowland. He'd shaken hands with him maybe once. "Bob didn't mix Wayne with other social circles," Sarah Pratt said. "He wouldn't mix Wayne with the glittery crowd, or the political crowd. I always thought it was an uneven relationship."

This ate at Pratt. "I think that's part of it—he wanted to be part of the group," his friend David Schorsch said. "Matthews was part of that—he was buddies with the governor, he had Bill Clinton to his house, and all this kind of nonsense. It's understandable that you could fall into that."

Pratt said yes. Matthews told him Rowland wanted $68,500. The price didn't seem unreasonable at first; Rowland had paid $57,500 eight or so years earlier. But the market for Capitol Hill real estate had since collapsed. In fact, Rowland's sale price was $27,000 more than the average price paid for similar units at the time.

Matthews didn't care. He wrote Pratt a check for $68,500, and then an additional $5,000 for the contents, telling Pratt that the governor was "squeezing him for more money." The two men agreed to "fudge" Pratt's account books to make it appear as if the money was for antiques.

On June 12 Pratt signed off on the deal without meeting Rowland, without seeing the condo, and without attending a closing. Though no one noticed the transaction in Connecticut, real estate agents in D.C. were astounded. "I almost fell off my chair," said Pam Kristof, who had sold Rowland the apartment in 1989.

Pratt said that Matthews told him to destroy all the records of what they'd just done.

Joe Torsella spent a restless weekend wondering whether the Bill of Rights was ever going to happen. By the time Monday, March 10, came and went, the museum CEO's anxiety level had risen palpably.

Ten days had passed since he'd gotten North Carolina involved, and Bill Reese's option was due to expire the following Sunday. The Constitution Center was scheduled to open in less than four months. If the document ended up in the museum's holdings, Torsella and his staff would have to hustle after plans to conserve, store, and display it.

Torsella again called John Estey in Governor Ed Rendell's office. Look, he said. Our only chance to get this thing is about to expire. Could somebody please tell us what to do?

Torsella also checked in regularly with Seth Kaller, who had built a consortium capable of covering the $5 million asking price. The enthusiasm among the museum's benefactors had not waned.

Finally, on Wednesday, March 12, Estey called the National Constitution Center with news: North Carolina wanted the museum to acquire the Bill of Rights. "Go," Estey said. "They want you to buy it."

But then, an hour later, something shifted down in Raleigh. Estey called back: Change of plans. Don't buy it yet. Stand by a little longer.

At 4:15 p.m. Reuben Young and Andy Vanore, a lawyer from the North Carolina attorney general's office, held a conference call with Torsella, Laura Linton, and Steve Harmelin from the Constitution Center. After a couple of weeks of back and forth, the first hints of tension began to emerge. Linton mentioned the museum acquiring title to the Bill of Rights—a suggestion Young bristled at. "Under no circumstances will North Carolina transfer title of the document to anyone," he said.

To the museum officials, Governor Easley's office sounded like a house divided. On one hand they liked the idea of the Constitution Center fronting the money and avoiding the risk of the document disappearing. On the other they wanted to maintain precedent. Historically, the state had toed a hard line when it came to paying for its own property. And no one on Easley's watch wanted to concede title to the iconic parchment.

Attorney Steve Harmelin called Reuben Young back later that afternoon in a quest for middle ground. Legal title isn't the be-all and end-all, Harmelin told him. The museum's benefactors would probably agree to North Carolina keeping title to the document as long as it was on permanent display in Philadelphia.

But by that point officials in North Carolina were starting to harden against the idea of any kind of compromise at all.

On Thursday, March 13, just the opposite seemed to be true, however. North Carolina again signaled that day that the museum should buy the document. The answer this time was definitive enough that Pennsylvania Governor Ed Rendell e-mailed Richard Gilder to say that North Carolina had given its blessing, and that the Constitution Center would acquire the Bill of Rights for $4.5 million. (Bill Reese had already expressed his intention to drop out of the deal, eliminating his $1 million commission. Seth Kaller, meanwhile, had negotiated a separate $500,000 brokerage fee.)

Joe Torsella headed over to the museum's construction site that afternoon. There were just three days left until the sale option expired, but it appeared, finally, that the museum would pull it off. After two months of Bill of Rights intrigue, everything was finally coming together. For the moment Torsella could focus on the building—on the countless construction issues to resolve between then and opening day.

And then his cell phone rang. Hardly an unusual thing, but when he looked down, he didn't recognize the number.

It's funny how big things start small: The fax machine hums, out comes a note from Ed Rendell, and the next thing Torsella knew he was on the verge of buying a Bill of Rights.

So it was late that afternoon, too. The cell phone. The unfamiliar number. Torsella answered it, heard an unfamiliar voice.

"This is Bob Wittman from the FBI," the voice said. "What's the deal with the Bill of Rights?"

16

The Sky's the Limit

WHEN PEOPLE SPEAK of the Constitution as being an organic document, they're not being literal. But in fact, the Bill of Rights manuscript started out as part of a living thing. Parchment is made from the skin of a sheep or a cow.

After slaughtering the animal and removing its skin, a parchment maker limed the skin and scraped off the hair or wool with a blunt knife. The skin was then dried at room temperature while tautly suspended, usually on a wooden device known as a stretching frame. The craftsman then applied more lime to remove moisture and grease. The last step was to shave the surface smooth with a semicircular knife and pumice. A good piece of parchment is thin and strong and flexible, and it has an even, uniform writing surface. No two are exactly alike. North Carolina's Bill of Rights had discolored blotches unique to the animal it came from.

Paper eventually wears down from human touch, but parchment sustains no such damage. The oils from human skin are actually good for it, in a revitalizing kind of way. Parchment also responds to temperature changes in eerily alive ways. Even hundreds of years after it was made, a parchment will expand in heat and contract in cold.

Parchment is different in yet another way: Ink thoroughly permeates paper over time, soaking through the individual fibers of the pulp.

Not so with parchment. Ink never penetrates the surface. The fluid, elegant script on the Bill of Rights seems to almost levitate above the writing surface. Rub hard enough, and you can take words off.

Yet one more element of it is alive: the ideas and genius. At his brightest moment, James Madison came hard up against an unappealing but inarguable fact: Given access to great power and wealth, humans need to be protected from themselves, from their basest impulses. Put even the most pure-hearted man on a throne, with access to all the riches of the crown, and he changes. He becomes more interested in protecting his station than in running a government, or in securing the welfare of his subjects.

The Bill of Rights created a firewall against those impulses. It short-circuited tyranny.

Obviously, the men who composed and passed the Bill of Rights are long gone. But if you're so inclined—as many people in the business of selling old things are—you might think their collective genius lives on in that parchment, ready to be infused into anyone who pauses to study and appreciate it. No one is immortal, but maybe it's true that in such documents the life forces of the nation's founders live forever.

Yet somewhere along the line, North Carolina's original Bill of Rights ceased to be simply a collection of revolutionary ideas. Through the years its value as an artifact increased exponentially. The parchment became a thing with a bottom line, a number that could be entered into a ledger. A commodity.

And instead of appreciating all of those remarkable, world-altering ideas, some people began to look at the document and see only their desires and ambitions reflected back.

To a handful of other people, there was something more still.

As the twentieth century passed, the document accumulated a history that belonged only to the Shotwells: the history of their family. By the time it returned from California in 1937 with Charles Shotwell's remains, the Bill of Rights had been part of the clan for seventy-one years.

Looking at the document reminded Grier Shotwell of how the

nation was founded, but it also brought his father to life. He could show it to his daughters, Anne and Sylvia, and tell stories of the grandfather they hardly knew. Whatever claim North Carolina staked to it, the parchment also had become a Shotwell heirloom, as infused with familial consequence as a handed-down quilt or piece of china.

Grier had wire-rim glasses and a round, solemn face and became a partner in a law firm and chairman of the Indianapolis Board of Education and legal adviser to the Indiana Senate. He was a First Presbyterian Church elder and president of Long College for Women and a board member of the Marion County Tuberculosis Association. When he died in 1972, the *Indianapolis Star* headline called him a "civic and educational leader."

"He was very dedicated," said his younger daughter, Sylvia. "Both my father and mother were very community-minded. They gave back."

When the teenaged Shotwell girls went to the movies with friends on Friday nights, the parents alternated pickup responsibilities. To summon their folks, Sylvia's friends used the pay phone to send a predetermined signal: They waited three rings, then hung up. That way they got their dime back.

Not Grier. "My father said that was not right—you're cheating the telephone company out of ten cents," Sylvia said. "Daddy was born in 1896, so he was a Victorian. He was very principled, very strict in his thinking."

Grier hung the Bill of Rights in the living room of the tidy, 1930s-era gingerbread family home at 5855 Forest Lane. The living room was ideal; there was only one window, and little direct sunlight. Grier eventually added an adjoining porch, making the room darker still. His wife, Anne, sometimes complained how little light crept in.

Grier believed the family lore justified the parchment's presence. His father had bought it legitimately in Ohio, he believed. And North Carolina had treated his father badly.

Shotwell was a steady, matter-of-fact caretaker. "Daddy didn't talk about it a lot," said Sylvia, who was born shortly after her grandfather Charles died. There were no newspaper stories, no dalliances with North Carolina.

Think of it as a piece of family history rather than a piece of national history, and it is easier to forget that it meant something to people outside their modest midwestern lives. Visitors who admired it got a straightforward, ho-hum description: "Oh, that," the Shotwells would say. "That's our Bill of Rights." And then they would explain how it had been in the family forever.

To the girls, Anne (who had the same first name as her mother) and Sylvia, the parchment was as familiar as the views from their bedroom windows. "As long as I remember, it was just hanging on a wall," Sylvia said. "Nobody really ever talked about it."

Still, there was no denying the events of the world beyond. By 1939, the 150th anniversary of the document's creation, fascism was spreading in Europe. Held up against the dark goings-on overseas, the Bill of Rights looked immensely important. The parchment had become a proper noun. It meant something tangible. Power had corrupted minds in Western Europe, and people had to be saved from their darkest impulses. But America had its firewall.

Sylvia Shotwell was in her twenties when all of this finally hit her squarely. Her husband was a graduate student at Miami University, near Dayton, and he brought to Sylvia's house a friend who was pursuing a doctorate in history. He stared at the parchment for a long time, longer than most visitors. Finally, he said, "Sylvia, am I looking at an original? Do you realize what you have here?"

She was only beginning to see it.

When Grier Shotwell died, his wife, Anne, took the parchment to an apartment in Marquette Manor, a sprawling, continuing-care retirement community in Indianapolis. She displayed the Bill of Rights there until her death in August 1990.

At that point the document and the family reached a crossroads together. There was no plan in place for what would happen next, no logical line of succession. Anne and Sylvia were both married. Between them they had five children, and there was no fair way to hand the document down.

There were other, practical, considerations: The manuscript had been in their family for 124 years, longer than it had been in North Carolina. Sixty-five years had passed since Charles Reid had tried to sell the Bill of Rights back to the state. The manuscript had accumulated so much value in that time, the sisters no longer felt they could care for it and safeguard it. It didn't belong on a living room wall anymore. Some of the ink had begun flaking during the parchment's stay in Marquette Manor. Though the document wasn't exposed to sunlight, it hung on a brick wall that faced east. "I think it got hot," Sylvia said. "I think it deteriorated a great deal there."

The sisters wanted the document preserved by professionals. And if there was ever a time to sell, it was then. The marketplace for historic documents was bloated with moneyed investors.

The first thing to do was find help. What did a couple of ladies from Indianapolis know about selling a Bill of Rights? Sylvia mentioned to her sister, "I could ask Charlie."

Charlie Reeder wasn't an obvious choice. He sued doctors for a living. He also handled personal injury and civil litigation and product liability—the primary specialties of Holland & Holland, the four-lawyer firm located on the northern fringes of the city. But he was a friend. Reeder and Sylvia's husband, Robert, had been fraternity brothers at Miami University, and they still got together often. And the sisters, more than anything else, wanted someone with whom they felt comfortable.

Reeder had an acquaintance in the trust department at the Indianapolis National Bank, and the contact gave him a name: Jay Dillon, a rare-book and manuscript specialist at Sotheby's. That made perfect sense. Everybody knew Sotheby's was a world-famous auction house that sold all kinds of fancy objects. Sotheby's had the resources to produce a glossy catalog entry on the Bill of Rights and the wherewithal to bring together wealthy collectors who—if the Shotwells were lucky—might engage in a bidding war.

Dillon asked Reeder to send a photograph of the parchment to Sotheby's New York offices. Soon after he did so, two of the firm's experts, David Redden and Selby Kiffer, flew to Indianapolis.

Redden, a polished, urbane man in his middle forties, was then senior vice president in charge of Sotheby's books and manuscripts department. He had joined the firm as a young man and recently had become one of its most visible public faces. Redden had been the auctioneer for the junk-frame Dunlap Declaration of Independence. Both he and Kiffer had authenticated the document and been quoted extensively in the *New York Times* and *USA Today* about the incredible find. The latter newspaper reported that before even unfolding the document, the two men could tell from the threads of cloth in the paper that it was from the 1700s.

A few years earlier Redden had sold an unpublished seventy-two-page work of Albert Einstein in which the iconic physicist spelled out his world-changing theory of relativity. That went for $1.2 million, then an all-time high for any manuscript sold in the United States.

Kiffer, who had joined Sotheby's in 1984 as a part-time cataloger, had a lower profile but was nonetheless a mainstay. Just six months earlier he had been involved in the auction of the earliest known draft of Abraham Lincoln's "house divided" speech opposing slavery. The document had sold for $1.65 million—another record.

The Shotwells' timing was impeccable, the two men said. Sotheby's was on the verge of posting its strongest year ever for American manuscript sales, even as worldwide art sales were dropping. "The dollars are chasing Americana," Redden told the *Times* not long after his trip to Indiana. The headline of that story was "What's the Bid? Sky's the Limit."

Reeder and the Shotwells brought the Sotheby's employees into the bank vault where the sisters had stored the manuscript since their mother's death. The two men immediately recognized the document as an original. "They were so excited," Sylvia Shotwell Long said. "They just thought it was the biggest find."

"Aren't you excited?" Redden asked.

Sylvia shrugged. "We've known what it was," she said. The question was, What were they going to do with it?

The experts said the parchment was in decent shape—not great, not terrible. The ink was still mostly legible, so that was good, and the old, chipped wooden frame could be removed easily enough. But the glued-on backing could reduce its value. And they would have to re-search whether the parchment had indeed been legitimate war booty. Redden floated the idea that maybe the document had come from any of a number of states, since several were missing their copies.

There was work to be done. But Redden and Kiffer said the doc-ument was worth "in the millions." The estimate was based on the Dunlap Declaration's recent sale for $2.42 million. Redden and Kiffer wouldn't draw up an agreement—which would include a 20 percent commission for Sotheby's—until they'd fully investigated the document's history.

The Shotwells had known the document was valuable—but "in the millions"? Middle-class folks from the Midwest didn't usually think in those terms.

That night the Shotwells and Charlie Reeder popped open a bot-tle of Champagne.

Whether Sotheby's officials were equally enthused is debatable. The rare-books and manuscripts division is the ugly stepchild at the auction house, which makes most of its money in jewelry and fine art. Manuscripts are a hassle. Fakes are ubiquitous, cataloging takes more time and effort than for most other objects, and provenance is often muddy and tangled—a growing concern as states such as North Carolina aggressively pursue lost archives.

The Bill of Rights was one of those messy situations. Sotheby's researchers visited archives in several states, including North Car-olina, Georgia, and Delaware, and uncovered the flaws in Charles Shotwell's claim of legitimate ownership. The process dragged across months.

What happened next depends on whom you believe. Sotheby's officials claimed they ultimately declined to offer the parchment at auction because of lingering provenance issues.

Reeder, however, asserted that Sotheby's *did* offer to sell the doc-ument. Only instead of an auction, the firm wanted to conduct a private sale. Sotheby's would discreetly offer it to top collectors such as Ross Perot, the Texas iconoclast who in 1984 had purchased an early copy of the Magna Carta.

There was precedent for this sort of under-the-radar transaction. Sotheby's tried to quietly move the $4 Dunlap Declaration of Independence after the failed auction in 1993. In 1996, when another high-profile item failed to reach a reserve price—the Einstein theory-of-relativity document that had previously sold for $1.2 million—Sotheby's sold it privately for "significantly more," according to Selby Kiffer.

But there are other reasons why Reeder's version is more plausible—most notably, the firm's well-established reputation for treading at the far edges of legitimacy. Put another way: Sotheby's wasn't scared off by controversy.

Not even courtroom challenges had dampened Sotheby's fervid entrepreneurial spirit. In 1984 the firm had agreed to auction a collection of rare Hebrew books and manuscripts, some of which had survived Nazi Germany. The New York attorney general's office and the city Department of Consumer Affairs both filed court actions to delay the sale when Jewish groups contended that more than thirty of the volumes in the sixty-item sale had come from a Berlin rabbinical seminary closed by the Nazis in 1942. Those objects could not have voluntarily become private property, they claimed. But Sotheby's won the legal maneuverings, and David Redden auctioned the materials for $1.45 million.

In some cases Sotheby's voluntarily returned items it had no business auctioning. In 1995 someone brought in four Walt Whitman notebooks stolen from the Library of Congress at the start of World War II. The notebooks were proffered to Kiffer, who had acquired the nickname "Special Agent Kiffer" for several instances in which he'd reported stolen property to the FBI. Kiffer initiated the return of the Whitman papers.

But that sort of whistle-blowing was hardly the rule. Sotheby's in the middle and late 1990s became enmeshed in an art-smuggling scandal, followed soon after by a commission-fixing imbroglio with Christie's, which drove out Sotheby's top executives.

The manuscripts division, meanwhile, faced allegations that it had knowingly offered fakes as authentic. In his book *The Poet and the Murderer*, about a fake Emily Dickinson poem created by notorious forger Mark Hofmann, Simon Worrall detailed how Kiffer, among others, disregarded clear warnings about several Hofmann counterfeits before they went to auction. Worrall wrote that the buyer who had spent $21,000 on the spurious Dickinson poem had become suspicious and tried to learn more about its provenance. (Auction firms typically conceal the identities of consignors. If a bogus or stolen document turns up in a salesroom, money gets refunded, and the employees usually renounce their responsibility to patrol the industry.) Kiffer, whom Worrall mockingly referred to by his "Special Agent" nickname, tried to pacify the buyer by mentioning an expert named Jennifer Larson. "According to Kiffer," Worrall wrote, "Larson had not raised any concerns about the Dickinson manuscript. Of course. He had never asked her about it."

Sotheby's eventually refunded the $21,000. In 1985 Sotheby's employee Mary Jo Kline grew so frustrated with the auction house's offering Hofmann fakes that she refused to catalog anything he'd once owned, according to Worrall. "Three years after that," he wrote, "in a move that shocked the closely knit historical documents world, Kline's boss thanked her for her pains by terminating her. His name was David Redden."

The art-smuggling and commission-fixing controversies prompted policy and leadership changes. But no such overhauls occurred in the rare-books and manuscripts division. As recently as 2004, a prominent expert—Tom Taylor, Bill Reese's friend and the author of *Texfake*, a book about forgeries and document theft from the Texas State Library—accused Sotheby's of deliberately misrepresenting the provenance of documents that were almost certainly among those stolen from Texas.

The firm was clearly apprehensive about the provenance of the Shotwells' Bill of Rights. Sotheby's loves publicity, and Redden was a master at generating headlines. The free advertising on marquee items is often worth more than any commission. When the stolen Whitman notebooks were returned to the Library of Congress, Sotheby's hustled to announce their reappearance.

The Bill of Rights had the kind of history that would have read beautifully in a catalog and press release. Backstory is currency in the auction business. As the $4 Declaration story proved, the more intrigue and legend, the better.

It didn't happen. The auction firm went as far as to retain a prominent lawyer to work out the terms of an agreement with the Shotwells, including issues such as how to transport and insure the manuscript, according to federal investigators. But the sisters wanted Sotheby's to indemnify them against any legal action, and the firm refused. After a lengthy and enthralling romance, Sotheby's and the Shotwells broke up.

"The longer we talked, the more they backpedaled," Sylvia Shotwell Long recalled. "Which I understood; we knew we didn't have clear title. We just knew my grandfather didn't steal it."

When the deal fell through, Charlie Reeder tried Christie's and got the same response: The title problem was insurmountable. Reeder asked around again and wound up contacting Leslie Hindman Auctioneers.

The Chicago-based firm was a long slide down the auction-house food chain from the behemoths of New York City and London. Sotheby's rare-books and manuscripts department regularly auctioned six-figure objects. Hindman Auctioneers didn't have a rare-books and manuscripts department.

Leslie Hindman sold art at the lower end of the market—stuff that Christie's or Sotheby's might not handle because they didn't deem it important enough. She also dealt in objects in the $1,000 to $5,000 range: items from John Belushi's estate, midlevel Frank Lloyd Wright collectibles. Hindman's mid-1990s revenues hovered in the $10 million to $15 million range—compared to the $4.4 billion that Sotheby's and Christie's combined to generate annually.

On the plus side, Hindman was like the Shotwells: She was from the heartland. No British accents. No attitude. She was the doyenne of Chicago antiques, a plucky midwestern Martha Stewart whose bubbly deconstructions of auction-world mystique attracted upwardly aspiring middle-class shoppers. She was in her late thirties, blond and winsome. Freshness counts.

Hindman didn't mind being the underdog. She had bottomless supplies of ambition and energy—and was deeply competitive. She had also been lucky. In 1990 one of her prospectors had discovered a painting in a home in suburban Milwaukee that turned out to be an original, unknown van Gogh. When she auctioned it the following year for $1.43 million, she made international news.

Roughly 150 people called her offices afterward, saying they, too, had discovered masterpieces. "In this business, everybody thinks they have a van Gogh," Hindman said. "Lots of people think they own a Declaration of Independence."

One reporter asked Hindman how many she expected to be authentic. "None," she said. "I mean, really, none."

How could it be otherwise? How many valuable artifacts are really out there masquerading as everyday possessions in Des Moines and Toledo? How many average midwestern families really have million-dollar treasures hanging on their walls?

Leslie Hindman was wrong. One of the phone calls she took after the van Gogh auction turned out to be the real thing.

Hindman's first clue was that Charlie Reeder was a lawyer. The second was that he had an authentic-sounding backstory, and documents to support it.

Hindman trekked to Indiana to take a look. She justified this: Hindman routinely traveled around the Midwest, so she could at least stop in. You had to be willing to suspend disbelief, no matter how many far-fetched stories you heard.

She quickly realized what Reeder had. Sotheby's had authenticated the Bill of Rights, and it appeared to be worth more than her van Gogh. Hindman figured that if the Shotwell family wanted something for the document, who could blame them? "If I have something I've kept in my family," she said, "I would think somebody should give me something for taking care of it."

She cut a deal with Reeder for a 20 percent commission. The two midwesterners settled on a handshake. Her idea was to recruit a philanthropist to buy it and donate it to North Carolina. Everyone would win: The family would get paid, North Carolina would get the document, and a patron would get a tax break.

Like Sotheby's, Hindman thought it best to avoid the potential pitfalls of an open auction. Scott Peterson, a Chicago document collector and Manuscript Society member who is familiar with disputes over alienated papers, told her that North Carolina was renowned for pursuing lost archival materials aggressively—even for dragging people into court.

On the other hand, Hindman saw that North Carolina had been offered a chance to buy the document back from the Shotwells in 1925 and declined. And she took the family at its word that the document had come into their possession legitimately. "No one knowingly sells stolen stuff at auction," she said. "Why would they? All people in this industry have is their reputation. You wouldn't do anything that tarnishes that."

Over a period of months, Hindman peddled the Bill of Rights to the wealthiest potential patrons she could conjure.

She called Michael Jordan's wife, Juanita. The Jordans were an adroit choice: The Chicago Bulls superstar had strong ties to North Carolina, having played college ball in Chapel Hill. She had breakfast with Steve Forbes. "Why don't you buy this thing?" she asked him. She approached Oprah Winfrey's people. She queried the Daniels family, a legendary North Carolina clan that had long owned the *News & Observer* newspaper in Raleigh.

The provenance problem repeatedly tripped things up. "Too complicated," prospective buyers told her.

There were other issues: The federal government, it turned out, has complex tax laws for such donations. She didn't know whether North Carolina would be helpful on that front. "And nobody wanted to donate it just to be nice," Hindman said.

In late September 1995, Hindman's lawyer invited Charlie Reeder for a visit. Reeder stopped on the way to his vacation house on the

Great Lakes. The two lawyers hit it off. There was a big football game that Saturday: Ohio State against Notre Dame. Reeder, an Ohio native, was a passionate Buckeyes fan, and Hindman's lawyer loved the Fighting Irish. The two began chatting about the game, ribbing each other. Hindman had no idea what they were talking about.

When they got down to business, Hindman's lawyer said, Look, this Bill of Rights was more work than anyone anticipated. The provenance issues were prohibitive. Given all of the obstacles, Hindman wanted to raise her commission to 33 percent.

Reeder asked the sisters about Hindman's request when he returned home. This put them in an uncomfortable place. They were getting anxious. Since they had removed the glass from the frame at Sotheby's request, the ink on the parchment had paled. "In the bank it faded tremendously, and I'm not sure why," Sylvia Shotwell Long said. "It was absolutely a piece of work before we took it out of the glass. We got urgent about it, because we could see it fading."

But Hindman was asking for too big a slice. They couldn't give her a third of the Bill of Rights.

When that deal fell through, Reeder didn't know what to do next. Then his phone rang one day not long after. It was Leslie Hindman.

She apologized about the way things worked out and said she understood the sisters' decision. "Look, I shouldn't be making this call," she said, "but it seems like you need help, and I think I can help you."

There was a guy, a top dealer in antique furniture. He lived back East, in Connecticut. Hindman said that if it was all right with Reeder, Wayne Pratt would like to give him a call.

"He's very honest, very competent," Hindman said. "You can trust me on this, he's a good guy."

Reeder thanked her. This was a different approach, for sure, an antique-furniture dealer. But Pratt sounded impressive enough. And Reeder had nowhere else to go.

• • •

Years later, Leslie Hindman could still clearly recall telling Wayne Pratt about the parchment for the first time.

Pratt thought the document sounded intriguing and said he'd like to get involved.

"I said, 'You should,'" Hindman recalled, "knowing he's a big risk taker."

For months afterward Hindman kept checking in. "She kept bugging me," Pratt said. "She kept saying, 'Why don't you make some money on this?'"

17

Just a Regular Guy

FRANK WHITNEY BEGAN HUSTLING up and down hallways, banging on doors, on the eighth floor of the federal building in downtown Raleigh. It was just after 9:00 a.m. on Thursday, March 13, 2003.

Whitney, the U.S. attorney for eastern North Carolina, knew he had to move fast. When he reached Bobby Higdon's office, he lurched inside to find the chief of the criminal division on the phone. Their eyes met, and Whitney reflexively stepped back out. Whitney and Higdon didn't have a typical boss-employee relationship. They'd known each other since their undergraduate days at Wake Forest. Their friendship had taken root when they both became assistant U.S. attorneys in Charlotte more than a decade earlier; Higdon was the lead drug prosecutor and had supervised Whitney. They'd worked together long enough to finish each other's thoughts. So even though Whitney ran the show now, Higdon didn't hesitate to wave him off for a minute.

Back in the hall, Whitney reconsidered. *This one can't wait,* he thought. He peered back in and gestured to Higdon that it was urgent.

"Thomas just called," Whitney said after Higdon hung up. "He said they got a line on North Carolina's Bill of Rights."

Higdon looked baffled. He knew that Thomas was Thomas Walker, a former colleague in Charlotte who now worked for North

Carolina's attorney general. But a Bill of Rights? Who knew North Carolina even had a Bill of Rights?

Whitney recapped the discussions between Governor Mike Easley's office and the National Constitution Center. Easley had consulted the attorney general's staff, and they wanted to try to get the document somehow. But they couldn't do it alone. The manuscript was out of state, which meant they needed the federal government's help. Time was short. Someone was selling the manuscript up North, and there was an option that expired in three days.

Whitney wanted a meeting with everyone involved, and fast. He tasked Higdon to call the FBI and U.S. marshal while he got back to the attorney general's and governor's offices. As U.S. attorney, Whitney had the clout to get things moving quickly, and by 10:30 a.m. he'd assembled a roomful of high-ranking officials. Among them were Higdon and Banu Rangarajan from his criminal division; Paul Newby, an assistant U.S. attorney who specialized in asset forfeiture; first assistant U.S. attorney George Holding; Reuben Young from Governor Easley's office; Walker and Grayson Kelley from the attorney general's office; and U.S. marshal Charles Reavis, who holds property seized by the federal government. Whitney asked FBI agent Andy Thomure, who was in the office on an unrelated matter, to sit in until his boss, Special Agent Frank Perry, made it over. They all packed around a T-shaped configuration of tables in a cramped conference room outside Whitney's office, many of them standing after the few chairs got claimed.

Hardly anyone in the room knew a thing about the state's Bill of Rights, so Reuben Young filled in the background. Then Whitney took over. The objective was to get the document back by the safest means possible—possibly through the use of civil forfeiture laws, the same legal mechanism his office used to claim duffel bags filled with cash taken from cocaine dealers. The law permitted the government to seize property used in the course of committing a crime. The crime in this case, as Whitney saw it, was transporting stolen goods across state lines—which was what had occurred back in 1865 when the Union soldier left the state with the Bill of Rights.

Whitney gave little consideration to the National Constitution Center's offer to buy and bequeath the document. "You can't donate what you don't own," he said. His way, the state would get the parchment back with no strings attached to a museum he'd never heard of.

By chance, civil forfeiture was Whitney's area of expertise—a somewhat uncommon specialty for a U.S. attorney. A tall, burly man in his early forties, Whitney had a prominent jaw, a youthful jauntiness, and a folksy, self-deprecating demeanor, describing a book he'd coauthored, about money laundering, as "a tedious treatise."

Whitney directed Paul Newby, who also specialized in forfeiture, to get started on a seizure warrant. Bobby Higdon, meanwhile, began preparing a criminal investigation. He planned on convening a grand jury to consider charges against the parties involved in the document's sale. But that would happen only after the Bill of Rights was safely in hand. Whitney and Higdon didn't want to risk word leaking out to the sellers.

When the meeting broke up, Whitney had a couple of requests for Reuben Young. He wanted copies of anything that established the parchment's authenticity and its North Carolina provenance. And he wanted to know all about Wayne Pratt.

Special Agents Paul Minella and Rob Richards were eating lunch in the FBI's Raleigh offices that Thursday afternoon when their supervisor, Frank Perry, walked in. Lots of activity in the U.S. attorney's office, Perry said. He explained about the Bill of Rights and asked Minella and Richards to coordinate the FBI's role.

Minella and Richards looked at each other. This was a new one.

The two agents headed over to Frank Whitney's office, where the U.S. attorney explained his plan to seize the document. His staff was working on a search warrant for the Woodbury property of antiques dealer Wayne Pratt, Whitney said.

To Minella, this sounded problematic. The document had moved around some in the preceding months; Pratt had at least two stores, in Woodbury and Nantucket, and had more than one home. Did anyone really know where the manuscript was actually located?

What if Pratt's lawyer had the Bill of Rights? What if it was in a safe-deposit box?

Minella stepped out to call another supervisor, Mike Saylor, who was driving back from a meeting in Charlotte. Saylor agreed that dispatching agents to Pratt's property with a search warrant sounded sketchy. The problem was obvious: If the FBI misfired on the location, it wouldn't only be embarrassing—it would also give Pratt a chance to play defense and put the document in hiding.

Saylor offered to check with headquarters for input. He called back soon after with good news: Philadelphia was the location of the museum negotiating for the Bill of Rights. By chance, that city was also home base for Bob Wittman, the FBI's undercover specialist in stolen art and cultural artifacts. Since that was Wittman's thing, Saylor said, why not do a reversal?

"Reversal" is bureau-speak for a sting. In other words, instead of chasing down the Bill of Rights, Wittman would arrange for Wayne Pratt to deliver the parchment—thinking he had a sale.

FBI agents Minella and Richards reconvened at 3:30 with the U.S. attorneys. Minella laid out the plan and told everyone about Bob Wittman. "The document is probably not where you think it is," he said. "The only way to find it is to be there when it shows up."

When the meeting broke up, Minella dialed the FBI's Philadelphia office.

Frank Whitney and Paul Newby postponed everything else on their calendars that day. This was a full-on race-the-clock affair—which was a drill they knew well. Sometimes they received word of an imminent shipment of cocaine, and if they didn't prepare a warrant and act on it within hours, the opportunity would pass. This job carried the same buzz of immediacy.

Whitney's staff had contacted U.S. District Judge Terrence Boyle early in the day to let him know something important was coming. Then, shortly before 5:00 p.m., Newby sent the seizure warrant over for Boyle's signature. North Carolina archives staffers with long memories might have spotted a pungent irony in this. In the 1970s Boyle, then a lawyer in private practice, had taken on a high-profile case involving a dispute over a couple of eighteenth-century documents. His client: manuscript dealer B. C. West Jr.

Newby had never heard of B. C. West, but he knew about the precedent-setting case soon enough. "Judge Boyle knew the North Carolina law very, very well," Whitney said, "so he knew what we were doing was not fiction. He knew we were not doing something that was abusing the law."

Joe Torsella's mind churned when he answered the phone and heard Bob Wittman introduce himself. The call caught him flat-footed; he'd been immersed in the minutiae of construction plans, standing amid cranes and heavy equipment.

For a moment Torsella wondered whether the call was legit: Can the FBI just call you on your cell phone and start asking questions? It seemed so informal. And how did this guy find out about the Bill of Rights, anyway?

Torsella steadied himself. Of course he could tell Wittman about the parchment. But they ought to include Steve Harmelin in the conversation; he was the museum's general counsel and the point man on the negotiations.

Wittman could hear the surprise and hesitation in Torsella's voice. Wittman couldn't blame him; he himself had heard about the missing parchment only within the last hour. The FBI agent had been driving north from FBI headquarters on Interstate 95 when the call came from his partner, Jay Heine.

Wittman had called Paul Minella in Raleigh. Funny thing, Wittman had thought after he'd heard the story: His parents had been antiques dealers.

This kind of thing didn't surprise him anymore. He was busy for a reason: Valuable old objects could bring out the worst in people. When he returned home, Wittman called attorney Harmelin and arranged to meet first thing the next morning, Friday, March 14.

Even more than Torsella, Harmelin heard alarm bells during that phone call. He immediately assumed the worst: Maybe the museum was in trouble for trying to buy the parchment. Harmelin immediately went into damage control mode. He consulted a few trusted

Dilworth colleagues, both for their opinions and to alert them to potential trouble. Then he called Rubin Weiner into his office again and assigned the associate another Constitution Center–related research project: Figure out whether they should be worried about Wittman's newfound interest.

The most likely scenario, Harmelin figured, was that Wittman would want to hear what had happened so far. And then Harmelin would turn over any relevant information—including Wayne Pratt's contact information. That was probably as far as it would go, but he wasn't taking any chances.

Harmelin assumed the FBI's sudden emergence meant the end of the Constitution Center's Bill of Rights quest. There was no time to feel disappointed yet, but after all the hope and intrigue and excitement of the past couple of months, they would probably feel the regret when the entire affair had blown over.

Bob Wittman was not the man Steve Harmelin had pictured during the course of a long night of wondering what was going to happen in the morning. Harmelin had played out various scenarios, some of them involving cinematic, bullying G-men.

He knew he'd been off the mark as soon as Wittman and his partner, Jay Heine, arrived at around 9:00 a.m. in Harmelin's office on the thirty-second floor of the Mellon Bank Center, a landmark building in downtown Philadelphia. Wittman was a genteel, round-faced man in his late forties with silver-tinged dark hair. He had a smooth, calming voice and a disarming sense of humor. He began talking about undercover work as if he were a Kansan laying out plans for a day of corn harvesting.

That laconic charm was Wittman's stock-in-trade. In covert work rapport was everything. He had to make people feel comfortable. He had to fit into a room like well-worn furniture. Wittman had several undercover doppelgängers: greedy buyer, corrupt art professor, discreet middleman. All of his characters had the same goal—to get thieves to trust him just long enough for him to betray them.

Wittman also played his parts well because he knew a lot about antiquities. He was born and raised in Baltimore, where his parents—his father American, his mother Japanese—ran a shop filled with Asian antiques. Being around the objects, working on weekends, learning from his father how to haggle, Wittman developed a natural affinity for the vases and pots. But he wasn't inclined to follow his parents' career arc. After spending the early part of his post-college life as a newspaper editor, Wittman hooked on with the FBI in 1988.

Each of the bureau's new hires is assigned to a training agent, and on the property-crime squad Wittman's mentor was Bob Bazin, who handled the art theft cases in Philadelphia. Their year together was productive. The agents recovered objects from two different thefts: a Rodin statue called *Man with a Broken Nose* and the world's second-largest crystal ball, swiped in the middle of the night from the University of Pennsylvania's Museum of Archaeology and Anthropology.

The work spoke to Wittman in a way that carjackings and bank robberies never would. And when Bazin retired, Wittman volunteered to take his place. It wasn't as if agents were lining up for the assignment; crimes against cultural property had long been considered a sort of twee distraction from the heavier lifting of anti-terrorism and drug-smuggling cases. Wittman, though, took the work to a new level: He convinced the bureau to send him for formal training at Philadelphia's Barnes Foundation and at the Gemological Institute of Santa Monica, California. He not only grasped the differences between a Miró and a Braque; he came to love the Impressionists—the works of Monet, Renoir's seascapes and countrysides—and Picasso.

Wittman also gained a technical proficiency that enabled him to credibly pose as an avid collector or broker. He could crinkle his nose up against a three-hundred-year-old canvas and riff authoritatively on its craquelure. He could distinguish etchings from aquatints.

Over the next fifteen years he developed an uncanny knack for tempting thieves to sell him looted antiquities. In one of his more memorable recoveries, in 1997, he posed as an ethically compromised art history professor in Madrid. Thieves were offering Pieter

Brueghel the Elder's *Temptation of Saint Anthony* for $1.2 million, and there were many more masterpieces to come if that first deal worked out: a Goya, Camille Pissarro's *Landscape at Eragny*—stolen paintings collectively worth tens of millions of dollars.

Sipping glasses of Spanish wine with mobsters in a Madrid hotel, Wittman so charmed his targets that they invited him to join their cabal as a full-time consultant. Wittman feigned enthusiasm but stalled for a couple of weeks while the sting came together. The day of the operation, Spanish police fanned out across the hotel posing as tourists, maids, and bellhops. Wittman, nattily attired in a sports coat, examined the Brueghel in his suite under black light, declared the painting authentic, and informed his new friends they were under arrest.

He recovered five Norman Rockwell paintings swiped from a private gallery in Minneapolis, three of which had been moved to a farmhouse in Brazil. Wittman posed as the buyer in a sting that landed Geronimo's eagle-feather war bonnet, valued at $1.2 million, and in the recovery of the 1862 Tiffany presentation sword awarded for Admiral John Worden's heroic command of the USS *Monitor* during its historic Civil War battle with the CSS *Virginia;* that piece had been stolen from the U.S. Naval Academy in 1932.

Wittman became something of a celebrity in Peru for the recovery of a two-thousand-year-old piece of body armor made of gold, copper, and silver and worn by the ancient Moche people. The "backflap"—asking price, $1.6 million—was looted from the Royal Tomb of the Lord of Sipán and traveled from Peru to New York via Panama. Wittman twice met the smugglers at the rest stop at exit 7A on the New Jersey Turnpike—a neutral, anonymous site chosen to soothe the criminals' jangled nerves, even though Wittman was wired and his colleagues were watching from a nearby van. That seizure brought a Peruvian Order of Merit for Distinguished Service, awarded by the nation's president.

Wittman had never worked on a historic document before. But when you really got down to it, he figured, the Bill of Rights couldn't be all that different from other valuable relics.

• • •

Wittman pattered on for a while, getting to know Harmelin and Torsella. He was happy to spin yarns of 3:00 a.m. meetings with machine-gun-toting art thieves. He knew people wanted that the first time they met him. Eventually Wittman circled back to the Bill of Rights.

"So what does the FBI want?" Harmelin asked.

Wittman explained that a federal judge in North Carolina had signed a seizure warrant for the parchment the previous day. His job was to retrieve it.

Harmelin didn't hesitate: Of course they would help. He knew exactly where the document probably was. Wayne Pratt owned an antiques shop in Woodbury, Connecticut, that was apparently right on the main drag, one of the largest in town. "Do you want the address?" Harmelin asked.

Wittman shook his head. They didn't know if Pratt really had the document, so a search warrant was useless. They were going to negotiate a sham purchase. A sting.

Harmelin was surprised the FBI would take things that far. Was that really necessary? Pratt was a reputable guy, an appraiser on *Antiques Roadshow*.

They're not who you think they are, Wittman said. The lawyer, John Richardson? He'd tried to sell the parchment back to North Carolina several years ago and had made some threatening statements when he did it.

No, Harmelin said, that couldn't be true. He recounted how, during their meeting at the Yale Club, Richardson had vehemently denied any link between the Bill of Rights and Carolina—and had opposed the idea of getting the state involved in the purchase.

Wittman nodded. Of course Richardson didn't want North Carolina involved. He seemed to have known all along the document had come from Raleigh, and that officials there considered it stolen property. Wittman had proof.

During the summer of 1995, when Wayne Pratt and John Richardson had first teamed up to broker a Bill of Rights sale, they read Charles Shotwell's letter from 1924 and decided the most logical first step was to try to sell it back to North Carolina, or to someone connected to the state. The two men had very little invested in the document at that point and liked the idea of making a quick commission. Perhaps they could convince a philanthropist to purchase and donate it to the state—with the bonus of a big tax write-off.

One potential benefactor was the Z. Smith Reynolds Foundation, an influential private institution in Winston-Salem devoted to the wide-sweeping goal of improving the quality of life in North Carolina. The foundation, created in memory of the youngest son of the founder of the R. J. Reynolds Tobacco Company, awards about $20 million annually to nonprofit groups concerned with community causes. The contact person there was Tom Lambeth, the foundation's director for the past seventeen years.

Pratt and Richardson couldn't have found more of a straight arrow if they'd called Boy Scouts International. Once dubbed North Carolina's "do-gooder in chief," Lambeth had been a giant in the arenas of philanthropy and education dating to the 1960s, when he helped manage the successful campaigns of Terry Sanford for governor and John F. Kennedy for president. As director of the Reynolds Foundation, he steered money into programs that tackled poverty, social justice, the environment, and education.

Lambeth, in short, wasn't the kind of guy who skirted official channels. In October 1995 he phoned Betty Ray McCain, secretary of North Carolina's Department of Cultural Resources, which includes the state archives, to let her know about the Bill of Rights offer.

Several generations had passed since word of the document last surfaced in North Carolina, and McCain, for one, knew little of its backstory. She was a political appointee, not a trained archivist. But there was no doubt that both she and her boss, Governor James B. Hunt, would reap some political capital if the Bill of Rights returned home on her watch. Both McCain and her deputy, Betsy Buford, a special-projects administrator, were known as exceptional fundraisers; with a little time, they could easily pull together the six- or seven-figure sum it would take to buy the parchment.

McCain summoned her top people—Buford, state archivist David

Olson, and top deputy Jeff Crow—for a confidential discussion. They decided to get the man representing the seller on the phone. They had no idea where this would go and wanted to keep things quiet. But they were eager to hear what attorney John L. Richardson had to say.

Although Pratt and Richardson's strategy for brokering a deal in North Carolina made intuitive sense, it also carried elements of risk. Richardson had done his research. He knew how North Carolina officials had spurned Charles Reid. He knew that since then the state had aggressively pursued several of its lost and stolen records. He knew about B. C. West Jr., the manuscript dealer the state had taken down in court.

Richardson also knew that if he never revealed the present-day possessors or whereabouts of the Bill of Rights, the Carolinians would be unable to chase after it.

Anyway, there was no way to gauge the mindset of the people running the archives until you talked to them. Maybe they'd never heard of B. C. West. That case had taken place nearly twenty years earlier. Maybe the new guys were softer than their predecessors.

Or maybe Richardson could appeal to their vanity. The Bill of Rights back in Raleigh would make bold headlines. It would be a feel-good story. There was no way to know until you asked.

The first conversation took place on a mid-October afternoon in 1995. Betty Ray McCain and David Olson were both on the line. Betsy Buford sat with them in McCain's office, located in a blockish four-story building on Jones Street in downtown Raleigh. There were pleasantries, and then Richardson laid out the situation. He wanted to do right by everyone involved, but he couldn't say much of substance. "It was a very bizarre conversation," Olson said. "Right away he was saying, 'I know a lawyer who knows another lawyer who knows another lawyer, and once you get through all those layers of lawyers you get to the person with the document—and wouldn't it be nice if we could get you back your Bill of Rights.' In my forty-year career, it was probably the most bizarre thing I'd ever heard."

Olson divined a clear message through this verbal hall of mirrors: Richardson wasn't going to give North Carolina the chance to sue anyone. "He was clearly being very careful," Olson said. "He knew darn well we'd go right to court." Like a sailboat in tricky crosswinds, Richardson began tacking between friendly advocate and cagey adversary working off a John le Carré script. He said he would insist on confidentiality for the seller and wanted the process to move briskly. To Olson, Richardson sounded like a relatively sophisticated lawyer accustomed to the delicate parry and thrust of negotiation.

Richardson eventually began nibbling around the delicate topic of money. He knew the state was opposed to buying its property back, so he suggested the state think of any theoretical payment as a sort of service charge—a finder's fee, or storage expense, or caretaker's stipend—rather than an outright purchase. Olson asked what kind of money Richardson was thinking; the lawyer replied that negotiations would start at $3 million. The air left the room for a moment. The number reinforced the document's significance— not that lifers like Olson really needed any reminders. A couple of years earlier, around the time of the bicentennial celebration of the U.S. Constitution, his staff had created a sort of permanent shrine to the missing Bill of Rights. The exhibition covered three phases of the manuscript's life: its creation, its disappearance during the Civil War, and the state's 1925 correspondence with Charles Reid.

Throughout the courtroom struggle with B. C. West, the parchment had loomed as the big prize on the horizon. Sarah Koonts, the collections management supervisor for the archives, remembered taking a graduate-level class at North Carolina State taught by David Olson. "He openly talked about the Bill of Rights as the goal of all North Carolina archivists, to get it back," she recalled.

Olson was an anomaly in the annals of North Carolina state archivists in one sense: He was a Yankee. He grew up in Nebraska and had been state archivist in Michigan for ten years before coming to Raleigh to take over for the retiring Thornton Mitchell in 1981. But Olson drank the Kool-Aid. He fully embraced the institutional doctrine that state records are forever state property (unless formally disposed of), and that North Carolina should never pay a cent to get them back.

Prior to the conversation with John Richardson that day, Olson had walked down the hall and studied the Bill of Rights exhibit again. Standing there, absorbing the unlikely series of events that marked the document's journey, Olson had one of those moments of knee-buckling clarity. "You realize, hey, this matters," he said. "You're not only representing the agency but the people of the state and all the professionals who went before you. You only have two or three of these kinds of issues in the course of your career."

Olson was so worked up that early in the call with Richardson, he'd felt his nerves jangling. The proximity to the Bill of Rights—as opaque as Richardson's presentation was—certainly felt tantalizing. "I do a lot of fishing," Olson said later, "and it was like you could see that lunker that you've always aspired to, but can't quite catch."

Now it was closer than ever. But Olson couldn't imagine any scenario in which he would authorize a $3 million payment. He hoped Richardson might see there was no way to legitimately sell the Bill of Rights at all, much less for that kind of money. Maybe, he thought, the document's present owner could be convinced to give it back.

Toward the end of the conversation, however, things got testy. Olson asked Richardson how he would demonstrate title to the Bill of Rights, considering it had never legally left North Carolina's custody.

Richardson seemed to expect this. "I know you have that little case down there," he shot back. The sarcasm was unmistakable. He was clearly referring to B. C. West.

If North Carolina wasn't interested, Richardson said, he had a potential buyer in the Middle East.

"Well, maybe they could use a Bill of Rights over there," Olson blurted, as cavalierly as he could manage.

Despite the terse exchange, the two sides agreed to keep talking. Richardson promised to follow up soon. After hanging up, Olson, McCain, and the others huddled. Olson, for one, wasn't overly concerned about Richardson's closing gambit. "I think that was just bullshit," he said. "It was very obviously a threat intended to provoke some kind of reaction—to get us to swallow our pride and our principles and come up with some money."

Olson was familiar with the old sales ploy—better act now, there's another buyer waiting in the wings—and the Middle East bit sounded totally over the top.

Still, the officials spent some time chewing on the question of making some kind of payment for the document. And not long after the meeting broke up, Olson went to see Andrew Vanore, a lawyer in the attorney general's office. Olson wanted to know his options: Could they buy back the Bill of Rights if they chose to go that route?

Vanore said that paying for the document was indeed an option, but he preferred using the courts. But John Richardson's evasiveness had left them with no such option at that point. "If we only had somebody to sue," Vanore said.

All they could do was to wait and see what happened next.

John Richardson didn't take long to follow up. On October 24, 1995, a three-page letter slithered out of the fax machine in Betty Ray McCain's office. Whatever Richardson took from the phone call, it wasn't a sense of hopelessness. The lawyer wrote that he had enjoyed the talk and hoped to quickly move toward a sale with "maximum confidentiality." Then he reiterated that he had no direct relationship with the possessors of the document, and that there were "at least three levels of intermediaries between me and those people."

The letter was at once evasive and coercive; it was filled with oblique language, yet it was unmistakably direct. Richardson never once used the words *Bill of Rights;* he referred to the document as "the article." He omitted gender, noting that his client "views itself as a facilitator." And he never referred to anyone as an owner, instead alluding to "the people who now have the article."

This seemed calculated: If no one actually claimed to own the Bill of Rights, there was no way—and no need—to pass title.

"[W]e are constantly encouraged to 'move faster,'" Richardson wrote, "and we are reminded that the people who have the article have alternatives available to them.

> Unfortunately, we have no way of knowing how much of this is posturing and how much is real . . . We are warned that they are nervous and, if they believe their identity may be disclosed against their will, they may act in a manner which will not be in any of our interests. Again, we have no idea about the extent to which any of these warnings should be taken seriously but, to the extent we can maintain a high level of confidentiality and expedite the process, we can minimize any potential adverse impact.

With those ominous preliminaries out of the way, Richardson proposed a sale between the present possessors and "a party you would identify." Then he spelled out the steps required to consummate such a deal: The article would have to be authenticated and its value determined, North Carolina would have to come up with the money to buy it, and the buyer and seller would have to agree on the terms of the transaction.

Richardson suggested the Carolinians pick an authenticator. If the expert was acceptable to "our side," he would make the parchment available for inspection "under appropriately controlled conditions."

As for the appraisal? The two sides would hire five appraisers, each of whom would independently judge the document's value. The highest and lowest numbers would be eliminated, and the purchase price would be the average of the remaining three. The experts would be instructed not to factor "questions of ownership" into their appraisals.

Richardson also wanted to establish a floor and a ceiling for the sale price—amounts above or below which a deal would be unacceptable. Richardson reminded McCain that bidding started at $3 million and noted that he'd seen estimates as high as $10 million.

He encouraged McCain to obtain the funds from one benefactor, or a small group of donors, to avoid the time lag involved with a large-scale fundraising campaign. And he wanted North Carolina to indemnify his clients—to absolve them of any legal exposure.

"As indicated above," he wrote, "we continue to hear stories of impatience and threats of pursuing alternative courses of action attributed to the present possessors of the article." Richardson signed off, "Best regards."

As 1995 drew to a close, the keepers of North Carolina's archives agonized over potential Bill of Rights strategies. Should they buy it back? Tell John Richardson to go to hell? Neither option seemed quite right. Instead, they merely tried to keep the conversation going. McCain and Olson followed up on Richardson's letter by telephone.

This time they discussed getting the document authenticated. David Olson found this a promising direction; he hoped someone could get a look at the parchment and somehow confirm that it really was North Carolina's copy. He produced the names of three potential authenticators, and Richardson promised to report back quickly.

The attorney's next correspondence, on January 16, 1996, came by fax and said that the choice of longtime historian and scholar Leonard Rapport as authenticator was "acceptable to people 'up the line.'" Richardson would arrange and pay for Rapport to inspect the document. "We appreciate the progress we are making," he wrote. "We continue to be concerned that inaction will jeopardize the project, and we encourage you to keep it on a fast track."

After authentication would come appraisal. Richardson suggested simplifying that process: Each side would name two experts, and the sale price would be the average of the four—subject, as before, to floor and ceiling figures. He proposed establishing those two numbers before Rapport's inspection. Richardson also wanted assurances that North Carolina could cover the ceiling price.

But Richardson also seemed willing to yield some ground. "The floor price previously advanced by the people 'up the line' when we started this process was $2 million"—not the $3 million he'd quoted previously. "We will reconfirm that price as soon as possible—after we are able to show convincingly that we are making progress."

Richardson offered one final nudge. "You should give me your ceiling price as soon as possible so we can make sure we can go forward," he wrote. "As discussed, if the ceiling is too low, the piece will go elsewhere."

Despite these promising developments, however, the process fizzled out after this second letter. No one in Raleigh heard from Richardson again. "It just dried up," Olson said. "It just stopped, and we kind of weren't surprised. I remember feeling a little relieved that we didn't have to make any kind of decision about what to do. I don't think anyone involved was interested in any kind of Faustian bargain for this.

"It was like a veil opened briefly, and we got a quick vision of something, and then it dropped closed again when it was clear we weren't going to be writing a big check."

Olson opined that Richardson viewed any further contact with North Carolina as simply too risky. "Any negotiation like this takes a great deal of trust," Olson said, "and there wasn't a lot of trust either way."

Olson ultimately would have advised Betty Ray McCain not to agree to pay for the Bill of Rights—not even by couching the compensation as a finder's fee, he said. "Any way you cut it," Olson said, "that's money changing hands. In this case, there isn't any gray area."

But he felt twinges of regret. Olson wondered whether he would ever hear of the parchment's whereabouts again. But at least the document appeared to have survived the decades intact. Olson consoled himself with the thought that Richardson might never find a buyer, given the cloudy title. If Richardson sold the manuscript to someone who kept it in a vault and took it out only after midnight and never told a soul, there wasn't much anyone could do. But any responsible patron would realize the legal morass into which he or she was descending.

The wait for the Bill of Rights stretched beyond Olson's tenure as state archivist. By the time the document suddenly resurfaced once more, he had developed heart problems, moved into a different job, and was on the verge of retirement.

Richardson's letters went into the files in the archives building, where they stayed until early March of 2003. After Jeff Crow unearthed them, copies began to multiply across Raleigh and eventually find their way up to Philadelphia.

When Richardson wrote them, in 1995 and '96, the stakes must have seemed ridiculously low. He was a well-connected Washington lawyer and Democratic Party insider—the husband of the IRS commissioner. Raleigh was hundreds of miles away, and he probably imagined he was dealing with a group of fusty, small-town bureaucrats. The Bill of Rights was a lark—an intriguing long shot with a huge upside.

Who knew where it would all lead? Who could have guessed?

18

Deception

STEVE HARMELIN AND MUSEUM CEO Joe Torsella had always felt that there was something strange in the way John Richardson was peddling the Bill of Rights. There was the Nixonian secrecy, and the refusal to cooperate with brokers on the routine matter of producing a conservation report. There was the enigmatic provenance. And there was the too-strenuous denial of the North Carolina connection.

Now FBI agent Bob Wittman was sitting in Harmelin's office, showing them copies of letters John Richardson had written, offering to sell North Carolina its own Bill of Rights.

Harmelin spent a moment digesting this. And Richardson had even tossed off those subtle threats? Surreal.

Harmelin flashed back to the Yale Club meeting. No wonder Richardson had declined to produce the names of his alleged experts—the ones whose findings contradicted Ken Bowling's. Harmelin realized that there almost certainly were no such experts.

Wittman was concerned that Richardson and Pratt might follow through on the threats—or indeed might try to hawk the document to some oil magnate in the Middle East. That was why the FBI was opting for the sting, Wittman said; pry too hard, and the parchment could be in peril.

Harmelin cringed. He'd insisted at the Yale Club on contacting North Carolina—blowing open Richardson's carefully constructed shroud of secrecy. And what happens? The next day Pratt takes the parchment back. Had Harmelin unwittingly shoved the document into oblivion?

Harmelin was still fitting all the pieces together when Wittman dropped another bombshell: He wanted Harmelin to be the point man in the sting. Harmelin's task would be to call Richardson and tell him that the museum officials had decided they couldn't stand to lose out on the Bill of Rights. The Constitution Center was not only prepared to pay the full asking price—it would also back off on the demands Harmelin had made at the Yale Club in order to make it happen.

"The only way that we'll be able to keep this document safe and in the country is if they're convinced that you will, in fact, purchase it from them," Wittman said. "If we're unsuccessful, I have little doubt that this document will leave the country and not reappear for another century."

Wittman said that he would do the negotiating if necessary; that was his usual role in these types of covert productions. But Harmelin had already met Richardson, had already gotten to know him. The most logical thing was for him to pick up where he'd left off.

Harmelin's and Torsella's eyes met for a beat; they both wore one of those "What just happened here?" expressions. This was not the kind of thing they'd contemplated getting involved in. They were a lawyer and a museum guy opening a not-for-profit historical center. Did it really make sense for them to be in the middle of an FBI operation?

Harmelin thought about the entity that they had hoped the National Constitution Center would become, all the work that had gone into getting it to this point. The project was far bigger than him, of course. Hundreds of people—employees, donors, volunteers—were counting on him to guide the project through whatever legal snares lay ahead. And yes, beyond all that, Harmelin had to admit: The whole idea scared the hell out of him. Part of him wanted to stop the conversation right there, say thanks but no thanks, I don't want to get involved.

Instead, he asked to speak with Torsella privately. The two men walked out into the hall. Later they would joke that they got stuck in the doorway together trying to hustle out of there, like in the old TV sitcom gag.

But at the time there was nothing humorous about the situation. First things first: A sting could expose the museum to a lawsuit filed by Wayne Pratt and John Richardson and God only knew who else. With millions of dollars at stake, that seemed all but inevitable. The publicity could be ugly if something went wrong. Donors could desert them. It was even possible they could get sued and the Bill of Rights could disappear anyway. At so many levels their involvement made no sense.

If they had kept going down that path, Harmelin and Torsella might have convinced each other to send Bob Wittman off with their best wishes. Instead, they examined it from the other perspective. What if Wittman was right—that the museum represented the best chance to recover the document? Were they really going to let a Bill of Rights disappear to who knows where? After coming this far, after unspooling so much of the story, could Harmelin and Torsella really turn their backs on the whole thing now?

The two men tried to think of it from a historical perspective. If the sting were successful, it *would* be a remarkable moment for the museum. The Constitution Center wouldn't own a Bill of Rights, but it would have an incredible story about rescuing one. "What's the worst case, Joe?" Harmelin said. "The National Constitution Center gets sued for trying to help the FBI get back a Bill of Rights? We couldn't *buy* that publicity."

Harmelin was also peeved about Richardson's letters, and about the Middle East threat. He was deeply patriotic—American history meant more to him than to most, because of all his family had been through—and the United States was about to go to war in Iraq. The letters made him want to help.

Torsella called the board chairman, John Bogle, to inform him of Wittman's request and tell him they were considering helping the FBI. Bogle said that if Harmelin and Torsella were comfortable with it and thought that was the right thing to do, he trusted their judgment.

Comfortable wasn't the word Harmelin would have chosen. As general counsel, his job was to steer the museum away from risk. Some job he was doing. But the more he thought it over, the more he and Torsella realized there was no way around it. "If this document gets back to North Carolina," Harmelin said, "at least we've done something."

They walked back into his office and announced their decision to the FBI agents. "I appreciate that," Wittman said to Harmelin, smiling. "You'll sound more like an attorney than I will."

In the age of color-coded terror alerts, the notion of FBI agents chasing after old broadsheets sounds charmingly nostalgic. But in fact, law enforcement has faced increasing pressure in recent years to stem the flow of public documents disappearing into burglars' hands. Clearly, the spike in the value of old papers has made public archives look very tempting to criminals.

The thefts are rarely brazen daylight productions involving masks and guns. More typically, the perpetrators are men like Charles Merrill Mount, who was a familiar face inside the National Archives and the Library of Congress in the 1980s. An eccentric character with a British accent who strode around on routine business in dress clothes and carrying a cane, he'd published three biographies of renowned artists.

In the mid-eighties Mount contacted Edward Bomsey, a dealer in suburban Washington, about selling some old documents. Mount seemed to be down on his luck—the suits appeared to be fraying at the cuffs—but the stuff he had for sale was interesting, so Bomsey became a regular buyer. They often met in a hotel bar to do business, so Bomsey was surprised, upon returning home from a business trip in August 1987, to find a package from Mount sitting in his pile of unopened mail. Bomsey ripped it open and found far more valuable material than he'd seen from Mount before; in particular, he was astonished to find old, rare Indian treaties that were clearly worth a lot of money. Bomsey put the package down and began to unwind by watching the local news. In his jet-lagged haze, Bomsey caught the mug shot of a man who'd just been arrested in Boston. Bomsey stared at the screen. It was Charles Merrill Mount. "It was kind of like, you ever see those cartoons?" Bomsey recalled. "The guy gets hit in the head and, *boiing!* That just knocked the stuffing out of me."

Mount turned out to be Sherman Suchow, born and raised in Brooklyn. While conducting research in the National Archives and Library of Congress, he'd been slipping historic papers into his suits. Not long before mailing the package to Bomsey, Mount had entered the Goodspeed Bookshop in Boston with some rare letters written by Abraham Lincoln, Winston Churchill, and others, which he sold on the spot for $20,000. After he left, the bookstore owners became suspicious and called the FBI. Agents called in a manuscripts dealer named Kenneth Rendell, who identified the letters as items he'd sold to the Library of Congress in the 1970s.

Mount had called the Goodspeed again several weeks later, offering some Civil War and World War I documents. When he arrived, the FBI was waiting. Back in Washington, agents opened two safe-deposit boxes Mount had secured and found hundreds more stolen papers. Slipping away with a few pages at a time, Mount had pulled off the largest known theft of historic American documents ever.

Bomsey called the National Archives the next morning and brought in everything Mount had ever sold him. "It cost me several thousands of dollars out of my pocket and I wasn't getting the money back," Bomsey said. "But I did what I felt had to be done, what anyone would have done when faced with the notion that you're going to have hot stuff in their collection, things that were stolen from *my* National Archives."

The case sent a shock wave through the archival community and prompted the Library of Congress and other institutions to reexamine their security systems. But the thefts continued at a striking rate.

NOVEMBER 3, 1998, SPRINGFIELD, ILLINOIS—A weeping Sean Brown was sentenced Monday to four years in prison for stealing [nearly 600] Lincoln-era documents—described by prosecutors as "about as serious a white-collar-type crime" as there is.

Brown, 29, of Springfield . . . was employed to search for Lincoln-era documents as part of the Abraham Lincoln Legal Papers research project.

DECEMBER 7, 2001, NEW HAVEN, CONNECTICUT—It was a summer job, and the duties for Benjamin W. Johnson were simple: to move boxes of documents at Yale University's rare books library.

But the treasure of half a million rare books and several million manuscripts housed at the university's Beinecke library proved to be too much temptation for Mr. Johnson, a 21-year-old University of Wisconsin student, according to the Yale police. Now he stands charged with stealing about 50 items worth more than $1.5 million from the library, including a letter from George Washington to French General Rochambeau, documents signed by Abraham Lincoln, Thomas Jefferson and Benjamin Franklin . . .

AUGUST 1, 2002, PHILADELPHIA—A former federal archivist driven by what he called a passion for history and a psychological compulsion to collect received a 21-month prison sentence yesterday for stealing hundreds of historic documents from the National Archives branch in Philadelphia.

"It went from a period of conflicting ethics to criminal activity," Shawn P. Aubitz told U.S. District Judge Jan E. DuBois. "I have a mental illness, a compulsive need to amass collections for self-esteem and approval." . . . DuBois, saying the stolen items were part of the nation's heritage, told Aubitz he "made victims of all Americans."

MARCH 4, 2005, LEXINGTON, KENTUCKY—Four Lexington 20-year-olds accused of stealing rare books from the Transylvania University library have been indicted by a federal grand jury on charges of robbery, conspiracy and theft of major artworks.

. . . [Warren] Lipka used a stun gun on the special collections librarian. Then he and [Eric] Borsuk tied her hands and feet, according to the indictment. The men left the library with the manuscripts and sketches . . . [Among the items taken was a 1425 manuscript from Winchester, England.]

MAY 27, 2005, WASHINGTON, D.C.—A Virginia man was sentenced yesterday to two years in prison for stealing more than 100

Civil War-era documents from the National Archives, including some he tried to sell on eBay.   WRITTEN

Howard Harner, 68, took letters authored by Jefferson Davis, Robert E. Lee and other historical figures. Federal prosecutors sought a lengthy sentence to help discourage trafficking in stolen American history.

DECEMBER 9, 2005, LOUISVILLE, KENTUCKY—Donald Eckard, a retired 70-year-old man with no criminal history, allegedly stole 53 items from the Filson Historical Society.

. . . Included in the documents Eckard took from the society's collections were nine letters written by Jefferson Davis, John Quincy Adams, Thomas Jefferson and Andrew Jackson, authorities said yesterday.

. . . Eckard has agreed to plead guilty to nine felony counts of art theft as part of a plea agreement with the U.S. Attorney's office.

JANUARY 29, 2008, ALBANY, NEW YORK—A veteran state archivist said he stole hundreds of historical artifacts from the State Library—including two Davy Crockett almanacs—to pay for home renovations, tuition and his daughter's $10,000 credit card bill.

The advent of the Internet in general—and auction sites in particular—has exacerbated the problem. "eBay, in my view, is the greatest fence in the world," said Bill Reese, the rare-books and documents dealer. "It's a recipe for selling stolen goods: It's anonymous, and they're utterly unresponsive to the security operations of the Antiquarian Books Association."

True to his lawyerly instincts, Steve Harmelin started the next day by calling a meeting to discuss how best to guide the National Constitution Center through the days ahead. He and a handful of his Dilworth Paxson colleagues chewed over potential areas of exposure for several hours.

To FBI agent Bob Wittman, the conversation was tedious—too many quarterbacks, too many game plans. He'd worked on cases that had spilled across several years and multiple layers of smuggling rings; by comparison, this one was simple. There was one seller. There was a seizure warrant. Let's go get it done.

Finally unable to restrain himself, Wittman cut in. The problem, he said, was that the attorneys were discussing the pending negotiations with John Richardson as if they were legitimate. "Dude, it doesn't matter what you say or don't say," Wittman said. "It's all bullshit."

All that mattered, in other words, was that Harmelin convince Richardson to show up with the Bill of Rights.

If Wittman had run the investigation from the start—if he'd heard about the Bill of Rights when it first came up for sale—Harmelin would no longer have been in the room. Wittman would have posed as the museum's buyer and met Wayne Pratt at the Yale Club.

And if things hadn't been so rushed, Wittman would have been trying to assemble a criminal case against Pratt and his lawyer for the interstate transportation of stolen property. To win a conviction for that crime, he had to be able to prove that the property was stolen, and that the person transporting it across state lines knew that it was stolen. That second element was the most difficult to prove. "Generally we try to get a middleman like Steve out of it as fast as possible because what you're trying to do is prove elements of a crime," Wittman said. "It's not just about bullshitting a guy; you're bullshitting them for a reason."

In this case, though, everything was different. Officials from North Carolina wanted to retrieve the Bill of Rights first and worry about everything else later. There was already a civil seizure warrant in hand. Wittman had arrived at the tail end, like a closer coming in to finish a baseball game. "Things were happening quickly, because there was a different goal in this case," Wittman said. "It would've been different if I'd had more time." In particular, Wittman said he would have tried to figure out what Richardson knew about the document's history.

That afternoon Harmelin collected himself and picked up the phone. When John Richardson answered, Harmelin did his best to sound breezy and relaxed and excited. Good news: The Constitution

Center's officers had decided they want to buy the Bill of Rights, he said.

Richardson sounded surprised and pleased.

Harmelin explained that the museum would pay the full $5 million asking price—less $1 million, because Bill Reese had waived his commission. Reese had agreed to a smaller fee from the museum, Harmelin said. This, too, was fiction, of course; Reese had no idea what was going on.

The museum's sudden about-face might have seemed implausible but for one key factor: the timing of Harmelin's phone call. Reese's option expired within days. Reese was the museum's conduit to the parchment. Harmelin mentioned the deadline as a way of encouraging Richardson to think that the museum was worried.

Richardson was thus free to believe that he'd simply outlasted the museum officials. Once they saw that Richardson wouldn't budge, they'd caved in.

Richardson had several conditions. He and Wayne Pratt wanted to remain anonymous. They wanted a confidentiality agreement. And they wouldn't provide any proof of the Bill of Rights' disputed provenance.

Fine, Harmelin said.

Joe Torsella, the museum chief, and Bob Wittman sat at Harmelin's conference table, listening intently.

Then Richardson asked: What about an indemnity clause?

This had been an obstacle as far back as the Yale Club meeting. Richardson wanted the Constitution Center to shield both him and Pratt against any future litigation. In other words, if North Carolina tried to reclaim the Bill of Rights, the museum alone had to take up the fight—and couldn't come asking for its $4 million back.

This was the same guarantee Pratt had given the Shotwell family. Only in that case he had used indemnification as a bargaining chip to drive down the sale price.

For a moment Harmelin couldn't suppress his lawyerly outrage. "You've got to be kidding," he barked. "We're a not-for-profit; we're not going to give you an indemnity."

This *was* an audacious request. Granting an indemnity under those circumstances would be supremely irresponsible. Harmelin could never put the museum in a position to lose the document *and* its $4 million.

The negotiations were bogus, but still: Harmelin was in an awkward spot. He was a seasoned negotiator. His gut told him that Wittman's advice—just agree to what he asks for—wasn't warranted in this instance. It just wouldn't sound plausible for him to give in easily on this request.

Well, then, we're not going to sell it to you, Richardson replied.

Harmelin had been a corporate lawyer with expertise in financial transactions for more than thirty-five years. He'd handled mergers and acquisitions and advised various companies' boards of directors. He'd dealt in nonprofit governance issues and lectured on financial transactions. He'd served as treasurer for U.S. Senator Arlen Specter's last four reelection campaigns, and as board chairman of a New York Stock Exchange company.

Harmelin embraced a big stage. At Dilworth Paxson he was known as the "gravitas partner." When something significant happened—layoffs, war, the 9/11 attacks—Harmelin was the one who stood and addressed the entire firm. As the United States prepared to launch an invasion of Iraq, everyone at Dilworth Paxson knew to expect a stirring speech from the gravitas partner about our boys in tents out in the middle of the desert.

But neither his extensive experience nor his taste for dramatic speechifying had prepared him for this surreal conversation. Harmelin said he'd need to confer with museum officials and call back.

Harmelin didn't need much time. After huddling with Bob Wittman, he called Richardson back with a solution: The Constitution Center had a benefactor—a donor who had made millions during the Internet boom—who was buying the Bill of Rights on the museum's behalf. That gentleman, Bob Clay, was also willing to personally indemnify Richardson and Pratt.

Harmelin promised to furnish the philanthropist's tax return. In fact, Clay would be at the closing to say a few words of appreciation. "You can meet him and see for yourself," Harmelin said.

After some initial skepticism, Richardson consented to that arrangement. After they hung up, Harmelin put the agreement on paper. "In order to avoid the risk of having the rights granted to Peter Tillou and William Reese expire, our client, the National Constitution Center, has determined to purchase your client's original manuscript of the Bill of Rights at the price originally discussed," Harmelin wrote.

"Please let me know a convenient time and location next week to close this transaction by delivery to me of the Bill of Rights in exchange for a certified check in the amount of $4,000,000. If that is not possible, we are available to close immediately, including tomorrow or Sunday. For sales tax purposes, we would prefer to close in our offices in Philadelphia, but are available to close in your offices in Washington, D.C."

Harmelin faxed the letter that afternoon along with a bill of sale and related papers. Everything seemed to be going smoothly so far. Richardson seemed a bit leery, but not so much that he wanted to abort the deal.

Richardson's and Pratt's lives had been intertwined with the parchment's since 1995. They had endured all the vicissitudes of the prized document's history and present-day realities. It wasn't a question of whether these were the right buyers. There *were* no other buyers.

Instead, what Pratt and Richardson must have begun to think about was the money—*finally,* after all those years, the money. In their minds, maybe they started spending it.

That same afternoon Bob Wittman approached Joe Torsella. I need you to go get $4 million, Wittman said. A cashier's check.

Torsella recoiled. A *real* check? Wasn't that taking the charade a bit too far?

Wittman shook his head. "The document won't arrive," he said, "unless they think it's all real."

One of the endemic risks in undercover work is risking real money. During the FBI operation that netted the Peruvian battle armor, Wittman's mentor, Bob Bazin, had initially spent $175,000 in taxpayers' money on a headdress from the same smugglers. The buy was purely an attempt to win their trust. The smugglers seemed pleased—but then vanished for three years, and FBI officials considered the $175,000 lost. When the smugglers reemerged and Wittman began negotiating to buy the armor, he had to deposit another $800,000 into a private account and send a statement to the sellers confirming that the money was available for withdrawal. This was all to build confidence, to make sure the smugglers arrived with the goods.

In this case, Wittman said, he wasn't worried: Richardson would never hold the check in his hands.

Torsella spoke to Adare McMillan, the museum's CFO, who in turn wrote a letter to First Union National Bank authorizing a $4 million withdrawal, payable to Wayne Pratt.

As the Friday afternoon pushed toward evening, Harmelin's fax machine hummed, and two documents rolled in. The first was a letter from Richardson, confirming the pending purchase of the Bill of Rights. The second came at about 4:00 p.m.: a letter from the Department of Justice that Harmelin had sought that morning. "We request that you work with the FBI to arrange for the presentation of these documents for sale to you," assistant U.S. attorney Michael Schwartz wrote. "It is understood that your cooperation may necessitate playing a role designated by the FBI and engaging in subterfuge to assist the FBI in locating the documents."

Wittman had orchestrated this earlier. He'd watched Harmelin overthink every scenario, trying to avoid any potential legal problem, and had called Schwartz. "We need a letter," Wittman said. "I'm going to have Steve call you for it."

The letter, Wittman admitted later, "wasn't worth the paper it was written on. We don't indemnify or hold anyone harmless."

The FBI agent didn't mention this to Harmelin, who seemed pleased with this reassurance. At 4:45 p.m. Richardson called back. He'd received the bill of sale. There was no need to worry about closing over the weekend; they could consummate the transaction the following week. Let's work out the logistics on Monday, Richardson said. He was going to Arizona and thus might not attend the closing, but didn't believe his presence would be necessary.

Richardson asked again: We agree that the museum is not asking for proof of provenance, correct?

That's right, Harmelin said. No proof required.

Ski trips seemed to trigger major happenings in Wayne Pratt's life.

He was in Lake Louise when he and Sarah conceived their first son, James. He once nearly died in Jackson Hole, Wyoming. Skilled skiers there tend to leave the groomed slopes and head for backcountry powder, carrying an avalanche beacon and shovel. It's high country—the mountain tops out at 10,540 feet—and is known for steep, harrowing drops. Up near the top, Pratt had trouble catching his breath. He had a bad heart valve and wasn't supposed to push too hard, and he struggled mightily to make it back down.

And in March 2003 the long-awaited Bill of Rights deal had come together. Pratt and his family alighted at Beaver Creek, a plush resort in the Colorado Rockies where he'd rented a ski-in, ski-out condo. The boys would spend the days in ski school while Wayne and Sarah followed a guide, ostensibly so they wouldn't need to burn time getting reoriented to the mountain's 776 groomed acres.

There was another reason, too: Sarah was always pushing Wayne to do tougher black-diamond trails than he was comfortable with, and sometimes he got testy and jokingly accused her of trying to kill him. But if a *guide* took them out, even to somewhere beyond his comfort zone, that was different. Wayne willingly plunged in.

Pratt felt equally well disposed with the Bill of Rights. He had a prominent lawyer watching his back, and finally the deal was almost done. That Friday, March 14, John Richardson faxed Wayne Pratt a copy of the bill of sale. Pratt signed it, had it notarized in Eagle County, Colorado, and faxed it back.

Richardson, meanwhile, decided at the last minute to rearrange his schedule, delaying a trip to Phoenix and Los Angeles until after the Bill of Rights deal. He would attend the closing. This deal was that important.

Richardson did not shuffle his schedule around lightly. He was an important guy with a lot going on—particularly in the past few years, as his prominence in the Democratic Party had grown.

Not so long ago he was best known as the husband of Peg Richardson, the IRS commissioner. In contrast to Bob Matthews, John Richardson tended to work best behind the scenes. But he had served on Washington Mayor Anthony Williams's transition committee after Williams was elected in 1999. That same year the new mayor appointed Richardson chairman of the eleven-member D.C. Sports and Entertainment Commission. This was a dynamic time for Washington sports: The commission arranged an uptick in major events and planned to upgrade Robert F. Kennedy Stadium in order to lure Major League Baseball to Washington, and to bid on the 2012 Olympics. The commission wanted to run a Grand Prix auto race. In summer 2000 Richardson, Williams, and several other commission officials attended baseball's All-Star Game in Atlanta to pursue Washington's bid for a team.

Peg Richardson counted Hillary Rodham Clinton as a friend, so the Richardsons sampled the swankier national scene as well. In 1999 the couple attended a state dinner for Ghanian President Jerry Rawlings, hosted by President Clinton and attended by political luminaries (including Vice President Al Gore), sports legends such as Hank Aaron and Jackie Joyner-Kersee, and several Hollywood stars. John Richardson had also been a member of the Committee for the Preservation of the White House and was on the guest list for the revered building's two-hundredth-anniversary dinner.

He was, in other words, the kind of man who didn't expect to be on the wrong side of an FBI operation.

The FBI agent and the Constitution Center officials parted ways by 5:00 p.m. on Friday. Things had gone well, and on the verge of heading off for the weekend, Steve Harmelin and Joe Torsella started to relax. Harmelin teased Wittman about his attire, suggesting that he buy better shoes for the closing and wear his best suit.

Harmelin began quizzing Wittman about high-tech lingo, trying to get a sense of how the FBI agent would play as a dot-com mogul.

Harmelin was sure that Wittman knew what he was doing, but still: The thought of the FBI agent making idle chatter with Richardson and inadvertently betraying his unfamiliarity with Silicon Valley parlance was yet another source of agita for the anxious lawyer.

Could they maybe avoid talking IPOs and Web portals? he asked. "You're good," Harmelin said, "but you'll last about twelve seconds in front of somebody who really is a high-tech expert."

Wittman smiled. He'd been alone with smugglers and thieves selling multimillion-dollar objects. His work was notoriously grinding—so much so that the bureau tested undercover agents every six months to measure their psychological stability. "Before going into a room to do a deal, I'd ask myself, 'What if they ask this? What do I say if that happens?'" Bob Bazin, Wittman's mentor, said in Roger Atwood's book *Stealing History*. "You have to become this person that you're not, and you have to make it believable, and after a while you're not sure who you are anymore."

Wittman thought of it as sort of like acting, except "unlike actors, you only get one shot and you have to remember everything you ever said." In Madrid the Spanish gangsters who offered him the consulting job said they'd considered kidnapping a British expert. They were thrilled Wittman could save them the trouble.

Harmelin had no concept of the prickly spots Wittman had navigated through.

So, banter along for a few minutes with a D.C. lawyer? That wouldn't be a problem at all.

19

Special Delivery

STEVE HARMELIN CALLED John Richardson first thing on Monday morning, March 17. Harmelin was keen to settle the final details of the Bill of Rights acquisition. They agreed to hold the closing the next day.

They hadn't yet discussed where they would meet for the closing, so Harmelin took the initiative. Despite the tossed-off comment in his letter, he *didn't* want to go to Washington to get the document; the FBI needed a place to stage their operation.

Richardson hedged. *Christ,* Harmelin thought, *let him decide, and he'll want me to meet him in Iceland.*

Harmelin had to get Richardson to Philadelphia without generating suspicion. "We don't have to close in this office," Harmelin bluffed. "Pick anywhere in Pennsylvania you want to close. This is an important acquisition for the Constitution Center, and we have an opinion letter that we need to do this in a way that's free of state transfer taxes. And the only place you can do that, if you're a Pennsylvania lawyer, is in Pennsylvania. If you want to close with us, figure out a place in Pennsylvania and I'll be there."

Harmelin had no idea where the transfer-tax idea came from. It was totally spontaneous. He even surprised himself, but it worked: This time Richardson gave in and agreed to come to Philadelphia.

Harmelin felt satisfied, especially with this last minor clash of swords, that the brief negotiations had come off as reasonably authentic. Add in the meeting two weeks earlier at the Yale Club, and the talks had many of the starts and stops and complexities of a significant asset purchase.

At 9:41 that morning Richardson e-mailed Harmelin: "I believe we are making progress at this end . . . we are trying our best to arrange things so that we can close in Philadelphia tomorrow through the use of a broad general power Mr. Pratt would give to me."

The lawyers began tending to the final details. At 12:21 p.m. Harmelin's associate, Rubin Weiner, e-mailed a power of attorney form to Richardson and asked that the lawyer "please advise as to what time you will be coming tomorrow, so we can reserve a conference room."

Richardson responded soon after that he'd already come up with his own power of attorney. "Logistics being what they are," Richardson e-mailed back, "I recommend that you accept the form presently being processed if we are going to be able to close tomorrow."

By 3:00 p.m. the last of the paperwork was lined up. Richardson faxed six pages to Harmelin's office, including an indemnification form to be signed by Bob Clay, the museum's philanthropist. That document specified that Clay "agree to hold Seller completely harmless with respect to any claim of any type which may be asserted against Seller following the consummation of such transaction . . . including specifically claims that may be asserted against Seller by . . . any state or other government instrumentality . . ."

Another document covered the terms of the agreement, which provided even more legal cover for Richardson and Pratt. The National Constitution Center would acknowledge that Pratt "makes no representations and provides no warranties as to the previous ownership or provenance of the document."

The museum and Pratt would both agree "not to disclose . . . the terms of this transaction, including the identities of the principals and their representatives, except as required by law or with the express written permission of both parties."

That afternoon Torsella met an official from First Union National Bank in the lobby of the Mellon Bank Center to collect a new check for $4 million. The bank had to reissue payment because Richardson wanted the check made out to his law firm, Crispin & Brenner.

Torsella's errand gave him a few minutes to think about all that was at stake. The $4 million came from the museum's construction fund, so the money had to go straight back into the bank when the curtain fell on Bob Wittman's one-act production. As it was, Torsella's request had caused quite a stir down at First Union. Now the museum chief tried not to let his thoughts linger on the chaos that would ensue with the project if something went wrong.

That same Monday afternoon, March 17, Pratt stood in a notary public's office in Eagle County, Colorado. There, with two witnesses, he signed a power of attorney to John Richardson to "act in my name, place and stead in any way which I myself could do if I were personally present with respect to . . . an original manuscript of the Bill of Rights and the sale thereof by me."

This was it: the last of a seemingly endless string of details that Pratt needed to tend to.

Though he didn't want the Bill of Rights deal publicly disclosed, Pratt enjoyed telling the people close to him about the pending sale. For his eightieth birthday Pratt's father-in-law had bought the entire family a vacation at the Buccaneer Hotel on St. Croix. While the family relaxed in the sun, Pratt had exhaustively detailed the pending transaction for Sarah's father—to the point that it annoyed Sarah. "I was pissed off," she said, "that Wayne was totally monopolizing him."

Bob Matthews had no clue as to the machinations involving the Bill of Rights. He'd invested $100,000 and then essentially forgotten about it. He still wasn't sure the parchment was real, and anyway, he had plenty else to keep him busy.

Predictably, Matthews fully bounced back from his mysterious and nearly fatal illness on Nantucket. For a time he was a changed man. He slowed down. He did yoga. He invited a group of Tibetan monks to his Nantucket estate. According to one newspaper story, he attended Catholic Mass daily. "His faith really moved him after his near-death experience," said Chris DiPino, Connecticut's Republican Party chairman at the time.

But it came as even less of a surprise to friends and family that as Matthews's strength returned, his inner Buddha withered away, replaced by the speed-talking salesman of old.

Matthews focused in particular on his greatest potential prize: the 550,000-square-foot New Haven building that he'd bought from the Southern New England Telephone Company for a half-million dollars. The attention paid staggering dividends. In January 2000 Matthews astounded the New Haven real estate and business community by selling the building to Massachusetts investors for $27.5 million. He later bragged to the *Hartford Courant* that the deal was "my best flip" and that he'd actually acquired the building for free because the phone company had leased the space back from him after he'd purchased it. "I gave them a check for a half-million; they gave me back a check for a half-million," Matthews said.

Buoyed by these and other successes, Matthews found new and creative ways to leverage his ties with public officials in New Haven and Hartford. That same year he promised officials from a fledgling Pennsylvania-based meatpacking company that he could deliver $10 million in public aid if the firm agreed to move to Connecticut— actually, into one of his buildings. In particular, Matthews touted his relationship with Governor John Rowland, who had cruised to reelection in 1998. Rowland even phoned Pinnacle Foods on Matthews's behalf while the two men played golf one day at the Country Club of Waterbury. Duly convinced, Pinnacle signed Matthews up as a consultant and paid him $2.7 million in company stock.

The deal didn't fly—Connecticut officials balked at that level of assistance—but Matthews didn't hold a grudge. In 2001 he opened his estate in Palm Beach to Rowland for a four-night vacation, gratis.

Matthews's generosity with politicians didn't go unnoticed. New Haven–based journalist Paul Bass wrote that Matthews "has been the Jay Gatsby of the Rowland era—the flaunter of turn-of-the-21st-century new wealth built by mingling personal friendships with the lust for money and power and the high life . . . If Jay Gatsby lived in

Connecticut today, he, too, would probably have a hard-to-get '1-CT' license plate on his BMW parked illegally in front of one of his office buildings."

Pratt, forever looking from the outside in on Matthews's political dealings, marveled at what his friend was able to pull off. Still, Wayne had occasional clashes with the newly supercharged Matthews. There was a piece of furniture—a secretary—that the two men had bought together a few years earlier for $55,000. After Matthews recovered from his illness, Pratt lined up a buyer willing to pay roughly five times what they'd put into it. But Matthews had kept the item in his home and had come to believe that he was the primary owner—by his own admission, the coma had left his memory fuzzy in spots. As Pratt recounted the story, Matthews demanded most of the profit from the sale. "Come on, this is ridiculous—this isn't what we agreed to," Pratt told him.

Matthews relented, but Pratt wondered about his friend. Bob's vow to radically and permanently overhaul his life? "That lasted about four months," Pratt said, the sarcasm unmistakable. Instead of being mellower and more grounded after his mortal struggle, Matthews seemed edgier than ever.

Pratt once took Matthews to a client's house to look at a chandelier Bob was considering buying. The client was an older, wealthy man—someone Pratt admired. The meeting went poorly. "Bob started doing his dance around—'how about I pay you this much, how about that much,'" Pratt said.

The client insisted on $20,000 and then refused to show Matthews anything else in the house. "Afterward he said to me, 'Wayne, don't ever bring him back to my house,'" Pratt remembered.

Pratt thought about that encounter many times. *Whoa,* he thought. *That's someone who reads people at a whole different level.*

But there were still the Fourth of July parties and the yacht trips, and though the economy wasn't quite as white-hot after airplanes crashed into buildings in New York City and Washington, Bob had not forgotten how to tell a story and throw a party and make people laugh.

In 2002 Connecticut voters elected Rowland, then chairman of the Republican National Committee, to a historic third term. His opponent, Bill Curry, repeatedly attacked Rowland for handing out lucrative state contracts to some of his administration's most generous donors, but none of it stuck. If Rowland finished that four-year term, he would be the state's longest-serving governor since 1784. The *New York Times* labeled him "Connecticut's unbeaten and perhaps unbeatable governor."

And so in different regions of Connecticut—but not so far apart at all—John Rowland, Wayne Pratt, and Bob Matthews all soared through the prime of their lives on separate but parallel courses. They were smart and charismatic and had enjoyed the fruits of a booming economy, and they had seized opportunities that had taken them farther than perhaps even they had expected to go.

Soon, all three men would have one other thing in common: They would all have the keen attention of the Federal Bureau of Investigation.

At 3:30 on the afternoon of March 17, 2003, close to the time that Wayne Pratt was notarizing his documents in Colorado and Joe Torsella was staring at a bank check for $4 million, a man named Joe Constantino climbed into a car in Woodbury, Connecticut. Constantino was one of Pratt's tenured employees. Thirteen years earlier, when Pratt lived in Marlborough, Massachusetts, Constantino was a runner; one of his routes took him past Pratt's house. Jogging by one day, he noticed the antiques dealer struggling to remove a piece of furniture from a van.

Constantino didn't want to halt his workout. He hit his turnaround point and circled back, but when he passed Pratt's house the second time he saw the dealer still struggling. This time he stopped. He wound up helping to move a number of bulky objects, and when they were done Pratt fished a $100 bill out of his pocket and asked him if he could come back the next day.

Constantino had been a fixture ever since. When Pratt moved to Connecticut, Constantino kept his job even though it meant commuting 170 miles every day from Sturbridge, Massachusetts, where his family lived.

He loved going on house calls with the boss. As they moved through a home, Pratt constantly pointed out features of certain pieces, explained what was great and what was merely good, and why. Constantino thought of Pratt as a friend, a boss, and a teacher.

Constantino had on many occasions transported valuable antiques and paintings, so he wasn't particularly fazed on that March afternoon to have a $4 million parchment inside a box on the seat next to him. His job was to drive down to the edge of Philadelphia, stay overnight, and then head into the city, to a downtown law office. The delivery wouldn't take place until early the next afternoon, so Constantino could have waited until that morning to leave. But there could be traffic, weather, who knew what.

Constantino drove to Mt. Laurel, New Jersey, about seventeen miles from Philadelphia, just across the Delaware River, and checked into a hotel. He kept the box containing the Bill of Rights in his room while he slept.

20

The Thump on the Door

*L*OOK AT YOU, Steve Harmelin told himself. *You're a mess.*

It was 3:00 a.m. on Tuesday, March 18. He hadn't slept at all. Harmelin kept padding around through the dim light of his house, trying not to wake his wife. He was ready to abandon the idea of sleep. All he could think of was everything that might go wrong later that day. He kept running through every point of negotiation, wondering whether, in some imperceptible way, he'd tipped John Richardson off to Bob Wittman's plan.

Harmelin wandered into his den to watch television—which on that night proved to offer cold comfort. The news channels unspooled nonstop coverage from Iraq, where the American invasion had been launched only a few hours before. As the small hours stretched toward dawn, he flipped channels fitfully, watching the drama unfolding halfway around the planet.

As TV cameras panned across blank voids of Middle Eastern desert, or zoomed in on troops in chemical-warfare suits, Harmelin felt guilty for feeling so anxious. *That* was peril. He should have known the difference. He had felt at least a frisson of the uncertainty and fear those American soldiers felt. He'd served in the Coast Guard Reserves as a young man, from 1964 to '69. He'd been required to report to Philadelphia's Navy Yard one weekend a month and two full weeks every summer. Harmelin remembered the volatility, the feeling that the world was cracking loose and sliding like avalanching layers of snow. Riots roiled the streets. Harmelin's officers taught him and his fellow reservists to defend port areas. He struggled to hold a defensive stance during drills while regulars—posing as rioters—pelted him with tomatoes and eggs and spit in his face.

Obviously, it could have been worse. He'd known plenty of reservists who had gone to Vietnam. Coast Guard types were in demand for their acumen with the small, speedy watercraft that the military favored in the Mekong Delta. Harmelin had tried not to think about it, but then on sleepless nights you could trick your brain for only so long. You run your life differently when on any given day you could be sent off to war.

He reminded himself that nothing like life and death was at stake now. *What the hell am I nervous about?* he asked himself as the screen flickered. *Look at you, and look at what they're doing. You oughta be ashamed of yourself.*

The sun rose behind a cloud cover over the slopes of Colorado's Beaver Creek Resort the morning of March 18. It was well below freezing, but mostly wind-free—more or less exactly the sort of crisp late-winter day the Pratt family had envisioned for their annual ski vacation.

But Wayne Pratt didn't want to ski. His thoughts were too far away. Because he couldn't be in Philadelphia in person, he wanted to keep vigil near the phone, wanted to be there when John Richardson called. In the meantime he would keep tabs on the coverage of the Iraq war's opening salvos.

As Wayne and Sarah sat talking that morning, Pratt's phone rang. It was Peter Tillou, the venerable Connecticut art and antiques dealer—he of the refined sensibilities and argyle socks. Pratt knew from conversations with broker Seth Kaller that Tillou and Bill Reese had waived their $1 million commission agreement. Kaller had said that the National Constitution Center would compensate them. But with a $4 million sale pending, Tillou (who knew nothing of the FBI plans) apparently felt jilted. He thought he deserved a larger cut of the proceeds.

Pratt was unmoved. He explained that he wasn't making much of the $4 million—his lawyer was getting most of it. And anyway,

Tillou had bailed out. Pratt, annoyed by now with this cabal of dealers, told him to talk to Reese and Seth Kaller.

When Pratt hung up, he turned to Sarah. "This," he said, "is going to be the biggest pig-fuck I've ever seen in my life."

Sarah headed out to ski. She felt a little guilty, but there was no point in hanging around. She was actually excited to be on her own, to not have to negotiate runs with Wayne. Pratt settled in to channel-surf. He, too, was excited—though maybe a bit more cautiously. Mostly, he felt eager just to have this whole business done.

John Richardson was running late. The closing was originally scheduled for 1:00 p.m., but Harmelin pushed the meeting back an hour when he learned Richardson's train from Washington was running behind.

The delay gave Harmelin and the FBI more time to prepare. Agents waited at Philadelphia's Pennsylvania Station–30th Street Station, looking for Richardson. From the train the attorney would make his way to Market Street and enter the art deco lobby of the Mellon Bank Center. He would take the elevator to the thirty-second floor, to the Dilworth Paxson reception area, and then turn right and walk about a hundred feet to the Kalish Conference Room, named for the late Harry A. Kalish, one of the firm's founders.

The airy room, about twenty-five feet long and fifteen feet wide, features a dark wood table in the center, ten high-backed swivel chairs, a large photograph of Kalish in owlish glasses, and some artifacts from Kalish's life, including a photo of him serving as a major in the South Pacific during World War II. Large windows offer expansive views to the south and east. The latter vistas include the Benjamin Franklin Bridge, the Delaware River, and New Jersey beyond. If not for the buildings obstructing the view, one could have gazed down on the construction site of the National Constitution Center.

Harmelin's associate Rubin Weiner removed the closing documents from an accordion file and lined everything up on the table. Joe Torsella, the museum's CEO, handed Harmelin the cashier's check for $4 million. The lawyer reminded Torsella of the plan: Harmelin would only show the check to Richardson. "I promise you," Harmelin said, "it will never leave my hand."

And then all that remained to do was squelch jangly nerves with gallows humor. "If you lose that $4 million for us today," Torsella said, smiling, "you're going to have to move out of town."

As far as everyone else at Dilworth Paxson knew, Harmelin had organized a business luncheon that day in the Paxson Conference Room, situated kitty-corner to the Kalish Room. Harmelin had reserved the room and hired a caterer to deliver a spread of sandwiches. The meeting's five attendees, all dressed in business attire, looked ready to do battle over some disputed merger. They were actually FBI agents Jay Heine, Thomas Duffy, Stephen Heaney, Diana Huffman, and Michael Thompson.

Wittman had assembled this team to protect the document and everyone involved in the operation, including Richardson. Wittman had to be ready for any eventuality. During the sting that netted Geronimo's war bonnet, the seller toppled with a heart attack when FBI agents burst into the room.

The subterfuge wasn't aimed only at John Richardson. Dilworth Paxson's reception room—elegantly appointed with recessed lighting, antique maps and documents, and a large window with panoramic views to the south—was often a meeting point for lawyers headed to the elevators to grab lunch. Law firms are notoriously gossipy, and in the preceding days Harmelin's mind had looped with endless waking nightmares. In one, Richardson is sitting in the lobby, the Bill of Rights next to him, when a couple of lawyers bump into each other and one says, "Hey, you see those FBI agents back there?"

But by the time Richardson boarded the elevator, the seal of secrecy, as far as Harmelin knew, was unbroken. Harmelin felt ready, sleepless night notwithstanding. Still, when a receptionist downstairs phoned in Richardson's arrival, everyone looked at each other. Wittman had expected word from the FBI agents at the train station that they had seen Richardson disembark and head over. But probably because of sheer numbers of passengers—and random chance—the agents hadn't spotted the lawyer.

Harmelin hoped that was going to be the day's only hitch.

John Richardson arrived empty-handed.

That was the first thing everyone in the room noticed. No box, no container of any kind. The only document he carried was a note from his managing partner, William H. Crispin, authorizing him to accept a check made out to the law firm Crispin & Brenner.

Harmelin hadn't believed Wittman when the FBI agent suggested Richardson might arrive sans parchment, to check out the scene first. In fact, Wittman didn't expect it to happen either. "I had never seen anything like that in a normal sale situation," he said. "I'd only seen that in criminal cases—with drug cases, things of that nature."

Harmelin thought about Richardson's calls and e-mails of the past few days, repeatedly reconfirming the arrangements. Richardson really *was* suspicious. Richardson shook hands with the room's three other occupants: Harmelin, associate Rubin Weiner, and historic-documents dealer Seth Kaller, who was there to authenticate the parchment.

Do you have the document? Harmelin asked.

Richardson said he would bring it up once he reviewed the paperwork and the check. Harmelin tried not to be distracted by this twist, even though he didn't have Wittman in the room for guidance. The plan called for Wittman, playing the role of Bob Clay, the museum's benefactor, to enter after everyone was settled. Harmelin had told Richardson he was bringing Clay to the closing, but Wittman didn't want anyone unfamiliar in the room at first. He wanted Richardson to get acclimated and comfortable and see that everything was in order.

There was the obligatory small talk—yes, the weather was spectacular for March, and Amtrak's service had been predictably unpredictable—as Richardson thumbed through the closing documents. Richardson asked to inspect the certified check. Harmelin held the $4 million close enough for him to read. "As soon as the document's here and we verify that it's real, you'll get this," Harmelin said.

Richardson nodded. He walked over to a corner, pulled out a cell phone, and called Joe Constantino, who was sitting in a nearby coffee shop, with orders to bring up the parchment.

Shortly thereafter Bob Wittman strolled in. "Bob Clay," he said to Richardson, and stuck his hand out. The two men began chatting.

Constantino appeared inside of ten minutes, but to Harmelin the wait was excruciating—like watching a film in ultra-slow motion, frame by frame. Wittman, though, felt confident. He'd spent many hours in the company of people selling stolen or smuggled property and had developed a finely tuned radar for anxiety and suspicion. Richardson appeared relieved to find everything in place—most notably the check. Wittman detected no edginess; Richardson chatted and laughed easily. He was buying into it.

As the FBI agent subtly steered the conversation toward the document and its history, Constantino walked in, carrying a cardboard art box wrapped in twine. Working carefully, he opened the box and placed a green, acid-free sleeve on a corner of the conference room table. Constantino zipped open the protective cover and slid the Bill of Rights out onto the table.

Most of the room's occupants remember this moment clearly, the prickly circumstances notwithstanding. Weiner had never seen an original Bill of Rights. Seth Kaller, the documents dealer, had viewed the parchment twice before, in meetings with Richard Gilder and Lewis Lehrman and at the Constitution Center offices. But Kaller never wearied of such treasures and leaned in to again take in the parchment's ambrosial presence. Even Wittman, the veteran of so many operations involving so many prized antiquities, felt a tang of exhilaration. "It was an amazing moment," as he later put it.

Harmelin asked Kaller to inspect the Bill of Rights. Kaller immediately recognized the broadsheet as the one he'd seen twice before. After examining the parchment and signatures again and scrutinizing the back for the first time, Kaller pronounced the manuscript authentic.

With these preliminaries complete, Wittman gave a brief speech. This was a wonderful day, he said, because this Bill of Rights was destined to be a crowning centerpiece for the new museum for now and for generations to come. Wittman thanked Richardson for the chance to be part of such a remarkable opportunity.

When Wittman was finished, Harmelin turned to Rubin Weiner. Since everything was in order, the time had come to bring in Joe Torsella to sign the closing documents, Harmelin said.

This was a cue for both men to leave. Wittman wanted them out of the conference room on the outside chance there was a struggle. Since there was no obvious excuse for Seth Kaller to slip out, the broker would simply have to stay out of the way as best he could.

Wittman, wearing a hidden recording device, wanted about ten more minutes to try to elicit incriminating comments from Richardson while Harmelin ostensibly fetched Joe Torsella. Wittman still believed that he could construct a criminal case. He was fairly certain Pratt's courier had moved the document across state lines within the last twenty-four hours. But Wittman would have to prove that Pratt and Richardson knew it was stolen. The trick was to get Richardson to say as much.

"The idea was to get evidence," Wittman said. "And when a guy's looking at a $4 million check, he's not thinking about what he's saying. That's when you get the best admissions. That's when they tell you everything, because they're happy."

Wittman would have asked Richardson, for example, whether he knew the experts at the First Federal Congress Project. Wittman knew that Charlene Bickford would have told him that no private party could own a Bill of Rights because the originals are all public property. Maybe Wittman could get Richardson to acknowledge having such a conversation.

As he talked, Wittman drifted gradually toward the Bill of Rights. He wanted to position himself between Richardson and the manuscript when the other agents came through the door.

Once he got what he was looking for out of Richardson, Wittman planned to signal his colleagues on his cell phone.

Harmelin, however, mistakenly thought it was his job to call in the troops. After exiting the Kalish Conference Room, he veered left, toward the Paxson Conference Room, the one he'd reserved for the business lunch. The distance between the two doorways was only about six feet. As he walked past, he thumped his elbow against the door. Just a single whack, and then he kept walking, hurrying a bit to make his way clear.

Within seconds, five FBI agents poured out, headed toward the conference room Harmelin had just left.

The journalist Mark Bowden once wrote, "Any nation is, at heart, an idea."

The Bill of Rights takes the idea on which this country is built—liberty for all—and inventories that concept. It is freedom's laundry list. The document has served the country remarkably. When our flaws became exposed—during the fight for women's suffrage and the Red scare and the civil rights movement—the Bill of Rights was always there to remind everyone what the United States is about.

North Carolina's copy had an amazing history of its own. In 1789 the manuscript crossed a countryside that had struggled first for independence and then for unity. The parchment vanished in 1865 at the close of an epic war, hours before a great president was assassinated. It zigzagged around the United States, adorning the walls of modest midwestern homes and office buildings before vanishing into the dark recesses of a bank vault. The parchment materialized again, passing through the hands of celebrated dealers of old things. And then, with the first bombs in Baghdad opening another divisive era in American history, the Bill of Rights was about to reemerge in dramatic fashion back into the public eye.

One hundred and thirty-eight years on the move. No wonder the Shotwells and North Carolina officials had fretted over the ink lifting off and peeling away.

Still, the document is merely a vessel. The ideas expressed by the fragile artifact are indestructible. The genius is in the words, not the medium.

But as time passed, the parchment became more valuable to some people than the ideas it contained. It was, in a sense, very much like a treasure map. For the people who held it in their hands when it was created, the value was not in the map itself, but in the treasure it led to.

Now? The map is its own treasure. And we know from repeated experiences over the millennia what happens to some people around great treasures. The spirit grows weak. An unimaginably valuable object thrown up for grabs begets all manner of base human behavior, starting with greed and deceit and betrayal, and continuing on down the line.

Beyond some faded ink and the harm from being glued to a board, the parchment didn't physically change much. But it had been transformed. It had become a commodity. And at that point the world-changing ideas spelled out in the calligraphic flourishes of the late eighteenth century were incidental. The writing could have been in hieroglyphics. The parchment became indistinguishable from any other rare object that commands a seven-figure price: a rare, historic highboy, or a folk art painting, or a historic building.

Some hoped it would bring a windfall. Others saw it as a stepping-stone, a boon to their careers—a chance to bask in its reflected glow.

A few people stood apart, detached from any self-interest. They looked at the Bill of Rights and saw something fiercely important. They wanted the document to survive so that others could read those words as originally set down and find inspiration in the fading ink, maybe find some motivation to do some good in the world. Wasn't that the ultimate value of such a historical relic? To remind us of something important about humanity? About ourselves?

There was another tiny glitch in the sting. Steve Harmelin had forgotten to tell Rubin Weiner that he wasn't really supposed to go get Joe Torsella. Not knowing that this was part of the ruse, Weiner walked down the hall to Harmelin's office and poked his head in. "They need you," he told Torsella.

Torsella's eyes widened. "Shit! Are you sure?"

Weiner said yes.

Torsella's mind churned. Something had gone wrong. He wasn't supposed to be involved. Maybe they needed him to fake some part of the transaction, or maybe Richardson had sniffed the whole thing out and was already gone, Bill of Rights under his arm, all this planning for naught.

Torsella slipped down the hall, his heart thrumming.

When the five FBI agents burst into the room, Wittman draped his body protectively over the Bill of Rights.

One agent announced "FBI" and showed a badge. Two of them grabbed Constantino and backed him against a wall, and the others surrounded Richardson. The idea was to separate everyone from the parchment. The agents feared above all else that somehow the document would be damaged. Michael Thompson, the group's supervisor, had told Harmelin that he'd recently had a nightmare in which three agents were holding one side of the document, and Richardson the other, and the ancient relic slowly began to tear. As a supervisor, Thompson normally wouldn't storm the room with the others. But he was a North Carolina native, and this was the Bill of Rights, and he was about four months from retirement.

Richardson reflexively stepped back. He was too stunned to make any kind of move, even if he'd been so inclined. The FBI agents, per typical protocol, avoided handling the important piece of evidence, so for a time the broadsheet simply remained on the tabletop, untouched, while the room churned around it.

Agent Thompson held the seizure warrant in front of Richardson's face, and Wittman announced he was conducting an investigation into the interstate transportation of stolen property.

When Joe Torsella appeared in the doorway moments later, he found FBI agents in control of the room; clearly, the seizure had happened after all. He glanced around, looking for Richardson. Torsella had been unable to square the lawyer's impressive resumé with what he considered a shabby effort to sell a national treasure. Torsella spotted the person he assumed was Richardson sitting in a corner, looking stricken, his face crimson.

Bob Wittman told Torsella that everything was fine, he wasn't needed. The museum chief stole a final glance at Richardson, then turned and found a relieved Steve Harmelin waiting down the hall.

Wittman and Heine signed a form that made official the agency's possession of the relic. One of them wrote, "North Carolina copy of the United States Bill of Rights"—a fact that was still in dispute. Someone noticed the supposition and crossed out the state name.

Richardson made no effort to talk the FBI agents into letting him keep the document. Nor did he have anything useful to contribute at this point to Wittman's investigation: Obviously, he wasn't about to say anything much at all. Later, when Wittman played back the sting in his mind, he was annoyed that Harmelin had summoned the agents prematurely. Wittman thought Harmelin might have panicked. "We missed the chance to get good evidence," the FBI agent said. "I was kind of pissed about that."

Wittman handed Richardson a copy of the seizure form and had a couple of agents escort him out. And so instead of a check with six zeros beneath the First Union logo, Richardson headed down from the thirty-second floor with a far less valuable piece of paper bearing the United States Department of Justice letterhead.

Meanwhile, Joe Constantino explained to two other agents that he worked for Wayne Pratt and had driven down from Connecticut with the Bill of Rights the day before. Then he, too, was set loose.

Eventually, the FBI let Harmelin back into the conference room. He'd assumed the agents would whisk the parchment away. But he hoped for one last peek at the object of everyone's obsession those past few days and months without John Richardson standing next to him.

But first, there was a celebration. Harmelin detected some relief in the high-fives and backslaps—this was a Bill of Rights worth millions, after all—but also a measure of exhilaration. All that planning and tension, the adrenaline, the high stakes—it all bubbled up and out. As Harmelin put it: "We were like a high school basketball team that just won the state championship."

• • •

A little after noon, Colorado time, Wayne Pratt's phone rang. Sarah was out skiing. The timing was right. This should be the call he was waiting for: John Richardson, announcing he was standing in downtown Philly with a check for $4 million.

It's funny how big things start small: an offhand conversation with Leslie Hindman almost a decade earlier, an inquisitive call to Indiana, and the next thing you know you're enmeshed with a revered, iconic relic.

And so it was that morning, too. The ringing phone. An unremarkable event, yet the arc of his life would change significantly afterward.

Pratt answered, but it was not the voice he'd expected.

Joe Constantino's voice was shaky, and he was talking in a blur. "Jesus," he was saying. "I don't know what just happened."

21

Blow-back

WHEN THE STING OPERATION was finished, the Bill of Rights lingered for a while. The FBI agents allowed Steve Harmelin to send an e-mail to the rest of the law firm, inviting everyone into the Kalish Conference Room. No one showed up at first, thinking it was a joke. Then word seeped out about what had just happened.

Torsella and Harmelin had envisioned the Bill of Rights as a centerpiece in the National Constitution Center. Hundreds of thousands of people would walk by it every year, run their eyes over the smooth curves of its letters, absorb its lofty, world-changing ideas.

For now, they would have to settle for the two hundred or so employees at Dilworth Paxson. The showing lasted almost an hour. The gravitas partner explained what they'd just done, and Torsella told the assemblage about Harmelin's leading role. There was applause and excited murmurs. And then the FBI packed up the document and headed out.

Sarah Pratt skied all morning before heading back to the condo for lunch at around 12:30. She wanted to check on Wayne, too, since by now he'd likely gotten his call. "Hey," she called as she walked into the condo.

She instantly knew something was wrong.

"Can I have a word with you in the bedroom?" her husband said.

Sarah told the guide to have a seat and a drink. Wayne closed the door and told her what Constantino had just reported. "You're kidding, right?" she said. Knowing that he wasn't.

Wayne had had the same reaction when Constantino called. "Joe," Pratt had said. "This is not the time for a joke." But even as he said it, he knew better. *Holy shit,* Pratt had thought. *What did I do? What the hell happened down there?*

He'd told Constantino not to worry, he would figure out what to do next. Pratt had immediately dialed John Richardson. Not thinking clearly, he called Richardson's home, where Peg Richardson answered. She hadn't talked to her husband yet and sounded shocked.

Then Pratt had dialed Richardson's cell phone, had caught him at the train station. Richardson sounded angry and flummoxed. "We're going to have to get an attorney," he'd said.

In Beaver Creek, Sarah Pratt tried to soothe her husband. "OK, let's think about this," she said. She pointed out that he wasn't going to make *that* much money anyway—Richardson would have been the big winner. Wayne would just have to wash his hands of it.

But she wondered: "Are people going to be coming here?"

Wayne didn't think it was that type of situation; they hadn't tried to arrest Richardson, and Pratt couldn't imagine they would be in that kind of trouble. Constantino called back, still talking too fast, bubbling over with anxiety. Pratt told him to go home, they would figure everything out later. When he hung up, he encouraged Sarah to go skiing. "There's nothing you can do," he said. "Just go back out."

Her afternoon session, though, had none of the exuberance of the morning. Sarah did a few halfhearted runs and told the guide she'd had enough.

Pratt, pacing around the condo, called Bob Matthews's New Haven offices. He asked Matthews's secretary to interrupt him in a meeting—the call was urgent.

"What do you want to do?" Matthews said after he'd heard the story.

"John Richardson said I should get an attorney."

"Don't do anything," Matthews said. "I'll check into it."

Before they signed off, Matthews lamented the possibility of losing $5 million. "No, *we* were not getting $5 million," Pratt said, reminding him of their lawyer's and brokers' fees.

That night the Pratts obsessively flipped between the news channels. There was no word of the seizure, and grasping for positives, Wayne began to think that nothing would be said of the FBI operation, that at least he could deal with the matter privately. But then he saw it the next morning on CNN, scrolling across the bottom of the screen: *FBI sting nets an original Bill of Rights.* A little later there was footage of agents displaying the document. Pratt looked at his wife. "Oh, shit," he said. "They're gonna make a big deal out of this." The sting was the only story that had managed to penetrate the war coverage.

Sitting there, Sarah remembered Wayne bragging to her father in St. Croix about selling the Bill of Rights. She picked up the phone to call and tell him, "In case you see this on the news, here's what just happened."

Phones jangled across Pennsylvania and North Carolina on Tuesday afternoon, March 18. The FBI called Bobby Higdon, the criminal chief in the U.S. attorney's office in Raleigh, who called Reuben Young in Governor Mike Easley's office. Though he later claimed to have masterminded the sting, Easley was confused; according to his own account, he thought this was only an initial meeting with the sellers. "Governor, we got it," Young said.

"What, got what?" Easley asked.

"The document, they brought the document and the FBI seized it right on the spot."

"Naw," Easley replied. "You know they weren't crazy enough to bring it to the first meeting."

Young also phoned John Estey in Governor Ed Rendell's office in Harrisburg, Pennsylvania, and then his wife, Pam, who worked in North Carolina's Department of Cultural Resources. He told her to not speak of it until the news became official.

Frank Whitney, the U.S. attorney, had taken his family to Sunset Beach, a barrier island off North Carolina's coast, for his daughter's school vacation. He was anticipating the phone call and was driving into the parking lot of a Food Lion grocery store when his cell phone rang—FBI agents in Raleigh calling with the news. He was so excited he wanted to shout out the window. He later compared the sensation to the scene in the movie *National Treasure* when Nicolas Cage realizes he's holding the actual Declaration of Independence—a case of art unwittingly imitating life. But the operation was still a secret, so Whitney didn't even tell his family what had just happened as he parked the car; he related only that an FBI undercover operation had been a success.

Around 3:30 in Raleigh, Bobby Higdon called Joe Torsella to say he planned to convene a grand jury and launch a criminal investigation. Higdon asked Torsella to avoid speaking to the media.

Torsella, in turn, e-mailed John Estey in Governor Rendell's office, apprising him of the news. Estey replied just before 5:00, saying Rendell would "keep quiet."

Estey also mentioned something that excited Torsella: North Carolina Governor Easley had called Governor Rendell to thank him for his help. Estey had heard only one side of the conversation, but he thought Easley had offered to loan the Bill of Rights to the Constitution Center.

Around that same time Bobby Higdon called Reuben Young in the governor's office and told him the document appeared to be North Carolina's copy and was "in good shape given what it's been through"—and the FBI was planning a news conference for the following day.

Once she received the go-ahead at 6:30 that evening, Pam Young called her associates—Libba Evans, North Carolina's secretary of cultural resources, and Jeff Crow, head of the archives—with the big news. Crow was shocked. Young said they would hear the details at a meeting at 10:30 the following morning.

After the flurry of communications died down, Torsella and Harmelin went to the Four Seasons Hotel, just the two of them, to have a drink. Sitting in the bar, they shook their heads and grinned and said, Damn, wasn't that quite a thing.

• • •

Bob Wittman and his team moved the Bill of Rights to the FBI's Philadelphia headquarters and locked it in the office of Jeffrey Lampinski, the city's top-ranking agent. They unveiled the parchment at a news conference the following afternoon. Governor Ed Rendell was there, and Joe Torsella, and Steve Harmelin, and documents dealer Seth Kaller. The FBI gave the National Constitution Center officials hats and T-shirts emblazoned with the agency logo. Bob Wittman, who was working two other undercover cases at the time, stood in the back of the room to avoid being photographed.

Attendees strained for superlatives. Many experts pegged the parchment's value at $30 million; a few went as high as $40 million. "The reality is that this is priceless, absolutely priceless," Lampinski said. "It's in the category of the Constitution, the category of the Magna Carta."

"This is an historic moment," Rendell gushed.

"This document is clearly one of the most important documents in history," Kaller said.

Another special agent, Joseph Majarowitz, later described the sting as "one of the greatest recoveries of historic information and intellectual property the FBI has ever made."

Torsella's picture appeared in newspapers all over the country, and all week he heard from classmates he hadn't talked to in more than a decade. But Torsella was mostly pleased that the Bill of Rights was getting attention. For a few days Americans had reason to think about the document and its contents. "That, in the end, is what we're all about," Torsella said.

In Raleigh, political leaders immediately weighed in. "This is so much more than a collector's item," Attorney General Roy Cooper said. "It represents freedom."

"North Carolina's stolen 'Bill of Rights' has been out-of-state for nearly 140 years but never out-of-mind," Governor Mike Easley said in a press release. "It is a historic document and its return is a historic occasion . . . I am confident that, very soon, schoolchildren and citizens across our state will soon be seeing their 'Bill of Rights' on display . . ."

Wayne Pratt, reading and watching, smoldered. He believed he had purchased the document legitimately. Reading Easley's comments, he thought, *Fuck you; the children of North Carolina should thank me for finding it.*

He was also anxious about the ramifications of the sting. But mostly he was in disbelief. "If the FBI wanted it," he said later, "all they had to do was call me. I'd have given it to them. I didn't have it hidden anywhere."

Pratt hired Hugh Stevens, a lawyer based in Raleigh, on Richardson's recommendation. Pratt's plan was simple: He would have Stevens turn over everything he had about the Bill of Rights to the federal government, including Richardson's thousand-page research dossier, and tell them, "If you can prove it's yours, you can have it, and I'll take a tax write-off. If not, give it back so we can sell it."

As bad as things initially looked, the situation was eminently manageable. Pratt could operate completely below the radar. The seizure warrant was sealed in a Raleigh court, so no one outside his small circle of family and employees knew he was the seller. And he wasn't worried about criminal charges.

In the week that followed the sting, FBI agents did some basic caretaking on the Bill of Rights. Wittman ordered a conservation report and a protective case for the manuscript. Near the end of March, Bob Wittman and fellow agents Michael Thompson and Jay Heine flew the document down to Carolina. In a show of the esteem in which the agency held the parchment, the FBI director lent his plane for the special delivery.

The event was so freighted with reverence, Wittman decided to have a little fun. Humor was part of his way of dealing with stress. Herb Lottier, director of protection services at the Philadelphia Museum of Art, once described Wittman as "an entertainer as well as an investigator." Once, as the guest on *USA Today*'s interactive chat feature, he closed by advising readers to "take some time to visit a museum—but don't take anything."

Before leaving, Wittman bought a small Bill of Rights reproduction at Independence Mall and put it on top of the protective sleeve containing the real parchment. When they landed in Raleigh, Wittman and Heine launched their prank: They opened the box to great fanfare, and then pretended to fumble the Bill of Rights onto the floor. The U.S. marshals looked aghast—"They about crapped their pants," Wittman said—until the FBI agents roared with laughter.

Once the joke died down, though, the earnestness returned. U.S. attorney Frank Whitney keenly awaited the document's arrival in Raleigh. He said that when he finally touched a corner of the parchment, he shivered.

Bob Matthews had long thought of the Bill of Rights as a sort of roadhouse gamble. He wasn't convinced the document was real and had never even met a member of the Shotwell family; attorney Charlie Reeder didn't want the sisters interacting directly with Matthews or Wayne Pratt. Matthews referred to them as "those mythical sisters." With the document, he figured, maybe you lose $100,000, maybe you make a couple million.

"I made an investment," he later recounted. "I thought it was a neat opportunity. I wasn't 100 percent sure it was real, but if it was, I really wanted to be a part of it. It's the kind of thing you tell your kids about."

The document's long, anonymous history in the Shotwell house "makes it sort of sexy," Matthews said. "I love the thrill of finding the deal."

When Wayne Pratt called after the sting, Matthews said, that was "the first time that I really knew in my heart that that was an original Bill of Rights."

Pratt invited Matthews to his house in Woodbury after returning from Colorado, hoping to mount some kind of joint legal challenge to the FBI seizure. They were partners in the deal, after all.

But Matthews behaved strangely. He resisted Pratt's attempts to coordinate a strategy and seemed to be backpedaling in terms of his involvement with the parchment. "I'm just an investor," Matthews said. "I wasn't a partner in this."

Matthews later recalled driving to Pratt's shop, livid, after getting word of the sting. Pratt was still in Colorado, so Matthews tracked down Marybeth Keene, who claimed he started bellowing: "What did you get me into? I get half a document, [and] you didn't check it out?

"I didn't do anything wrong," Matthews complained to her. "I'm a passive investor. You guys hired the lawyer. You hired the experts. I've depended on you for your expert opinion on what it is."

Matthews brought up the thousand-page research dossier that John Richardson had supposedly compiled: "I thought you hired this guy, John Richardson, to make sure everything was done right."

Keene handed him documents related to the sale, including Richardson's bill. Matthews told her it was ridiculous that the lawyer was going to make so much money and argued that the attorney's 30 percent cut should have come from Pratt's half of the profits. He complained that Tillou and Reese were signed up for $1 million. Nothing Pratt had done seemed right anymore.

"Wayne, you did this deal," Matthews said he told Pratt. "You bought it. I gave you half the money. You were running with the deal. And what did you drag me into with this whole mess?"

Neither man could have guessed exactly how much of a mess the parchment purchase was about to become. On March 25, a week after the sting, the U.S. attorney's office notified attorney Hugh Stevens that Pratt was the target of a criminal grand jury investigation; he faced up to ten years in prison if indicted and convicted.

Stevens, meanwhile, filed a request for the court to unseal the seizure warrant. The news media were waiting when the judge approved the request, and Wayne Pratt was publicly unmasked as the man selling the Bill of Rights. Stevens quickly issued a statement saying that he'd advised his client to avoid answering journalists' questions.

Even before Pratt's name became public, the FBI and others had begun seeding outrage over the attempted sale of a national icon. "A courier appeared with this document in a cardboard box, if you can believe that," Lampinski said in one instance. (According to Pratt, such cartons were commonly used in his business for transporting fine art.)

News reports conjectured that the owner had threatened to destroy the document during negotiations with North Carolina—not sell it overseas, as John Richardson had actually done. No one bothered to point out that David Olson, the North Carolina archivist, thought this to be a mere bluff.

The release of Pratt's name only plumped up the point sizes on the boldface headlines. His prominent standing in the antiques world—a *Roadshow* appraiser, no less—and the possibility of criminal charges made for titillating news. The *New York Times* reported that Pratt and Matthews had tried to sell the document "at a carpetbagger profit." The *Christian Science Monitor* noted, "The controversy probes . . . whether Pratt broke the law when he tried to sell the original American edicts." The time between the theft and the attempted sale became conflated in the stunted rubric of newspaper headlines. A *Cape Cod Times* headline read, "Nantucket Dealer Tied to Stolen Document."

Down in federal court in North Carolina, Hugh Stevens, a highly regarded Raleigh attorney, gamely tried to make Pratt's case. Stevens contended that he'd seen no proof that the document was North Carolina's and argued that Pratt had bought the document legitimately.

But by that time the water was rising too fast for any lawyer to hold back. With criminal charges pending, Pratt's bank called in his loans, giving him thirty days to pay them off. Pratt managed to head off that near catastrophe but still had to endure an audit. The bank required him to hire a forensic accountant to establish that the business was on solid footing.

Scores of random e-mailers hammered him for dealing stolen goods and demanded he give up his claim to ownership and return the Bill of Rights to North Carolina. *Antiques Roadshow*, meanwhile, announced it was dropping Pratt from its lineup of appraisers for summer 2003—an ironic twist, given that Pratt's *Roadshow* appearances contributed to making the story so sexy.

The antiques community trembled with schadenfreude. "Wayne is a polarizing figure," said David Schorsch, Pratt's friend and fellow dealer. "There are people who love Wayne and people who hate Wayne. There were a lot of people in this business who were going,

'Ha ha ha'"—Schorsch rubbed his hands together in mock glee—"'look what happened to Wayne!'"

Pratt's stature, and legally mandated silence, rendered him unable to publicly fight back. The U.S. attorney's office would be in no hurry to decide on criminal charges; merely dangling the possibility was a powerful cudgel.

This was a popular tactic. In 2001 FBI agent Bob Wittman had cooperated with Brazilian authorities and threatened an art dealer there with criminal charges in the United States to pry loose three Norman Rockwell paintings that had been swiped from a gallery outside Minneapolis in 1978. The dealer, who had been quietly offering them for sale in the United States, surrendered the paintings willingly in exchange for dropped charges. The bigger the businessman's reputation, the greater the leverage.

"All of a sudden," Pratt said, "we went from being on top of the world to shoveling shit. We were going to go out of business. We were putting all of our money into this, so we couldn't buy anything, and nobody would deal with you because they were afraid of you. We had all of our money going to attorneys, and they're telling me not to say anything, and people are asking, 'What's going on? Did you steal it?'

"The only thing that kept us in business was we're good at what we do, and we have good customers. The majority of my customers knew about the Bill of Rights."

Barely hanging on, Pratt staggered into the summer of 2003. He began drinking heavily in his darkened living room. "You could cut it with a knife, the doom and gloom," Sarah Pratt said.

For Sarah, the implosion of the Bill of Rights deal inflicted far more collateral damage than she'd imagined possible. The parchment had been in Wayne's life longer than Sarah had, but she'd never fully grasped its story. She knew little of the historic-documents world.

At the time the Pratts were investing many of their resources in a dream house in Woodbury and had two young boys on their hands. Even before the recent debacle, Wayne wasn't much help around the house; Sarah had to hassle him just to take the garbage out. And his travels in pursuit of antiques often took him away from home, to the degree that he sometimes missed the boys' birthdays.

As Wayne slumped in his chair, Sarah confronted him. "Get a grip," she said. "If you're going to do that, do it in the bedroom, not in front of the children." But she refused to let him succumb to his ennui, eventually ordering him to stop drinking. With her encouragement, Wayne fired Hugh Stevens, who perhaps underestimated the impact of making his client's name known to the public. (Pratt called him "the biggest jerk in America.") In his place Pratt hired Thomas Dwyer, head of the prominent law firm Dwyer & Collora in Boston. Dwyer charged more than $1,000 an hour. But he was a Boston guy like Pratt, down to the missing consonants, and he offered a 20 percent discount.

Pratt's dyslexia kept him from grasping all the nuances of the legal briefs and updates. Sarah got into the habit of talking to Dwyer and his associates every Friday "to find out what was really going on."

Because she had her own business, PBS allowed her to continue making appearances on *Antiques Roadshow*. "I felt like somebody in the family has to do it," she said, "just to keep the flame burning."

She had been adamant from the start about not working at Wayne Pratt Antiques. When Sarah was at Sotheby's, a husband-wife team unsuccessfully ran a department, and she wanted to avoid the "petty politics" that came with that. But she also didn't like the looseness of her husband's enterprise. "I don't like your working style," she told him.

Bob Matthews, meanwhile, was conspicuously quiet—even unreachable. Pratt called several times over the first couple of weeks after the debacle in Philadelphia, hoping to coordinate on their legal strategy. He also missed his friend's camaraderie. But Matthews wouldn't return his calls.

A mile or so north on Route 6, fellow Woodbury dealer Wayne Mattox was finding that people were confusing him with Wayne Pratt. This was not unprecedented. Mattox had noticed that when Pratt joined *Antiques Roadshow,* first-time visitors sometimes asked whether he was the guy on TV. Likewise, when Mattox started writing his online column, people occasionally told Pratt that they enjoyed his writing.

The mix-up had been amusing—and often beneficial for Mattox, who had a lesser profile. Now it was a problem. Visitors seemed less friendly. "A lot of people," Mattox said, "started treating me differently."

"Pratt was getting destroyed," Mattox recalled. "Before all the facts were in, I heard lots of people attacking him about it. Everybody was talking about him dealing stolen goods. That was a phrase I heard a lot in town—so many times that I tended to take the other side."

Mattox knew nothing more than what he'd read in the papers, but he was aware that southerners had sold off many treasures in the Civil War's aftermath. Maybe that's what happened with the Bill of Rights, Mattox said. Who knew whether it was really stolen? he told people. "Antiques dealers tend to be hard on each other," he said. "When there's blood in the water, the fish tend to swim differently."

But when Mattox heard the full story, of Peter Tillou and Pratt's apocryphal tale of the hardware store in upstate New York, he sounded chagrined. Both he and his parents had worked with Tillou, and Mattox thought highly of him. "If Pratt made that mistake, that's a big mistake. It's one that, in hindsight, I'm sure he'll wish he didn't make."

For at least part of the time that Bob Matthews didn't return Pratt's phone calls, he had a good reason: He was out of town. Within a couple of weeks of the sting, Matthews traveled to Raleigh, North Carolina, where his lawyers had set up an appointment with the U.S. attorney's office. While Pratt hid in a foxhole, Matthews approached the enemy with a white flag. Matthews wanted to lay out the story of the Indianapolis family that had owned the Bill of Rights and his involvement with its purchase. Matthews wanted to fully cooperate and explain whatever they wanted to know.

His unexpected appearance caught everyone off balance. Matthews hadn't cropped up in the criminal investigation, and Bobby Higdon, the office's criminal chief, hadn't even heard of him.

But once Matthews started talking, Higdon quickly grasped what was happening: Matthews wanted to circumvent trouble. He explained that he'd put some money in the document but was merely a passive investor—not an active seller. Matthews explained how Wayne Pratt had pulled the trigger on both the Indiana deal and the Constitution Center transaction—the one that ended in the FBI sting. Matthews hadn't even been aware that the second one was going down and had been shocked—*shocked*—to hear what happened. By the way, Matthews said, he respected that Higdon and his associates were federal employees: Matthews had actually been tight with President Clinton, had visited the Oval Office and Lincoln Bedroom, and he knew a number of senators as well.

Higdon could have guessed what was coming next: Matthews hoped for favorable treatment in return for his cooperation. He was an entrepreneur—he was in construction and software in addition to his core business as a real estate developer—so he had interests to protect. "He's a wheeler-dealer," Higdon recalled, "and he was going to make sure that when the wheel turned, he was on the right side of it."

Not long after meeting with Higdon, Matthews finally called Wayne Pratt back and told him he would stop by. He sat down in Wayne's house and explained what he'd just done. "I got a get-out-of-jail-free card," he said.

Matthews had a point: They had bought something together at Pratt's behest, and Matthews hadn't had any role in trying to resell it. The next thing he knew, the FBI was displaying the thing on CNN. Who wanted any part of something like that?

Still, Pratt—not thinking too objectively at that point—was stunned. "What are you doing? We were working on this together."

"You'll be all right," Matthews said. "I told them all about you, and they're gonna love you. I didn't hurt you."

Pratt doubted that. He had criminal charges looming. All he

could think was, *Holy shit—ten years in jail for this? And then you come tell me you've got a get-out-of-jail-free card?*

In Pratt's fragile state of mind, Matthews's act of betrayal was unforgivable. Pratt was an old-school guy. He was loyal. He kept the same clients for years, in some cases decades. He and Marybeth Keene had worked together for a quarter-century.

"I always thought Bob's done well enough, so if I was really in trouble at some point, he'd help me," Pratt said. "Then when I really needed him it was, 'Fuck you.' But I didn't know that until then."

Peter Tillou was among the witnesses before a federal grand jury convened in Raleigh in summer 2003 to consider criminal charges in the case of North Carolina's Bill of Rights. U.S. attorney Frank Whitney's office assured him he wasn't the target, but Tillou paid a lawyer $8,000 to come along anyway. Auctioneer Leslie Hindman flew down from Chicago to testify. She spent more than $10,000 on an attorney.

Tillou blamed Pratt for the expense and stress. "He was such a rat," Tillou said. "Bill [Reese] is the one who was the big loser financially because he put so much into the research. We were so misled. We thought this could have been an unknown copy."

Reese, who wasn't called to testify, found the whole thing painful to watch from afar. "I think Peter really trusted Pratt," he said, "and obviously it became graphically clear that that was a bad idea. He was furious with Pratt."

Reese had been in Mexico when Seth Kaller called with the news of the FBI sting. The tall, lanky Americana expert with the booming voice couldn't believe the situation had come to that; an FBI sting sounded ridiculously excessive. Later, though, when he saw John Richardson's letters to North Carolina officials in 1995 and '96— the ones with the ominous language—he understood why it happened. "To me, that was remarkably sleazy stuff," Reese said. "Once I knew about that post facto, it didn't surprise me what North Carolina did."

• • •

As time passed, Bob Matthews began to feel differently about his involvement with the Bill of Rights. In the weeks after the FBI sting, he claimed to be nothing more than an outside investor. He was like someone who puts cash into a money market account and lets a fund manager handle the investing. Wayne Pratt and the state of North Carolina were the only two parties that initially claimed in court to own the parchment. But in late spring 2003 Matthews's lawyers showed up in Raleigh to enter his claim as well.

Why the change of heart? It's possible that Matthews felt differently about his involvement with the document once he learned he faced minimal exposure to criminal charges. But his deposition a few months later suggested an even more compelling reason. He had noticed in newspaper accounts that experts pegged the parchment's value at $30 million, sometimes even $40 million.

This got Bob's attention. He'd spent $100,000 and had stood to make $500,000 to $1 million on that investment. A nice deal, but nothing like his George Street building, which he'd bought for a half-million dollars and sold for $27.5 million.

Forty million dollars? *That* would be his greatest flip ever. Matthews just had to figure out how to engineer it. His buddy Wayne Pratt didn't appear to be an obstacle. Pratt's struggles continued through the spring, and by the time the long, heavy days of summer arrived he wasn't sure how much longer he could fight on. His bills ran into six figures, and his lawyers promised a long, pitched battle. The Pratts were simultaneously building their home in Woodbury. "I kept thinking, I don't know whether we're ever going to be able to live in it," Sarah Pratt said.

Every major court development sparked a fresh news cycle about the stolen parchment. Driving her kids to school, Sarah Pratt groped for the radio dial when NPR aired updates.

That summer, as Pratt's legal bills approached $700,000, Matthews called Wayne. Their friendship had been frayed since Matthews's Raleigh visit, when he'd scored his get-out-of-jail-free card. Their usual summer party scene in Nantucket had fizzled as Pratt wallowed in his troubles. But this time Matthews said he felt badly that Wayne was having such a hard time and wanted to help his old buddy out: He wanted to make Wayne a deal. Bob wanted to fix all of his problems by buying out Pratt's share of the Bill of Rights.

It was a relatively simple deal: Matthews would reimburse Pratt for his half of the document—the $100,000 he'd paid the Shotwells—plus the $2,500 for the conservation work, plus up to $1.1 million for his legal fees. Matthews would make him whole again.

In return, Matthews would own the entire Bill of Rights—assuming, of course, he could outflank the state of North Carolina in court. From there, his plan was to donate the parchment to a nonprofit institution. Matthews's reasoning: "If we were successful with the civil suit, the document A) could be worth $40 million, or B) we could get an IRS ruling and have a deduction for, I don't know, $5 million to $15 or $20 [million]."

The deal was contingent on Pratt being cleared of all charges. If the U.S. government indicted him for transporting stolen property across state lines, the deal was dead.

Pratt said he'd have to discuss the proposition with his lawyers. When he got on the phone with the attorneys in Boston, they told him that Matthews had presented an intriguing idea. But they told Pratt to hold off, to let the court proceedings play out for at least a few more weeks.

As the legal drama unfurled in the South, the National Constitution Center opened on schedule on Independence Day 2003. Supreme Court Justice Sandra Day O'Connor attended the festivities along with Pennsylvania Senator Arlen Specter, Governor Ed Rendell, Philadelphia Mayor John Street, and others.

But the museum remained oddly susceptible to unforeseen drama. During the opening ceremony at the front entrance, the dignitaries pulled red, white, and blue streamers intended to trigger the drop of a large screen. Instead, a 650-pound piece of wood-and-steel staging toppled onto the guests of honor.

The frame narrowly missed O'Connor but struck Street and Specter and cracked museum CEO Joe Torsella on the head, knocking him to his knees. Steve Harmelin, the museum's general counsel and fellow FBI conspirator, helped Torsella to the hospital that day.

Still, the show went on. Miniature cannons fired streamers over the crowd, fireworks boomed from the building's roof, and four military jets buzzed overhead. Then the museum opened to a crowd of several thousand people.

Investigators later discovered that due to some construction oversight, the bolts intended to attach the massive frame to the stage had never been installed.

22

The Great Divide

BY LATE SUMMER OF 2003, the pieces were in place for a climactic moment in U.S. District Court in Raleigh, North Carolina. As Bob Matthews angled to buy out Wayne Pratt, his attorneys looked to fatally cripple the federal government's case in the seizure of the Bill of Rights.

On August 8 Matthews's legal team moved to get the sting declared illegal. New Haven attorney Michael Stratton zeroed in on a mistake in the seizure warrant. Hurriedly assembled in a single day in March, the warrant had asserted that the Bill of Rights was located in North Carolina—not in Pratt's Connecticut shop, its actual location.

In addition to overcoming this error, the federal government faced the task of proving the property was stolen—a daunting challenge, given the amount of time that had passed since it vanished. Judge Terrence Boyle set a date of September 11 to hear evidence.

On September 4 Bob Matthews returned to North Carolina for a deposition. After swearing to tell the truth, he brought up his near-death experience as a mitigating factor. "[I]t's affected my memory," he said, "so some of the things I'm going to say I'm not really sure [about]."

Then assistant U.S. attorney Paul Newby plunged in. He focused on one line of questioning: How involved was Matthews with the Bill of Rights? Did Matthews have any part at all in the Bill of Rights purchase, or the proposed sale?

NEWBY: With regard to the price of $5 million, did Mr. Pratt
  consult with you or seek your consent to that price?

MATTHEWS: I know he told me he was going to sell it for
  $5 million or $6 million, what do you think about that?
  I said, it sounds good to me . . .

NEWBY: So, if Mr. Pratt had sold it for $4.7 million, would that
  have been within your understanding of the agreement you
  had with Mr. Pratt?

MATTHEWS: I would have trusted Wayne to do the right deal. I
  mean, that's part of the deal.

NEWBY: And he would not have had to consult with you before
  lowering the price?

MATTHEWS: I mean, if it was only $250,000, I think he knows
  me well enough I wouldn't have been arguing for an extra
  $125,000. We're not nickel and dime kind of—

Though Matthews didn't yet grasp what was happening, the federal government had a strategy of its own. Newby was laying the groundwork to dynamite Matthews's claim to the document by proving that he never legally owned it.

The government had a trump card in pursuing this strategy: Wayne Pratt. Having endured the public relations beat-down of recent months, the antiques dealer was ready to capitulate. He yearned to clear his name and move on with life—so much so that he was willing to renounce his claim to the parchment and declare the state of North Carolina the rightful owner. "We didn't see any light at the end of the tunnel," said Marybeth Keene, Pratt's partner.

Believing Matthews had betrayed him, Pratt decided to exact a measure of revenge. He agreed to hand over the entire Bill of Rights—not just his 50 percent. He could do this, his lawyers believed, if the government could prove Matthews lacked what's known as "possessory interest." According to this legal principle, a person does not legally own something unless he or she possesses it and exercises dominion and control over it. Matthews had never once taken possession of the document, and he'd had no control over who examined, handled, or brokered the sale of the Bill of

Rights. He hadn't known that the National Constitution Center was the buyer. He'd even asserted, in the panicky aftermath of the sting, that he was merely a passive investor.

Matthews had unwittingly provided the basis for this strategy when he'd flown to Raleigh just after the FBI seizure in pursuit of his get-out-of-jail-free card.

Under questioning from Newby, Matthews conceded there was no written proof of his partial ownership of the Bill of Rights; there was only the money and the implicit understanding in his partnership with Pratt. "I know that Wayne Pratt, Inc., bought it," he said. "I mean, consciously, I know that. And I'm not an owner in that sense . . . But I always knew from ever that I gave $100,000 and that I had fifty percent of it."

There wasn't a bill of sale because the two men never put anything in writing, Matthews said. "Wayne is a friend of mine," he said. ". . . I trust him, and I can't imagine him not honoring his, you know, his handshake on the deal."

Furthermore, Matthews claimed under oath that Pratt had agreed to his buyout offer: Matthews would pay Pratt's legal bills in exchange for full ownership of the Bill of Rights. Matthews said he had proof: He had recorded their phone call.

Pratt denied accepting the deal, and Matthews never produced a tape. The two men were talking through their attorneys by now, and when Pratt's legal team reported back to Woodbury that Bob had furtively taped a conversation, Wayne was enraged. "When Wayne heard that," Sarah Pratt said, "that was the end—the end of any hope that Bob was acting in any way other than in his own interests. That was a turning point psychologically for Wayne."

A rift between the two old pals had opened. For decades Pratt and Matthews had shared business deals, lobster feasts in Nantucket, yacht races, spontaneous adventures on Matthews's airplane. They had talked through girlfriend problems and business troubles. Bob was the godfather of Pratt's older son.

Now, because of a single document—a twenty-six-and-a-half-by-thirty-one-inch piece of parchment—everything changed. Wayne profanely impugned his friend's motives and actions. Bob secretly recorded their phone calls—or claimed to. Both men sold out the other to government lawyers. The crevasse that tore open was vast, and it would never be bridged. By autumn 2003 Wayne Pratt and Bob Matthews were no longer speaking.

On September 10, 2003, the day before the court was set to hear evidence on the Bill of Rights dispute, Pratt withdrew his claim and conveyed full ownership to the state of North Carolina. He declared that Wayne Pratt, Inc., alone had bought the manuscript from the Shotwells, and that he had exclusive authority to convey interest in the document. He stipulated that the federal government's actions, including the FBI sting, were legal and proper.

As a result, U.S. attorney Frank Whitney moved to dismiss the case. As far as Pratt and the United States government were concerned, the Bill of Rights belonged to North Carolina.

Four weeks later the feds cleared Pratt of any criminal charges. Many media reports linked this development to Pratt's abdication of the Bill of Rights. Whitney insisted there was no such connection: The government simply couldn't prove criminal intent, he said. Ultimately, prosecutors couldn't get around one key fact: Before Pratt bought the Bill of Rights, he had hired attorney John Richardson to look into the legality of the acquisition—and that alone was proof that Pratt hadn't intended to commit a crime.

On September 11, the day after Pratt's stunning hand-over, Bob Matthews and his lawyer, Michael Stratton, scrambled to reconstruct their case. Stratton fired off a series of truculent legal briefs arguing for the document's return. "It is improper," Stratton wrote, "for the government to simply give the spoils of its illegal seizure to the State by stealing it in Philadelphia and bringing it to North Carolina."

Stratton claimed in another volley the following day that the government had also threatened Matthews with a criminal investigation, having ordered him to appear before a grand jury the week prior. "In fact," Stratton wrote, "[assistant U.S. attorney] Paul Newby made an offer that all claims would be dropped if Matthews quitclaimed his 50% share to North Carolina. Not coincidentally, this offer was made just before Matthews [*sic*] grand jury appearance. Matthews refused to be intimidated . . ."

Matthews, ever the salesman, emerged from his legal pillbox long enough to announce he was still willing to strike a deal. Stratton offered two options: The two sides could hold a trial in which a jury determined ownership percentages between Pratt and Matthews. Pratt's share would go to North Carolina; the court would then decide how to partition Matthews's share. Or, the state could purchase his share of the parchment for $1.5 million a year over the next six years, payable annually on December 1. Matthews would find it in his heart to donate the rest.

When those offers went nowhere, Matthews sued everyone involved: the lawyers, the FBI, the court. Two subpoenas went to his erstwhile allies, Wayne Pratt and Marybeth Keene.

Soon after Pratt signed away ownership of the Bill of Rights, Connecticut Governor John Rowland's political career—once, like the *Titanic,* thought to be indestructible—began to run aground. Despite winning a third term, he was coming under increasing scrutiny for accepting favors and gifts from people who stood to benefit from state contracts. Rowland initially lied about the fact that aides and contractors had done free work on his cottage on Bantam Lake. He'd paid several ethics fines for accepting free or discounted vacations, including the stay at Bob Matthews's place in Palm Beach. The U.S. attorney's office began sniffing around. As the holidays approached in Hartford, Rowland seemed perhaps too eager both to give and to receive.

Toward the end of 2003, federal investigators began probing yet another apparent sweetheart deal: Wayne Pratt's 1997 purchase of Rowland's condo in Washington, D.C. In December a *New York Times* reporter showed up in Woodbury to ask Pratt about the transaction. Pratt characterized the deal as "an investment opportunity that was presented to me," and then cut off the interview.

Pratt rushed upstairs to his office to make yet another call to attorney Tom Dwyer. He explained the whole deal: how Matthews had recruited him to be the straw man, and how a couple of years after buying the apartment for $68,500, Pratt had sold it for $37,500. Even though Matthews had covered Pratt's condo costs, Pratt had written off $24,773 in losses on his 1999 income tax return.

The once-untouchable governor was suddenly vulnerable. Pratt was caught in the middle and had fudged his taxes to boot.

Journalists began circling Bob Matthews as well. In an article in the *Hartford Courant* on January 6, 2004, Matthews denied any involvement in the condo deal. "Wayne's looking for a place to buy," he said. "He's thinking of moving to D.C. John's got a place in D.C.; he's thinking of selling that. I don't know if he called up John; I have no clue."

Pratt, of course, knew better. And Dwyer encouraged him to cooperate with authorities; they had Pratt on the bogus tax write-off. Pratt figured he'd better beat Matthews to the punch: "If a guy's gonna sell me out on the Bill of Rights," he said, "he's gonna sell me out on this, too. When he gets in trouble, he'll rat out anybody—or he'll find somebody to rat out."

One development surprised Pratt: As the media floodlights homed in on Rowland and his dealings, Matthews seemed flat-footed, blinking in the glare. It was as if the wand he'd waved to engineer all those astounding deals and Houdini-esque escapes had suddenly turned into a divining rod for trouble.

Newspapers began to plumb all of those scrapes that Bob had told Pratt about. The details sounded far different when they weren't coming out of Matthews's mouth. That fiancée back in the mid-1990s—the Rollerblade heiress, Jennifer Naegele? After Matthews had convinced her to award power of attorney to his associate, Steven Fournier, Bob went on a "spending spree" at her expense, burning through $5 million in thirty-nine days, she said. He'd purchased the yacht, a $158,000 wooden Indian, and the Mercedes he'd given her as a gift. He'd diverted $2 million into his insolvent Fort Lauderdale marina.

Naegele had broken off the engagement when she learned he was "hemorrhaging" her accounts—and when she confronted him, he tried to intimidate her by "threatening physical harm," she wrote in an October 2, 1995, letter to dozens of the couple's acquaintances.

Naegele felt hoodwinked. "Mr. Matthews repeatedly bragged to me, my parents and my family that he was worth $80 million to $100 million," she wrote. She concluded that the actual amount was less than $15 million. As part of their breakup, Matthews promised to repay Naegele for "loans" on the marina and yacht.

The former president of Fabricated Metal Products, whom Matthews had fired for awarding himself a bonus? Robert Hughes, in a sworn affidavit, charged that Matthews began withdrawing money at a rate of $200,000 to $250,000 per month to fund his "bankrupt real estate empire and lavish personal expenses"—and that Matthews falsely recorded millions of dollars in withdrawals as "leasehold improvements" to conceal the company's financial status from his lender, the Bank of Tokyo, and the FDIC. Hughes alleged a variety of other offenses, including that Matthews falsified vendor invoices so he could overcharge a parent company for capital improvements by more than $1 million—bringing in more tainted income. Matthews repeatedly threatened to fire Hughes if he revealed what Matthews was doing.

Matthews eventually agreed to pay $950,000 to settle Hughes's lawsuit. Matthews sold Fabricated Metal Products in 2001; the new owners shuttered the firm not long after.

And Pinnacle Foods, the Pennsylvania meatpacking company? As Connecticut officials began considering loans to entice the company to move north, Matthews and an associate helped several people— including relatives of two state economic development officials— make profitable stock purchases of $10,000 each. Meanwhile, Pinnacle Foods claimed in court papers that Matthews deceived them by "misrepresenting that his close, personal ties to the governor . . . and other state officials would allow him to easily obtain" millions of public dollars.

There was more. The *Courant* reported that in the early 1990s, Matthews had handed Waterbury's corrupt and soon-to-be-disgraced mayor, Joseph Santopietro, $25,000 in cash in a brown paper bag. Though Santopietro was convicted of taking bribes, among other crimes, Matthews, of course, dodged prosecution. He initially denied to federal investigators that he'd given the mayor money. But when presented with contradictory evidence in a second interview, he reversed tracks. According to the *Courant:*

> Matthews told investigators that it was the death of his father, between the two interviews, that had persuaded him to be forthcoming about the gifts to Santopietro. Matthews said that his father would have been so disappointed by the bag of money that Matthews was initially reluctant to acknowledge it. Matthews' explanation for the change of heart stuck in the memories of investigators, the sources said. So did his behavior: Matthews flirted with a prosecutor and entertained his inquisitors with magic tricks.

Not long after that, Matthews began declining requests for interviews and began pulling up stakes in Connecticut. He abandoned plans for a new 8,630-square-foot mansion overlooking the Steep Rock preserve in Washington, Connecticut. The blueprints required blasting away part of a mountaintop to accommodate a swimming pool and terraces. Mike Ajello, the town's zoning enforcement officer, found Matthews's workers clearing the land without a permit and stopped them. Matthews told the town he'd had no idea his crews were cutting down the trees.

Soon after newspaper reports hit that Wayne Pratt had bought John Rowland's condo, the antiques dealer decided for the second time in the previous six months to cooperate with the feds. He explained to investigators how Matthews had set up the deal. He told them he'd ignored Matthews's admonition to throw out his records of the transaction and handed over the canceled $5,000 check he'd written to Rowland for the apartment's contents.

On March 18, 2004—by coincidence, exactly one year to the day after the FBI sting—Pratt pleaded guilty in federal court in Hartford to filing a false tax return. Pratt avoided jail time by cooperating. "I am sorry for the mistake I made," he said in a statement, "by failing to file a completely accurate tax return."

"I did a stupid thing," he said years later. "I should have analyzed it more."

Pratt absorbed yet another public relations bullet, but it was done. Matthews later invoked the Fifth Amendment in the Rowland investigation—the Bill of Rights making a cameo appearance in the proceedings. Governor Rowland, meanwhile, was headed for impeachment.

"Bob was always getting himself into trouble, because he was a house of cards," Pratt said long afterward. "But he's been able to get in and out of trouble like nobody I've ever known. He's a crazy guy. Really crooked as hell."

What really stung was the way Pratt had defended Matthews for all those years. "He's your friend, so you tend not to pick up on stuff," Pratt said. "I can't believe now I didn't see it then."

As the months passed, North Carolina officials grew increasingly confident they would prevail in their legal battle with Bob Matthews. They believed that because of the precedent set in the B. C. West case, they simply had to prove the document was once North Carolina property—and to that end, they were making good progress. The venerable archivist George Stevenson Jr., studying photocopies of the parchment's docketing increased to ten times its actual size, identified the writing as that of Pleasant Henderson, a clerk in eighteenth-century Raleigh. Stevenson was already familiar with Henderson's handwriting from his previous decades on the job. He compared the docketing to several other examples from that era, including the docketing on the Eleventh Amendment, which was passed in 1793. The document's folds also matched creases in other papers Henderson filed.

In August 2003 Philander D. Chase, senior editor of the Papers of George Washington project, housed at the University of Virginia, examined the evidence and found that it "conclusively" proved the document's connection to North Carolina. An FBI handwriting expert, Ken Martin, weighed in favorably as well.

An even more compelling clue came later. While working on the case, Karen Blum, an ambitious young lawyer in North Carolina's attorney general's office, sometimes locked herself into the state archives after hours. One night she faced the task of typing the entire text of the Bill of Rights into a legal brief. To save time, she copied the text from the National Archives' website and pasted it into her document. Blum was loath to inadvertently introduce an error by taking this shortcut, so she compared the text, word by word, with a reproduction of the parchment the FBI had seized. Midway through the Sixth Amendment, she stopped. That particular amendment guarantees the right to an impartial jury "in the State and district wherein a crime shall have been committed . . ."

That was how it read in the National Archives text, anyway. When she looked at the photocopy of the seized parchment, it read, "in the State and district where a crime shall have been committed . . ."

Not *wherein*, but *where*.

Blum sat back, worried. Why was the wording different? Then anxiety washed over her. *Oh, my God*, she thought. *It's a fake.*

The archival staff had already gone home, so she scrambled around for another source. James Iredell, a prominent early North Carolinian, had published a 1789 tome called *Laws of the State of North-Carolina*. In effect, he had copied for the record everything the legislature had passed that year. Blum flipped to where Iredell had recorded the Bill of Rights. There it was: "where a crime shall have been committed . . ."

Again: *where*, not *wherein*.

Did North Carolina's copy differ by two letters? A momentary lapse by clerk William Lambert in 1789? That seemed a possibility.

Another thought occurred to Blum: Maybe this could help North Carolina's case. Maybe Lambert's goof could help the state prove that its copy was, in one small way, one of a kind. Over the next month Blum chased down text from the other states that had lost their copies of the Bill of Rights. It was true: The originals sent to New York, Pennsylvania, Georgia, and Maryland all included the word *wherein*.

Blum had stumbled onto an important find.

The pitched battle between Bob Matthews and North Carolina raged on for nearly two years until, on August 4, 2005, U.S. District Judge Terrence Boyle ruled in favor of the state. Boyle asserted that the mistake in the warrant involving the parchment's whereabouts was a "harmless" typographical error, and that North Carolina should "immediately" take possession of the Bill of Rights.

U.S. attorney Frank Whitney quickly mobilized state officials for a ceremony in the Capitol—the building from which the document had disappeared more than 140 years earlier. Before the hand-over took place, Whitney and his staff gathered around the Bill of Rights one last time. State archivists had told them they could touch the parchment as long as they avoided the ink, so the entire group of lawyers passed a finger over a corner before anyone else entered the room.

Then Governor Mike Easley walked in and called everyone over. "He says, 'Hey, we're never gonna get to do this again,' and he touches the corner," Whitney recalled. "Not knowing that all of us had already done it, Easley picks up the plastic cover and says, 'Go ahead.' And so we all came back and did it a second time." Whitney laughed.

The ceremony took place within two hours of Boyle's court order. There was no time for Wayne Pratt to fly in and take part. "Pratt did the right thing," Whitney said later. "We were prepared to make a very clear and loud congratulatory thank-you statement to him."

But it's unlikely that anyone in Raleigh regretted his absence. After all that had gone down in Connecticut between Pratt and Governor Rowland and Bob Matthews, Whitney and others no doubt felt squeamish about the notion of the antiques dealer standing onstage with North Carolina's top officials.

For Pratt, this was yet one more unwarranted snub. With the Rowland affair over and the Bill of Rights behind him, he had begun to rebuild his life. He'd spent almost three-quarters of a million dollars on lawyers. "Those were the worst two years of my life," Sarah Pratt said.

Friends were pained by Wayne's struggles. David Schorsch was blunt with Pratt. "You know what? Stick to what you know," Schorsch told him. "If someone comes to you and says, 'I want you to buy my friend's apartment,' you say, 'Well, I'm not really a real estate speculator. I buy highboys, I buy folk art, I buy block-fronts. Bring me one of those and I'm in.'

"The same thing with the document: 'It sounds like a great opportunity. Let's call in Seth Kaller, let's call in Sotheby's, let's call in Bill Reese, whoever the players are, and I'll take a finder's fee.'"

Schorsch shrugged. "It would have been a different world for him. If he had said those things in those two transactions, you wouldn't be talking to me now. Twenty-twenty hindsight, but I live by it."

Pratt still had loyal clients, still had his livelihood, and all but a few employees stayed on. "This is one of the few businesses where seniority is a benefit," Schorsch said. "Old-timers are revered, and there's no forced retirement. It's like the Mafia—you're in it forever."

Still, Pratt felt stung by his exclusion from the proceedings in Raleigh. He had an entire speech planned for the ceremony where the document was officially handed over. "I was going to say that, despite the unfortunate misunderstanding that came about, I was happy to be giving this document to North Carolina," he said. "I would've said that it was nice to have handled something as important as that, and I enjoyed it for the years that I had it, that I used to go up to the office, look at it, read it."

He would have joked about the FBI's involvement, let the air out of that balloon. In Pratt's mind that would have officially put the incident behind him forever. "That was what I needed," he said.

Pratt had fantasized about *Antiques Roadshow* covering the handoff. He'd imagined the event clearing the way for him to return as a guest appraiser. He believed his exclusion from the ceremony prevented him from being invited back on PBS.

Was this delusional? Probably. Pratt, after all, still had a sentencing awaiting him in the Rowland imbroglio. In 2006 *Roadshow* spokeswoman Judy Matthews declined to participate in any way with this book. "We don't want to get involved with anything that has to do with Wayne's business practices or problems," she said when asked for tapes of Pratt's appearances. "If you were interested in the program, or something positive about the program, it might be possible for us to help you. I'm sure you'll find other ways to skin this cat. But I'm basically handcuffed, to use an unfortunate metaphor."

And to those who knew Pratt, his planned Raleigh speech wouldn't have sounded terribly sincere. Pratt often complained bitterly about the Bill of Rights affair. "I've got two kids I've got to support, and I've got a business with fifteen or twenty people, so they could really turn the screws on me," he said. "I was pissed. I wanted to roll that paper up and light the thing on fire and tell them to shove it where the sun don't shine. I felt like I was stabbed in the back. But if I wanted to keep fighting it was going to be another $500,000 to $750,000, and *Good Morning America* would have my face on TV as the guy who stole the Bill of Rights."

Pratt frequently asserted that he had bought Pennsylvania's copy, which he often mistakenly referred to as Philadelphia's. "In my heart of hearts, I really don't believe it's North Carolina's," he said. "I really don't. If I had to bet my life on whether it was theirs or not, I'd say not. And that's not just me not wanting it to be theirs. There are too many things that go against it."

But Pratt couldn't, or wouldn't, produce evidence supporting that claim. He said he'd signed a document legally declaring North Carolina's ownership, and thus was bound to silence on its true provenance. "That's going to cause me trouble if I do that," he said. "By the time they get through with me, I'll be reinvestigated by the FBI on whatever they can come up with. If they want me, they'll go after me for driving down the road."

Pratt and his employees—Joe Constantino among them—often said that in the FBI sting, the government violated "everything that the Bill of Rights is about"—in particular, the Fourth Amendment, which secures "the right of people to be secure in their persons, houses, papers, and effects, against unreasonable searches and seizures . . ."

Pratt believed that federal and North Carolina officials prosecuted him in the media after the sting, subjecting him to a sort of bloodless auto-da-fé.

All of this allowed him to remain the innocent victim in his own mind. He also declined to blame John Richardson, despite having relied on the attorney's advice for nearly eight years, and despite the fact the FBI used Richardson's letters to North Carolina as justification for the sting. Pratt continued to chat with and sell antiques to Richardson in the years after the sting.

"Before I purchased this thing," Pratt said, "before I gave my consent to buy it, John Richardson was standing next to me, saying it was OK." But then he added that Richardson had copiously researched the document and suggested—yet again—that the document may well have come from somewhere other than North Carolina.

Those around Pratt were less sanguine. "Wayne was being advised by John Richardson," said Sarah Pratt. "You pay a lot of money to lawyers, they're supposed to know what they're doing."

Cindy Pratt-Stokes, Wayne's sister, went further. "I think his lawyer screwed him," she said. "I think everybody screwed him. Everybody was so afraid of the government. Nobody wants to tangle with the government, and nobody wanted any fingers pointed at them."

23

Another Way

PEOPLE HAVE RISKED MUCH, and in some cases lost everything, in the pursuit of old documents.

In 1735 Lorenzo Boturini Benaducci, a knight of the Holy
Roman Empire, traveled to Mexico to tend to some affairs on behalf
of a countess of Aztec lineage. Boturini became fascinated with the
exotic land and decided to dedicate his life to compiling its history.
There was amazingly little source material, though. Within twenty
years of the Conquest, the Spaniards had pillaged record offices and
temple libraries, decimating their shelves. One of New Spain's supposedly liberal governors had sold the few ancient documents left in
Mexican archives as "wrapping-paper, to apothecaries, shopkeep-
ers, and rocket-makers."

For the next eight years Boturini combed the Mexican countryside for papers the Spanish had missed. He slept in peasants' huts
and in forests and caves, eventually earning the locals' trust enough
to accumulate about five hundred documents—the largest number
of pre- and post-Columbian items ever gathered.

Unfortunately for Boturini, he had a second obsession: Our Lady
of Guadalupe, the Madonna who had appeared to a peasant in 1531.
Boturini craved papal sanction for the coronation of her image and
thought he could successfully make the case in Rome with the material he'd gathered. But Mexico under the Spaniards was a gothic
place. The local viceroy was irked that he'd been excluded from matters of such immense gravitas and was distrustful of Boturini's mo-

tives. In June 1743 the Spaniards arrested Boturini, charging him with entering New Spain without license from the Council of the Indies, and with introducing papal documents without a royal permit. The colonists tossed him in prison and seized his collection.

After being held for eight months, Boturini was expelled from Mexico and loaded on a ship back to Spain without his collection—the sole possession "which he would not change against all the gold and silver in the New World," wrote Alexander von Humboldt, who later took up a similar chase. Somewhere en route, British pirates intercepted the ship, seizing the few remaining manuscripts Boturini had managed to keep.

Back in Spain, the charges against him were dropped and he wrote his history, appending from memory a catalog of his collection. There was a brief moment of near glory: The work impressed the king, who appointed him historiographer general of the Indies—an impressive title that, unfortunately, paid too little for Boturini to return to reclaim his collection. He died not long afterward. Back in Mexico, his documents sat in the humid air of the viceroy's palace basement, slowly decomposing. Many wound up stolen.

Boturini's successor—at least in terms of tragic zeal—was the Right Honorable Edward King, Viscount of Kingsborough in England. An untrained layman, Kingsborough had just entered Exeter College in Oxford in 1814 when, on a foray into the Bodleian Library, he came across the Codex Mendoza, a collection of documents depicting ancient Mexican customs. The codex had a bewitching history. Don Antonio de Mendoza, the first viceroy of New Spain, had ordered its creation in 1549 so officials back home could better understand their new subjects. But pirates intercepted the ship on its way back to Europe. The codex was sold and moved through a series of owners, vanishing for more than a century, before reappearing around the time Kingsborough arrived at Exeter.

His lordship was haunted by the papers and moved to collect and publish everything else he could find. "Judging by the suddenness and intensity of his interest," Leo Deuel wrote in *Testaments of*

Time, "it was close to a mystical experience . . . One witness alleged that 'he thought of nothing else.'"

Kingsborough's fixation undid him. He published nine volumes of early Mexican documents—borrowing wildly to support the venture, which cost more than £32,000. But his family had no interest in the project, and the volumes were too expensive to sell. Creditors began hounding him, and Lord Kingsborough eventually served three stints in prison. During his final stretch he contracted typhus and died within days. Had he lived a few more months, he would have succeeded to the earldom of Kingston, a title that paid £40,000 a year.

Still another devotee of historical finds, Polish collector M. W. Shapira, staked his life in 1883 on his greatest find: two ancient Hebrew manuscripts of Deuteronomy, written in old Phoenician-Hebrew characters, said to date back to the ninth century BC. The finds—which Shapira put up for sale for a million pounds sterling—were a sensation when they were unveiled in London, crowds pouring into the British Museum for a glimpse. But after three weeks a prominent French expert declared the manuscripts fake. Other scholars eventually agreed, and despite Shapira's strenuous defense, he was drummed out of England in shame. Not long after, he committed suicide in a hotel in Rotterdam, Holland. Decades later, a few academics argued that the manuscripts may have been authentic after all.

For many such aficionados, these struggles yielded nothing more than being labeled an "autograph collector," the term that caught hold in eighteenth-century Europe. Such collectors were often lumped into a community thick with forgers, scissors-wielding letter mutilators, and thieves.

To serious scholars chasing the story of human history, the obsessive tendencies, celebrity chasing, and otherwise unbecoming behavior of many document collectors were deeply exasperating. "Doubtless the 'profane vulgar' consider me, and all other individuals of my autograph-hunting species, as members of the common horde of semi-lunatics who gather birds' eggs, butterflies, hotel-paper, teacups, and Japanese sword-guards," Adrian H. Joline sniffed in his 1902 book, *Meditations of an Autograph Collector*.

"They think that I carry about with me a gilt-bound volume and ask luckless magnates to write their names in it . . . When they wish to be particularly kind, they tear the signature from some letter or document of an eminent person and present it to me . . . [I]t jars me to reflect that, in the minds of the multitude, the school-girl with her scrap-book and the fiend with his awful album are all of a piece with *me!*"

Still, Joline didn't hesitate to own up to his own Mephistoph-elean leanings: "There is, however, one evil thing about the other-wise harmless habit of autograph collecting. It fosters envy, hatred, malice, and all uncharitableness."

Most collectors in the first half of the twentieth century revered a man known as A.S.W. Rosenbach. A brilliant but hard-living Phil-adelphia rare-book dealer, Rosenbach had an uncommon knack for selling great things. He rose to prominence in the early 1900s by dominating auction floors on both sides of the Atlantic, buying the most coveted manuscripts: Chaucer's *Canterbury Tales*, James Joyce's handwritten *Ulysses*, Gutenberg Bibles, Shakespeare folios. He also bought and sold great American documents, including the first printings of the Articles of Confederation and the Constitution and early copies of the Declaration of Independence.

Many elite collectors were Rosenbach clients: J. P. Morgan, Henry Huntington, Harry Widener, and a Hollywood mogul named Barney Balaban, the chief of Paramount Studios, whose fascination with historical documents had a personal bent. During his child-hood his family had escaped persecution in Eastern Europe by flee-ing to America. Out of fascination with and fealty to his adopted homeland, he purchased Civil War letters, Lincoln correspondence, a collection of presidential signatures.

In 1943 Rosenbach approached Balaban with an idea. The United States was deeply immersed in war. Between Pearl Harbor and the intensely single-minded focus on the Allied campaigns in Europe and the Pacific, patriotism had soared to stratospheric levels. What an utterly perfect time, Rosenbach suggested to his patron, to buy a Bill of Rights and donate it to a national institution. America was fighting for freedom around the globe, and the Bill of Rights, more than any other document, spelled out the very liberties that Balaban so cherished.

Rosenbach happened to know that the Library of Congress would gladly accept such a gift. Rosenbach suggested that Balaban even link the gift to the war bond drive, to inspire Americans to invest still more in the ongoing global struggle.

Balaban loved the idea. He and his brother John agreed to put up $27,500 for the parchment's purchase—provided they were recognized as the donors. The brothers were "thrilled beyond words, and are very grateful to you for giving us an opportunity to participate in this historic transaction," Barney wrote to Rosenbach. "It will be only a small repayment of the blessings of liberty which the Bill of Rights has afforded . . ."

Library of Congress officials were equally electrified. The staff there already considered Rosenbach a kind of manuscript shaman who possessed nearly mystical powers. In 1941 librarian David Mearns had asked Rosenbach to borrow his original Bill of Rights for an exhibition commemorating the 150th anniversary of the document's ratification. "I have known for some time that one of the engrossed copies . . . was in private ownership," Mearns wrote. "I have, however, only just learned that it is you who are the owner, although I might very well have guessed it!"

As the deal fell into place, Librarian of Congress Archibald Mac-Leish openly lusted for the parchment, declaring that the institution "would be profoundly gratified, and those who are responsible for its administration would be grateful beyond any words of mine to express."

MacLeish, a poet, essayist, and playwright who won three Pulitzer Prizes, noted that the Bill of Rights was the only great sovereign American document the library lacked. When the donation was finalized, he wrote to Rosenbach, "You know better than any man living what it means to us to have this copy."

At a ceremony on December 13, 1943, the 154th anniversary of the Bill of Rights' adoption, officials accepted the gift outside New York City's Subtreasury Building, built on the site of Federal Hall, the place where the first Congress had convened and the clerks had written out those ten constitutional amendments. A military band played. The New York chapter of the Sons of the American Revolution placed a wreath on the framed parchment. Officials awarded a reproduction to the grade-school winner of a Bill of Rights essay contest.

Amid all the pomp, one person interjected a note of wariness. Five days before the ceremony, Julian Streit of the U.S. Treasury Department, the agency running the war bond drive, had asked MacLeish whether the document ought to be authenticated.

"No manuscript can be authenticated unless its provenance is known," MacLeish had replied. "Dr. Rosenbach has not informed us of the provenance of his copy of the Bill of Rights."

MacLeish added, "The Library will be happy to receive it as a gift without the establishment of origin which it would desire were it purchasing the document."

In other words, if the Library of Congress were *paying*, MacLeish would want to know more. But it was a gift; who was he to inquire?

This don't-ask, don't-tell policy allowed MacLeish to ignore some larger, painful truths. The most cursory research would have revealed that all of the original Bills of Rights had gone to the thirteen original states and the federal government. There were no private copies, no extras.

Rosenbach's parchment had to be stolen property.

How could the federal government accept a Bill of Rights as a gift, and then sixty years later treat the sale of another original as a crime?

In 2003, obviously, the cast of characters was drastically different, the aggrieved state of North Carolina standing in for the covetous Library of Congress. Wayne Pratt lacked Rosenbach's ironclad credibility in the manuscripts marketplace. And Pratt and John Richardson undermined their efforts with their dubious tactics.

Even taking those disparities into account, however, the Rosenbach sale strikingly demonstrates how the playing field of historic
manuscripts has tilted in the decades since. The typical public archive in the 1940s was an unsophisticated government backwa-
ter run by a political toady. In his landmark 1960s study, *American State Archives,* Ernst Posner reported that "archival lethargy or
neglect" still prevailed in about three-quarters of the states. Thefts
were rampant. In his 1961 book, *Collecting Autographs and Manuscripts,* ostensibly a celebration of the hobby, dealer Charles Hamilton wondered of the document world, "When will this orgy of destruction and thievery end?"

By contrast, for nearly a century beginning in the 1860s, the marketplace was the single most potent force for preservation. As dealer
Mary Benjamin wrote (somewhat self-servingly) in 1946, "In America, with few exceptions, credit for preserving the records of the nation's past must go to private collectors."

Sir Thomas Phillips, who in the nineteenth century was called
"the greatest collector of manuscript material the world has ever
known," recognized the critical role of private collectors. His goal
was "not only to secure good manuscripts for myself," he wrote, "but
also to raise the public estimate of them, so that their value might
be more generally known and consequently more manuscripts preserved. For nothing tends to the preservation of anything so much
as making it bear a high price."

Library of Congress officials in the 1940s grasped this. Far from
considering Rosenbach an adversary, the librarians made him their
unofficial broker. Rosenbach represented the institution at the Biddle Sale—the object of Ken Bowling's obsession.

But as states solidified archival practices and holdings, the landscape began to shift. Professional archivists replaced political hacks
and developed more or less homogeneous conservation practices.

Contemporary caretakers were hard-pressed to countenance
their predecessors' blunders. As states began to appropriate lavish sums of money for cutting-edge vaults and high-tech facilities,
they contemplated the return of lost or stolen property. States such
as North Carolina, South Carolina, Virginia, Maine, and New Jer-

sey increasingly viewed archives as trophy departments and aggressively pursued lost papers.

"Some collectors regard these demands as rank ingratitude for their timely action in preserving important public records which the government had ignored for generations," Colton Storm and Howard Peckham presciently wrote in a 1947 tome called *Invitation to Book Collecting.*

A previous generation of Texas officials had refused to acknowledge pervasive thefts in the 1960s and '70s; now they circulate lists of missing materials. "All this Texas stuff, forty years ago nobody gave a rip about it," said Everett Wilkie, chairman of an American Library Association committee on theft and security. "Now people are spending all kinds of fancy money on it and everything's changed."

Wayne Pratt either grasped none of this or believed too deeply in his ability to rig the game. He made a supposition that the soaring value of historic documents was a boon for his Bill of Rights dealings. That's how it works with Nantucket baskets and Ralph Cahoon paintings. But for many manuscripts that were once public property, notoriety is bad for the marketplace. The more prices go up, the more government archivists take to the hunt.

The growing institutional fascination with old papers has led to unlikely skirmishes. Peter Force, a prominent early collector, wound up with many stolen Maryland documents that eventually landed in the Library of Congress. Later, when Maryland asked for their return, the library refused—even when state officials offered proof they were stolen. The library capitulated after an extended tussle, allowing the material to remain on "permanent deposit" in Maryland.

In 2003 officials in Exeter, Rhode Island, quarreled with Brown University's John Carter Brown Library over a regional broadside printing of the Declaration of Independence. Three years later the state of New Jersey tussled with the Northampton County Historical and Genealogical Society in Pennsylvania over a 1758 land deed. But private dealers feel they're most often targeted in such disputes, given their relative lack of resources. "If you sue the Library of Congress, you're going to have a lot heavier sledding than if you sue a private individual," rare-books dealer Bill Reese said. "Also, there's the question of how it can be spun in the media."

Edward Bomsey, the Virginia-based dealer who aided in the prosecution of Library of Congress thief Charles Merrill Mount, once bought at auction a 1783 letter. The document, written by the president of the Confederation Congress, introduced to Virginia's governor a resolution recently passed by Congress. Bomsey purchased the cover letter only; the bill itself was not included. Bomsey liked the free frank on the included vellum envelope.

"I took a photograph of the letter," Bomsey said, "and I put it up on my website. Then I got an e-mail from a gentleman who asked if he could have a digital version of the document, which I happily did. The next thing I know, I got a call from the Library of Virginia. They said, 'Thank you very much, but we think this is our property.' Now, I'm not an idiot. I live in Virginia. I don't want a state trooper knocking on my door. There's an irrational fear collectors have: If I don't cooperate, am I going to have my business records from the last thirty years audited? Am I going to have problems registering my car as a corporate vehicle? I don't know what the price of non-cooperation is going to be.

"I said, 'Can I mitigate my damages and keep the free frank leaf?' At least in the philatelic market this would be worth something and I could recoup some of my losses. They said no. Quite honestly, I don't know where I see the great history in this particular item. If it included the certified act of Congress along with it, I'd understand."

Bomsey felt discouraged by this approach. "We're dealing with so much gray—shades beyond belief," Bomsey said. "I worry that there are some archives that will subscribe to the *Finding Nemo* theory of replevin. Remember the seagulls? They said one thing over and over again: 'Mine, mine, mine, mine, mine.' What I'm concerned about is that if you all persist in going after things that are of less consequence, I'm going to think twice about what I'm going to put on the Internet and what I'm going to put into a digital photo. Things will be pushed underground; that is not a happy consequence for anyone."

• • •

There are alternatives to the shock-and-awe approach to archival repossession. Take Edward C. Papenfuse. He's something of an institution in Maryland. His place of work, in fact, is named the Edward C. Papenfuse State Archives Building. When it opened in 1986, the edifice boasted the second-largest installation of compact shelving in the nation. Papenfuse the man is striking, too: He's a balding fellow with a large gray beard, a studious demeanor, and an unusual take on his state's missing Bill of Rights.

Papenfuse buys into the prevailing theory that the parchment Barney Balaban donated to the Library of Congress was Maryland's original. He's unsure how it went missing but is disinclined to chase after it. "What I would categorically say is that, because it's at the Library of Congress right now, it's not a high priority," he said.

North Carolina's situation was different, Papenfuse noted. "That document was lost under suspicious circumstances, and you can't say that for a fact with our copy," he said. "If ours wasn't in a place like the Library of Congress, I'd be going after it hammer and tongs."

Yet Maryland takes a far different approach to retrieving lost property from dealers and collectors. Rather than suing people, Maryland's attorney general authorized Papenfuse to offer a "finder's fee, for the good-faith efforts of private individuals."

Put another way: Maryland operates as a partner in the marketplace rather than an adversary. And as a result, citizens come to the Papenfuse building to repatriate items rather than hiding materials or anonymously selling them on the Internet. This policy also tacitly acknowledges that in many of the recent major theft cases, manuscript dealers helped apprehend the guilty parties.

Ed Bomsey, who in 2008 became president of the Manuscript Society, has worked to codify this middle ground. He has proposed that archivists and dealers agree on a few principles developed by an attorney in his organization:

- States should, as a matter of policy, promptly advertise alleged thefts and document the materials taken.

- When items are clearly stolen and misappropriated, the collecting community should mobilize to repatriate the pilfered items.

- Documents that have been openly bought, sold, traded, and published in articles should be immune from confiscation if no theft or misappropriation has been alleged and proved.

- Collectors should be sensitive to a state's desire to fill in the blanks of history. If copies of documents are requested, they should be provided.

To deal with inevitable disputes, Bomsey proposed the formation of a "blue-ribbon panel" equally representing archivists, dealers, and collectors to mediate real or imagined questions of ownership.

So far, no such panel has come into existence.

Would any of these remedies have altered the odyssey of North Carolina's Bill of Rights?

Doubtful. The journey had all the ingredients of an explosive homecoming—inordinately valuable object, dubious seller, murky provenance. There is a historical poignancy to the story: In 1787 each of the thirteen states was asked to vote on the United States Constitution. At North Carolina's convention, in Hillsborough, delegates voted to neither reject nor ratify; instead, they pushed for amendments that would safeguard individual rights. North Carolinians still like to point out that they were an impetus for the creation of the Bill of Rights.

Many outsiders acknowledge that given the full breadth of the story, North Carolina's decision makers had few practical options. "I think any governor's going to try to get the document back," said John Estey, Pennsylvania Governor Ed Rendell's chief adviser. "From the perspective of someone working in government, for a governor, I think it's a no-brainer. No North Carolina voter would be pleased if the governor didn't do anything in his power to get it back."

There was also the matter of precedent. In both 1995 and 2003, the state considered easier and safer courses of action. But North Carolina's no-compromise, no-negotiation policy dated back to R. B. House's eloquent rejection of Charles Reid's sale offer in 1925 and threaded through the pivotal B. C. West case of the seventies.

State officials take pride in their truculence. In the aftermath of the West victory, archives chief Thornton Mitchell wrote that he was "not concerned about alienating manuscript curators . . . [because] the relationship between archivists and manuscript custodians had already been critically damaged."

"We've been viewed for years as probably the most strident users of replevin," said David Olson, North Carolina's now-retired state archivist. "Anyone would be wary. We have a long history."

Still, one question continues to baffle outsiders: Why did North Carolina's archive-obsessed mandarins never actively pursue their missing Bill of Rights? By the time John Richardson emerged offering the parchment in October 1995, after all, North Carolina had known of the Shotwell family's possession of the document for nearly a century. The manuscript hung on the wall of the same family's humble middle-class home—hiding in plain sight, like Edgar Allan Poe's purloined letter—for almost a hundred years, and no one ever bothered to travel up from Raleigh to seek its return.

Instead, the state archives issued an institutional shrug. In 1991 a Raleigh *News & Observer* article began, "North Carolina is giving up hopes of finding its copy of the Bill of Rights."

William S. Price Jr., then director of the Division of Archives and History, told the newspaper that North Carolina officials had heard nothing of the document's whereabouts since 1925, when Charles Reid offered it for sale. "If it exists at all," Price said, "it may exist in his family, and nobody knows what they've got."

Then again, nobody asked.

Sylvia Shotwell Long recalled one occasion, in the 1990s, when a North Carolina–based journalist called her sister to ask about the Bill of Rights. Anne, caught off guard, pretended not to know what the reporter was talking about. Otherwise, there was nothing.

The sisters were surprised to learn North Carolina had built a shrine to its wayward Bill of Rights. "What irritates me so is that

North Carolina supposedly didn't know where it was," Long said. "If they were really interested in getting it back, they knew where it was. To think they didn't do anything. It's amazing to me."

Wayne Pratt agreed. "You mean to tell me they couldn't find it?" he said, leaning forward in his office chair, wearing an incredulous look. "Come on. I could've found it like that." He snapped his fingers.

Postscript

WAYNE PRATT WAS BLEEDING.

The antiques dealer was standing outside his Woodbury shop one warm June morning in 2007, a wad of crimson Kleenex attached to his bottom lip. "Shaving," he said, grimacing. "As soon as I did it I thought, *Ah, shit, this is gonna be a bad one.*"

Pratt was taking a blood thinner. He was due for surgery on a bad heart valve in about a month. His store's landscaping had a middle-spring verdure—a lush spaghetti of vines sprawled across a huge trellis—but Pratt himself looked withered. We had been talking on and off for six months about the Bill of Rights—the first such dialogue he'd had with a journalist—and he had often mustered defiance and outrage. But in the bright light of morning, with blood oozing out, he looked wan.

Sarah Pratt had noticed the same thing. When I spoke to her that weekend, she said she'd recently perused family photographs from before the showdown with North Carolina and was stunned: Her husband still had color in his mustache and a full face.

Pratt blamed his health lapses on the Bill of Rights affair. "Every time I talk about this goddamned thing," he said, "I get all worked up again." The bleeding never seemed to stop. Over the next few hours he gingerly removed the makeshift bandage several times, only to have blood pool anew.

Camus wrote that there is no pain that cannot be surmounted by scorn. More than four years on, Pratt still bitterly derided the government officials who had organized and executed the sting. "Our fore-fathers would've hung that group of bastards from the highest tree they could find," he said. "I am so disappointed in our government over this—the way they handled it, the way they used all their powers in a way that's totally opposed to what's in the Bill of Rights."

Pratt professed an Orwellian distrust of the government. He thought he might still be under surveillance. An attorney had warned him his cell phone could be bugged. "You don't know," he said, shrugging. "You get paranoid."

Our conversations about the document had begun to stall out in cul-de-sacs of denial and deflection. When I spoke of needing more proof to validate his version of the story, Pratt countered that he could have sold the document to a private collector and been done with it. "Do I regret that?" he said. There was a fertile pause. "I think about it. But I didn't do that, and I get absolutely no credit for it.

"I didn't want to break my deal with the [Shotwell] family. I made a deal, so I was going to keep it. You know, I've made a lot of money in this business by keeping verbal agreements with people, and it's always come back to benefit me. The only thing you have going for you in this business is your word."

He also pointed out several times that if he were really such a bad guy, he would have scraped the docketing off the parchment, making it impossible to trace. He got no credit for resisting that.

Pratt saved his greatest fits of vitriol for his erstwhile best friend, Bob Matthews, to whom he hadn't spoken in four years. Winding down a conversation about Matthews, I asked Pratt to recount his old friend's repertoire of magic tricks. "Probably just the standard French drop," Pratt said. "But he's a showman, so he'd make it seem bigger than it was."

After thinking for a moment, he added, "You know, one of the best tricks he did was, you give him money, it disappears."

Pratt allowed himself a weary grin, then cut off the conversation. He had to get back to work, bleeding be damned.

In early July 2007 surgeons in New York replaced a valve in Wayne Pratt's heart. He went home to Woodbury a couple of days later and proceeded smoothly through his recovery. A few weeks on, he was getting strong marks from his doctors and had begun walking a mile a day.

On the night of July 25, he watched a Red Sox game with his friend and client Jerry Conway. Then Pratt went to bed and died in his sleep.

On July 1, 2004, John Rowland resigned as governor of Connecticut amid the threat of impeachment for receiving inappropriate gifts and favors. Six months later he pleaded guilty to a single conspiracy count for failing to pay taxes on money he took from people doing business with the state. And in March 2005 Judge Peter C. Dorsey sentenced Rowland to one year and one day in federal prison. Dorsey noted that the former governor had conspired to "deprive the State of Connecticut and its citizens of the intangible right to the honest services of its governor."

Despite Wayne Pratt's cooperation with federal prosecutors on the Washington condo purchase, Bob Matthews was never charged in the Rowland investigation, and he decamped to Palm Beach. "Without, it seems, a care in their gilded world, Palm Beach's new It couple has been working their way up The Ladder," a *Palm Beach Post* gossip columnist reported in March 2006. "Nary a week goes by without developer Bob Matthews and his wife, failed actress Mia Matthews, materializing at the head table of a charity dinner. Or on the cover of *Palm Beach Society* magazine. Or hobnobbing with England's Prince Andrew or Olivia Newton-John."

In May 2007, under the auspices of the newly created Matthews Hospitality Group, Matthews announced plans for the Palm House, a five-star condo project on Palm Beach Island. The town, concerned about overdevelopment, had recently halted all such new construction, but Matthews managed to squeeze in his plan just in time. "If town officials hold fast to a recent vote calling for a moratorium on condominium hotels," a press release said, "The Palm House may be the last real estate ownership opportunity of its kind there"—a "major coup" for the owners.

In August 2008 actor Jim Belushi sang the blues at the opening of the Point Breeze Club and Residences, a historic landmark on Nantucket that Matthews was converting into a private club and community.

But when the economy tanked later that year, Matthews's empire began to exhibit signs of distress. In May 2009, the *Palm Beach Post* gossip columnist reported on his website that Matthews faced the county's single largest unpaid residential property tax—$272,391 on his sixteen-thousand-square-foot mansion—and owed the IRS another half-million dollars in back taxes. Around the same time the bank that had provided $40.5 million in financing for Point Breeze moved to foreclose on the property, announcing that it was putting the resort up for auction in August, according to Nantucket's *Inquirer and Mirror*. The newspaper also reported that eight lawsuits had been filed against Matthews and the company he set up as the resort's owner, "revealing a pattern of contractors claiming to have been paid for only a portion of the work they performed on the project."

Meanwhile, Matthews continued his fight for possession of the Bill of Rights from afar. Although Judge Terrence Boyle had awarded custody of the Bill of Rights to North Carolina in 2005, the legal battle wasn't over. For jurisdictional reasons, Boyle didn't have authority to decide who actually *owned* the document.

Matthews and the state of North Carolina staged a lengthy standoff in Wake County Superior Court, in Raleigh. Motions and filings dragged across months and years, and the case appeared headed for trial.

But before the two sides could meet in front of a jury, Matthews's legal team slipped up: His lawyers had lined up a key witness—a military history authority—to testify. But they missed the court's pretrial deadline for inclusion of their expert witnesses.

The state's lead lawyer, special deputy attorney general Dale Talbert, pounced. He argued that the witness should be barred from testifying. A judge agreed, and Matthews's case was effectively gutted.

In early 2008 Matthews finally surrendered, signing his interest in the document over to the state of North Carolina. State officials accepted Matthews's conveyance in a letter that also asserted that the state had owned the manuscript all along and had never transferred title to anyone else. This was the same paperwork given to Pratt more than four years earlier.

Matthews was free to use this document to pursue a tax write-off. But it was unclear whether the IRS would grant any such benefit. In December 2008 he agreed to pay a $2,000 fine to Connecticut's State Ethics Commission for trying to use his friendship with Governor Rowland to help close the Pinnacle Foods deal.

In the years following the FBI sting, Ken Bowling of the First Federal Congress Project tried to solve the puzzle of the four copies of the Bill of Rights that remained missing. He hoped to determine, among other things, which states originally owned the manuscripts in the New York Public Library and the Library of Congress.

Bowling concluded that it was a simple exercise in logic. Most historians believe that New York's Bill of Rights burned in the 1911 fire in Albany; Georgia's manuscript, according to officials there, is misfiled somewhere in the state's own archive.

With those two effectively gone, Bowling homed in on the Pennsylvania and Maryland copies. His analysis hinged on one key presumption: that Maryland's copy was seen hanging on the wall of the legislative chambers in Annapolis in the 1930s. Bowling and his colleague Charlene Bickford both recalled Maryland archivist Edward C. Papenfuse telling them this was the case.

If so, the math was simple. The New York Public Library obtained its copy in 1898—before Maryland's went missing. Thus, New York Public *has* to possess Pennsylvania's copy—and the Library of Congress has Maryland's.

But in November 2007 a problem emerged: Ed Papenfuse reviewed his files and found no timeline for the Bill of Rights' disappearance from Annapolis. There was no indication the document had been displayed in the thirties, and in fact, Papenfuse said, it could have vanished anytime. Maryland might even have made the same mistake as Delaware: Officials might have signed the amendments into law and returned the parchment to the federal government in the 1700s. Maybe the document was stolen after being sent back.

Confusing matters, the Library of Congress website claims that its copy belonged to John Beckley, the First Congress clerk, but no one outside the institution seemed to believe that. "It would be one thing if an original of the Bill of Rights was actually found in Beckley's papers," Charlene Bickford said. "But that is not the case."

Indeed, if that copy yielded an obvious link to Beckley, the dealer A.S.W. Rosenbach would have advertised as much in the 1940s, when he arranged its sale. On the contrary: Rosenbach identified the document as "one of the original fourteen copies."

This proved the old axiom that with historic documents, nothing is ever as simple as it seems.

Unbowed, Bowling pressed onward with his quest. Working on behalf of the National Constitution Center, which was hoping to identify Pennsylvania's missing original, Bowling obtained permission to examine both parchments.

Bowling was shocked by what he found at the New York Public Library. "At some point someone took a razor blade," Bowling said, "and scraped away a huge section where the docketing was. The parchment in various places is half the thickness."

Bowling planned to ask a forensic expert to try to reconstruct the docketing. He was still hopeful. "Even with my eyes," he said, "I could see remnants of handwriting."

He even had a suspect in the theft: William Henry Egle, a nineteenth-century historian from Harrisburg.

Bowling believes that when the mystery is ultimately solved, both libraries should relinquish their parchments. But that seems unlikely. There is institutional prestige in possessing one of America's holy relics. And there is the matter of precedent. Libraries and historical societies all across the United States harbor alienated, possibly stolen, public documents. "They would be concerned the dam could break," Bowling acknowledged, "and they could lose their collections. This is a concern of all manuscript repositories and collectors."

Gerard Gawalt, the American history specialist in the Library of Congress's manuscript division, said the lack of markings on that institution's parchment makes it unlikely the library would ever surrender possession of it. More likely, if there were adequate evidence and sufficient political leverage, a sharing arrangement could be settled on. The Bill of Rights "is considered one of the library's top treasures," said Gawalt.

Gawalt, a forty-year veteran of public archives, is not in favor of simply pursuing replevin every time the Library of Congress comes across an alienated public document. There were too many fault lines over the centuries: wars, mismanagement, official purges of items. "Other than outright theft, which we prosecute, it's very difficult to go back 100, 150 years and say, 'That belongs to us,'" Gawalt said. "Some think you should go out and replevin all the papers that are now in private hands. That's complicated, and expensive, and not the responsible thing to do at this point."

Down in suburban Atlanta, Sylvia Shotwell Long and her husband of thirty-nine years had divorced within the past few years, and she wound up back in the workplace in her late sixties. Like her grandfather, she once thought the Bill of Rights might secure her retirement. "In the end," she said, "we were really lucky to have gotten anything for it—and in my mind, what we got was a token for our efforts in preserving it."

Still, Long knew what she was dealing with. Even when Sotheby's said the manuscript was worth millions, she was dubious. "The cards were stacked against us," she said. "There was no way we were going to be able to realize what the value was. If it's the state's, it's the state's. You can't fight city hall."

For years Long had been a homemaker, raising three children. When her kids entered their teens, she began teaching ballroom dancing and etiquette as part of an after-school program. For her latest job she worked as an administrator at a Massage Envy franchise store. In her free time she liked to play bridge with friends.

In 2005, when North Carolina won custody of the Bill of Rights, the *Atlanta Journal-Constitution* ran an article about the affair that portrayed the Shotwells in an unflattering light. The story "just made it look like we were such bad people," Long said. "It hurt me." That day she got the first speeding ticket of her life.

Conflicting emotions lingered. "I'm glad it's back where it needs to be and is getting cared for," she said. "But I have a little bad taste in my mouth. We got no thank-you, and we took beautiful care of the document, and it meant something to this family. My grandfather paid for it in a store in Ohio, and my father thought he came by it rightfully." Charles Shotwell bought the Bill of Rights under the assumption that the Union soldier had saved it from being destroyed, she said.

"I had a problem with the idea of taking it to the state of North Carolina and saying, 'Here, take it,' because of the stories of their treatment of my grandfather," Long said.

The Bill of Rights was the impossible heirloom—a keepsake ultimately as ephemeral as a daydream. Part of her knew that all along, but still. No matter what else was true, the parchment had been part of her family for 134 years. "Wouldn't it have been nice to have a letter?" she asked. "Something that said, 'Without your protection, who knows what would've happened? Who knows whether we would have ever gotten the document back?'"

Attorney Steve Harmelin received the Philadelphia Bar Association's annual Replansky Award in 2005, given to a business lawyer for significant professional and civic accomplishments.

Richard Gilder and Lewis Lehrman, the philanthropists who offered to donate $1 million toward the Bill of Rights purchase, were awarded a National Humanities Medal in 2005 for their work promoting the study of American history. President George W. Bush honored them at the White House.

The $4 Declaration of Independence that they had twice tried to buy at Sotheby's turned up at a July Fourth celebration hosted by hip-hop mogul Sean Combs. Combs, who had borrowed the document from Norman Lear in an effort to publicize his nonpartisan get-out-the-vote organization, referred to it as his date. "I don't really have faith in politicians or politics," Combs said, cradling the document. "But I have faith in the power of the people, and if we educate ourselves about the hustle we can make things right."

President Bush in 2006 nominated North Carolina–based U.S. attorney Frank Whitney to serve as a federal judge; the Senate confirmed Whitney later that year. Whitney said the Bill of Rights recovery was the highlight of his career as a federal prosecutor, calling the sting "one of the most amazing undercover operations that I have ever seen." Assistant U.S. attorney Paul Newby was elected to the North Carolina Supreme Court.

Bob Wittman successfully lobbied the FBI to form an Art Crime Team, spearheading its formation in early 2005. He supervised a dozen agents spread around the country in an effort to pinch off a burgeoning trade in stolen art and antiquities. Wittman became a frequent public speaker, appearing on the condition that attendees not photograph him. He addressed the likes of the J. Paul Getty Museum, the Philadelphia Museum of Art, and New York's Museum of Modern Art on theft and fraud prevention. "The real art in art theft," he told me, "is not stealing, it's selling. In the old days you could steal a painting in New York and run down to Atlanta and sell it. Today, the minute something is stolen, that news is all over the world." The same is true of old papers, with one key difference: Keepers of documents often don't know an item is missing for weeks, sometimes months.

Before retiring in September 2008, Wittman was featured in the *Wall Street Journal* and photographed for the first time—with his back to the camera, wearing a white fedora. He felt pleased about the Bill of Rights returning to North Carolina. "Things like that are going to last forever and are going to have an impact after I'm gone," he said. "In a really, really small way, I became part of the history of that object."

The National Constitution Center survived its opening-ceremony snafu and opened to uniformly glowing reviews. The *New York Times* opined that the museum was "destined to take its place among the nation's leading monuments." A Zagat's travel guide pronounced it one of the country's top fifty attractions.

"I think it has exceeded even my fondest hopes for what it could be as an interpretive experience," said Joe Torsella, who left to run for Congress, lost, then returned as president and CEO. "It's been sort of the missing piece on Independence Mall. It takes the story of Philadelphia and brings it to the present, and projects it into the future."

The museum commands a national stage. Former attorney general John Ashcroft launched a month-long tour in support of the Patriot Act there. Former president George H. W. Bush was elected chairman of the board of trustees for 2007. Barack Obama delivered a widely hailed speech on race there in March 2008 during his successful presidential campaign.

"There's a sense that for a long time Philadelphia was sort of sleepwalking through its history, missing out on its own incredibly rich heritage," Torsella said. "Now, as in the eighteenth century, we're having important conversations about the republic."

Torsella kept his FBI hat. Two years after the sting, he wore it on vacation at a Florida resort. While signing out beach chairs, Torsella asked where his family should sit. The attendant looked at him and said, "You can sit wherever you want."

What Torsella really wanted was the chance to exhibit the Bill of Rights he helped recover. He still hoped years later that that would happen. "I think it would be a nice gesture," he said.

Despite the Bill of Rights experience—and also because of it—the Constitution Center began collecting historic documents. In 2007 the museum, with Seth Kaller as its broker, acquired a copy of the Emancipation Proclamation signed by Abraham Lincoln. The museum devoted part of its fund drive to raising money for other such artifacts.

In surveys, visitors routinely ranked viewing the Constitution and other original documents among their top three experiences. Torsella recalled watching an elderly donor press his nose to a glass case holding the Emancipation Proclamation—exactly as a group of school kids had just done. "We've really come up against the idea that when people see the real thing, they have kind of this 'aha' moment when they realize that this was the work of human hands, and maybe they have some work to do, too," Torsella said. "There's something very arresting about the physical thing.

"If you had talked to us in 2002, we wouldn't have appreciated the effect these artifacts have. We think these things ought to be seen. It doesn't do America much good to have a copy of the Bill of Rights that nobody sees."

Bill Reese continued building his legacy as his generation's greatest bookseller. Reese said he was satisfied that the Bill of Rights belonged to North Carolina. But he was very much alive to one of the ironies of the story.

To Reese, it made no sense for a state to own a document and just tuck it away, out of sight. There is no scholarly value to the parchment—its contents are not unique, or heretofore unknown—so its greatest value is its ability to inspire. Perhaps people see the document and feel so moved they decide to run for higher office, or work on behalf of human rights, or join the armed forces in defense of freedom.

"If that document can act as some kind of inspiration to visitors and citizens, which I think it can, having spent my life among these kinds of things, then I think it'd be better off in the Constitution Center, where a million people a year, or whatever the number is, can see it," he said. "I thought—and still think—that that would be a great thing."

Sometime around 1996, a pipe fitter from Nashville, Tennessee, named Stan Caffey bought an old copy of the Declaration of Independence at a tag sale. To Caffey, it was obviously a contemporary reproduction—you don't find historic stuff at Tennessee tag sales—but he liked the way it looked, and he took it home and hung it in his garage. A decade later his wife, Linda, began hassling him to amend his pack-rat ways. She convinced him to donate a bunch of stuff—including the Declaration—to a local thrift store.

Michael Sparks, a music equipment technician from Nashville, later found the yellowed, rolled-up document while wandering through the Music City Thrift Shop. An employee had slapped a price tag on it: $2.48. Something about it struck Sparks as interesting. Mostly it was just an instinct—something like what Charles Shotwell might have felt more than 140 years earlier, when he decided to blow $5 on a souvenir of war.

Later, Sparks showed the document to experts and learned he'd purchased a rare printing of the Declaration from 1823. He spent a couple of thousand dollars on conservation work, and in March 2007 he sold it at auction for $477,650. No one sued or claimed to be the document's real owners. The thrift-shop staffers said they were happy for Sparks.

Manuscript dealer Seth Kaller connected Sparks to the auctioneer who sold the Declaration. Kaller had shown it to some clients, but the document eventually sold for more than they were willing to pay. "I got two hundred phone calls after that from people who thought they had a Declaration but who unfortunately didn't," Kaller said. "Or they thought they had a Bill of Rights, or a Gettysburg Address—those are the big ones." None of them were real. Kaller followed through anyway.

"Tomorrow," he said, "we could get a call from somebody who really has one."

In summer 2007 Christie's held an auction titled "Fine Printed Books and Manuscripts Including Americana." The sale was held in a large, somber, windowless second-floor room. The event moved at an astonishing speed. The auctioneer had barely knocked down one sale when he slid into the next. A framed Declaration of Independence hung front and center, suspended between black curtains. A ticker board high above the auctioneer's left shoulder listed current bids, converting dollar amounts into euros, British pounds, Swiss francs, Hong Kong dollars, and Japanese yen.

The poker-faced participants re-upped their bids simply by nodding. The winners often wound up paying more than Christie's pre-sale estimates. The auction house had assessed the reproduction of the Declaration at $100,000 to $150,000; the high bidder paid $300,000. Christie's had guessed that a set of letters from John F. Kennedy to an early lover, Inga Arvad, would sell for $20,000 to

$30,000. They went for $120,000. A John Wilkes Booth screed that set the stage for his assassination of Lincoln sold for $260,000.

Almost none of the sellers were identified in the catalog. Instead, a George Washington letter was "the property of a California collector." Another one was simply "the property of a gentleman."

Seth Kaller acquired several new pieces. The auction lasted less than two hours; the tally of money spent was somewhere around $2 million. And then the bidders wandered away, one by one, blinking as they stepped out into Manhattan's dazzling summer sun.

In December 2006 I asked Ken Bowling to accompany me to the Washington Capital Area Autograph and Manuscript Show in Alexandria. Among the scheduled attendees were Seth Kaller and Edward Bomsey, the Virginia dealer. I wanted to see the event through Bowling's eyes.

Inside the Old Town Hotel, twenty-five or so dealers were shoehorned into a tight L-shaped conference space. A police officer stood at the entrance. Lines of narrow tables held small exhibits, many with oversized dossiers filled with old paper. Bowling quickly looped the room, scanning the tabletops. "A lot of this is just autograph material," he said dismissively.

As Bowling prowled, I ran into Kelly Maltagliati and Mitchell Yockelson, a pair of officials heading up an effort by the National Archives to recover alienated government papers. The two had come to make introductions. "We're kind of like Starsky and Hutch," Yockelson said. He was short and pudgy, with graying hair. The bookish Maltagliati was an equally unlikely casting choice for a TV cop, even one from the 1970s.

Dealers had bemoaned the new National Archives program, predicting heavy-handed government tactics. But Maltagliati said they were looking to build partnerships with dealers. "You know, we don't want to have an adversarial relationship, or have people upset with us," she said. "These are the first people to see things."

Bowling had alighted a few tables away, across from an ursine fellow with a head of bushy hair, overgrown eyebrows, and a push-broom mustache. He introduced himself as Dennis. "This is really interesting stuff," Bowling said as I pulled a chair over.

Dennis had a large collection of early republic–era letters. Bowling explained his credentials. Dennis opened a large binder containing protective sleeves. "When you see what I have," he said, "you're gonna die."

Bowling watched the pages flip by with growing interest. "Can I ask where you're from?"

"Connecticut. You recognize that handwriting?"

Bowling shook his head. The person who penned the U.S. Constitution wrote this, Dennis said.

"Oh, wow," Bowling said, rolling his eyes, grinning.

The pages rolled by. Dennis lingered long enough for us to make out only a few words of each page. There was a receipt from Independence Hall. Significant letters to and from revolutionaries. Dennis noticed I was taking notes. "Wait, I don't know if I want you to do that," he said.

Before I could respond, Dennis flipped the page again and Bowling bolted forward. "OK, stop for a minute," he said. "I've been looking for this letter since 1970!"

It was a Biddle Sale letter—one of the couple of dozen he'd been tracking for half his life. Bowling suddenly seemed flustered. He began to explain the history of the 1940s auction, about how he'd hunted down a hundred of the letters but had never located the rest.

"OK," Dennis said, nodding. Then he quickly flipped the page.

"That's another one!" Bowling said, raising his hands in the universal stop signal. "Oh, my God, wow, I'm dying here," he said. "See, I wrote an article about this."

"OK," Dennis said.

Flip.

Bowling grimaced, but kept up the Ping-Pong of conversation. When Dennis reached the end, he looked at Bowling and said, "I'm your guy."

"We're each other's guy," Bowling replied. He offered to show

Dennis an article he wrote about the Biddle Sale and offered to explain some of the history of the documents in the folders. We shook hands, and Dennis handed us his business card, which read "American Historical Collection."

Bowling retreated to a seat in the hotel lobby. He looked elated. "Boy," he said, grinning. "Our man really didn't want us reading those letters, did he?"

I asked whether he would try to get a better look sometime. "Of course," Bowling said.

But a couple of years passed, and every time I checked in, Bowling had something else going on. I offered to drive him to Connecticut, but he demurred. Eventually I stopped asking. He always had too much going on, too many trips to other places, too many pages to edit yet on his documentary histories. He had Bill of Rights mysteries to crack.

For a while I thought that maybe Dennis was just one adventure too many for Ken Bowling—it was too much for one person to take on. But then I theorized that something else was going on: Maybe Bowling loved the thrill of the chase more than anything and simply didn't want to come that much closer to the end.

Maybe it was enough to know that more stuff survives out there, that the search *never* really ends.

Maybe that was what mattered most of all.

Wayne Pratt's family held a memorial service on September 1, 2007, on the sprawling grounds of Mill House Antiques in Woodbury. It was a sun-splashed late-summer day, and about 150 people—many of them antiques-industry heavyweights—wandered the grassy grounds and sipped wine before the speeches began. Margaret Milner Richardson, the former IRS commissioner, was there, though her husband was notably absent. As expected, Bob Matthews was also a no-show.

I came expecting to hear the story of the whiz kid turned kingpin: the full Wayne Pratt narrative arc, writ large for the occasion. Speakers included friend David Schorsch, longtime employee Joe Constantino, and Jerry Conway, Pratt's friend and client. Business partner Marybeth Keene, who had kept a picture on her office wall of Pratt playfully wearing a Nantucket basket on his head, recalled Pratt's raunchy humor. A former employee, Johanna McBrien, now the editor of *Antiques & Fine Art*, started crying even before she began her comments.

Pratt's sister, Cindy Pratt-Stokes, told how during their childhood, the well-to-do Morse family next door had a pond on their property, and Wayne—ever the entrepreneur—decided to harvest the water lilies that grew in it. He paddled out in an inner tube, dove to pick the flowers, and then sold them door to door. Eventually he even approached the Morse family. "Mrs. Morse gave Wayne a withering stare," Cindy recalled, "and said, 'Wayne Pratt, why should I buy water lilies from my own pond?'"

But she invited Wayne inside, and he eventually emerged with a victorious grin. "I can see him now," she said, "dashing down the back steps, smiling, with some cookies for me and no more water lilies—and probably a contract to sell her more in the future."

No one uttered the words *Bill of Rights* or mentioned Bob Matthews. Only old friend Ron Bourgeault, the owner of Northeast Auctions, elliptically referenced the troubles, suggesting that friends had taken advantage of Pratt.

It was almost possible, amid the dappled sunshine and the tenderhearted remembrances and the raw, freshly liberated emotions, to imagine that the entire Bill of Rights affair had somehow been a huge mistake, and that a good man had been victimized—perhaps even martyred—by overzealous state and federal officials and friends who had done him wrong.

But even before the memorial service had ended, something struck me: No one talked about his early years. There were no recollections of the boy wonder—the one who starred in *Objects of Desire*, the *New York Times*, and Pratt's own fanciful tales. Wayne buying a Windsor chair at age seven. Wayne strapping furniture to the track-team bus in high school. Wayne as a boy convincing the bank manager to let him open a checking account by flashing a wad of bills: *I have a business. I buy antiques.*

In fact, Tom Constantine, a classmate who spoke at the memorial service of Pratt's prowess in high school football and track, professed being surprised when Pratt had told him at a reunion that he'd gotten into antiques.

Sarah Pratt described her husband as an earthy, sentimental man who always seemed to be telling a tall tale, until you ran into someone else who confirmed the story. "His own life," she said, "was something of a fairy tale." Between fond recollections, Ron Bourgeault said Wayne "was no angel" and that he pictured Pratt sitting around in heaven with antiques legends Israel Sack and Hymie Grossman, "all of them trying to tell tales taller than the others."

I couldn't escape the impression that even the people closest to Pratt accepted the threads of fiction he wove into his colorful backstory. They loved him enough not to care what was really true.

Later, I called Cindy Pratt-Stokes, who confirmed as much. The story she told of Wayne's childhood was far different than his own auto-hagiography. Wayne was a sickly boy who suffered from rheumatic heart disease, an affliction in which rheumatic fever damages one's heart valves. He spent time in an iron lung. The Pratts acquired a phone—becoming one of the first families in the neighborhood to have one—because his tenuous health mandated that they be able to reach doctors quickly. Wayne's doctors prescribed penicillin—then a new drug with difficult side effects. He lost so many teeth that by the time he finished high school he was fitted with dentures.

The protracted illness rocked the family. His father had to quit a more lucrative auto-sales job—"in our family, we all could basically sell ice to Eskimos," Cindy said—to work at Simpson Springs, which had a better health insurance plan.

The pay was pitiful, though, and the family scraped by with the kids wearing neighbors' hand-me-downs. This penury, stretched across nearly a decade of his childhood, profoundly shaped Wayne. "He did not want to be poor," his sister said. "He had a drive after that to not want for anything. He did not want me to want for anything. When women were with him, they felt like the one and only princess of the world."

Viewed through this prism, Pratt's apocryphal tales had Sche-
herezade-like qualities. They helped him stay one step ahead of the
poverty of his past. Antiques suited him perfectly: Success hinged
on sales skills, precise memory, and whimsical backstory. What
was true of the antiques—the better the backstory, the greater its
value—was also true of the dealer.

There were antiques around during Wayne's childhood. But the
idea that he bought a Windsor chair at age seven—one of the most
ossified nuggets of the Pratt mythology—was sheer folly. "He was
a very sick little guy," Cindy said. "I do think that's stretching it a
little bit."

Cindy Pratt-Stokes was eleven years younger. She remembered
Pratt flexing his entrepreneurial muscles as his health improved. At
sixteen he ran a summer camp for children. He was good with kids.
She recalled a landscaping business for which he printed business
cards. He had a green thumb, and the town had a lot of doctors and
lawyers with yards.

But the stories in *Objects of Desire*, about Wayne's thriving childhood business? "I don't think that's totally accurate," she said. "My
brother embellished things."

How much?

Cindy sighed. "I'd hate to negate anything he said at this point,"
she said. "I like to figure everything my brother said was real and for
true. He had a great eye, he knew his stuff, and he could sell. I'd like
to leave it at that."

Like everyone else who entered his life, I heard Wayne Pratt tell
many stories. Some of them became implausible only after hearing
the larger story of his life. For example, the man constantly hunting for items with a "$20,000 difference" once told me: "It's never
the money to me—it's the object. You have to make a living, but I'm
more interested in the object."

Another time I asked him what he would have done if he'd been
convinced the document was North Carolina's. "People have asked
me that: 'If you had known, would you have still bought it?' I thought

about it, and I don't know if I would. But if I really thought it was theirs, I would've called them while I had it." John Richardson had done that, of course, in 1995—with disastrous results.

Pratt also described in detail the dedication ceremony he'd anticipated after the National Constitution Center bought the Bill of Rights. Sarah and the boys would be there, he said, and Bob Matthews and his family, and Richardson. Pratt would talk about how much fun it had been to hammer out the deal with the museum, and how happy he was to place such a prominent piece of history with such a worthy institution. Pratt said he'd approached *Antiques Roadshow* producers about doing a segment on the Bill of Rights, and they'd seemed interested.

Only later did I see the confidentiality agreement that his lawyer, John Richardson, had required of the museum. The sale to the Constitution Center would have been secret. There would have been no such ceremony, and certainly no television show.

Pratt wasn't the first self-made man who embellished. And he certainly wasn't the first antiques dealer to do it. But the stakes were lower with furniture. As David Schorsch told me, "Nowhere in the rules of antique furniture does it say you have to tell someone where an object came from. It's none of their business where it came from. Some people do, but you don't have to."

And Pratt's success on the industry's biggest stages made it easier for him to make truth pliable. If *he* said on *Antiques Roadshow* that a set of whale-bone dominoes had come from the *Minerva,* who doubted it was true? He was Wayne Pratt. Only in the world of historic documents did Pratt's extraordinary alchemy of salesmanship and storytelling turn toxic.

Pratt's involvement with the Bill of Rights ultimately has a *Rashomon*-like quality, with different onlookers divining different realities. Some see an innocent victim taken down by power-hungry government opportunists; others see a conniving carpetbagger or a scheming rat; still others view him as an ambitious, hard-driving entrepreneur who simply took bad advice.

What is the truth of the story of the Bill of Rights? Did Pratt get what he deserved? Did North Carolina state officials deserve what they got? Should the Shotwells have made a fortune off the document—like many other people who have bought and sold public documents over the past 150 years—or not a penny? Was A.S.W. Rosenbach the hero he was made out to be, or just a profiteer with good timing?

What is fair and just? With old papers whose stories swirl far back into the haze of war-torn centuries past, who is really qualified to decide?

Maybe, in the case of the stolen Bill of Rights, Wayne Pratt became a victim of his own mythmaking powers. He believed too fiercely in the power of his own legend.

Or maybe the authors of the Bill of Rights simply knew it best: Power corrupts. Maybe, when it comes to objects with values greater than we can fathom, we all need a firewall. We all need to be saved from our worst impulses.

No one was there to save Pratt from himself. He gambled that he could score a huge payday and lost, and his friends real and imagined melted away, leaving him alone to fall.

In September 2007, by coincidence just two weeks after Pratt's memorial service, North Carolina officials unveiled the Bill of Rights for public viewing for the first time in Raleigh. This was the third stop on a six-city tour.

In Fayetteville that February, the local newspaper had published a special section about the document in advance of an exhibition at the Airborne & Special Operations Museum. More than five thousand people showed up on opening day, some waiting three hours to view the parchment. Sarah Koonts, the collections manager, saw veterans choke up at the sight; here on ancient parchment were the freedoms they had fought to protect.

In Raleigh there were brief introductory remarks. The lights in the North Carolina Museum of History were dimmed. Then five of the state's Supreme Court justices pulled a cover off a large cherry case that had been custom-built for the Bill of Rights. The first wave of viewers numbered roughly a hundred. The daily newspaper hadn't run much more than a notice. The excitement level seemed to have receded some since the tour's launch.

The state had no further concrete plans to display the parchment. "I'm sure it will be on display at times, most likely in Raleigh, but probably not permanent display," Sarah Koonts said. "We have been advised against that, due to the very faded nature of the ink, particularly on the signatures."

This, of course, is the only way to go. The object has to be preserved. The document now resides in a secure microfilm vault on an acid-free mat, sealed between framed Plexiglas sheets that filter out ultraviolet light. The dimly lit room remains at a constant fifty-five degrees, with 45 percent relative humidity.

There the parchment will remain, out of sight and largely out of mind, interred in the cool dark, for months and years and centuries to come.

Acknowledgments

Funny thing about writing a book: I spent a hefty percentage of three years alone in a basement perspiring over this manuscript, and yet little I've done in life felt so much like a team effort. In particular, I'm deeply grateful to the people who read the manuscript and provided vital guidance. Bill Strickland and Peter Flax, both of them extraordinarily talented editors, each read two early versions and offered critically important input; Bill even lugged an embarrassingly overlong draft to Africa. Todd Balf and Dan White also read the manuscript and provided sharp insights. Thanks to Charles Monagan, editor of *Connecticut Magazine*, for assigning me the feature story that got this book going. My agent, Jeremy Katz, plowed through multiple drafts and brought his relentlessly upbeat manner to the foxhole throughout; as a friend, reader, cheerleader, and adviser, he gave more than I could have hoped for.

Susan Canavan, my editor, routinely offered keen insights and clear vision of where this book needed to go, elevating it far beyond where it started. And Webster Younce, the book's initial editor, ably guided me through the book's infancy. Thank you to Barbara Wood, copyeditor extraordinaire, for her eagle-eyed work. Thanks also to the preternaturally cheerful Liz Lee at Houghton Mifflin Harcourt for her helpfulness.

Many people generously offered up hours of their time to share memories, insights, arguments, or resources; to avoid redundancy, I've credited many of them in the sources section, but I appreciate their contributions no less. As far as I know, I was the first and only journalist to whom Wayne Pratt spoke on the record about the Bill of Rights and his problematic condominium purchase; he also opened his family, friends, and staff to my questions and requested nothing in return. I'm grateful for his cooperation.

Ken Bowling and Charlene Bickford at the First Federal Congress Project gave me broad access to their time, ideas, and resources and allowed me to dig through their stacks. Patrick Kennedy at the Troy-Miami County Public Library's Local History Library in Troy, Ohio, went far beyond the call of duty in assisting with my research, often cheerfully joining me down spur roads in my research that proved to be dead ends. Doug Slagel of Tipp City, Ohio, generously offered his time, hospitality, and Civil War bookcase during a reporting trek.

At the North Carolina Department of Cultural Resources, Michael Hill offered advice, expert guidance, and even a place to plant my laptop while roaming around Raleigh. He also forwarded newspaper articles and press releases involving the Bill of Rights. Thanks also to Jeff Crow, Dick Lankford, Boyd Cathey, and Sarah Koonts at the state archives.

I learned much about the larger, complex issues tackled in this book from conversations with state archivists Rodger Stroup of South Carolina, Joe Klett of New Jersey, and Ed Papenfuse of Maryland. Some of the nation's leading experts on archival issues provided input on the larger issues that they wrestle with: Susan Allen, chief librarian of the Getty Institute's research library; Jean Ashton, vice president and library director of the New-York Historical Society; Gary M. Stern, general counsel at the National Archives; Greg Giuliano at the Rosenbach Museum & Library; and Everett Wilkie Jr., chairman of an American Library Association committee that deals with issues of theft.

Dealers of historic documents largely avoided me throughout my reporting forays, wary of what I planned to write. I'm indebted to the businesspeople whose lives became intertwined with the Bill of Rights for eventually trusting me enough to talk. Also, Edward Bomsey was among the few dealers with no stake in the story who let me inside his world, and I'm indebted. Thanks also to Wayne Mattox, who provided insights into the world of antique furniture.

My gratitude goes out to the history department at Lehigh University for providing a capable student researcher in Evan Rothman, who located dozens of background nuggets and leaned heavily on the interlibrary-loan system to dig up hard-to-find tomes. Thanks to Christine Mattheis and Alison Granell for transcription and research help.

Evelyn Murray, my aunt, is an accomplished genealogist who tracked several family lines in hopes of identifying the soldier who took the Bill of Rights during the Civil War. Though that quest ultimately went unfulfilled, I appreciate her efforts. Also, thanks to my brother Steve for technical support.

Jonathan Dorn conjured ways to make my full-time magazine-editing schedule mesh with my book-writing needs. A big thank-you to him.

I'm grateful to John Murray for his wise counsel, his help with the on-the-ground reporting, and his spare room for my many forays up to Connecticut. He made the book better, and his company made creating it immeasurably more fun.

Finally, my wife, Ann Quigley, and our son, Vaughn, rode with me through every swell and trough: Ann read the manuscript and provided thoughtful feedback; remained steadfastly supportive through my struggles with time and energy and confidence; told me when it was time to back off, and then nudged me forward, shouldering greater responsibilities so I could soldier on. For all that, and much more, she has my enduring love and gratitude.

Sources

This book was largely constructed through interviews with the people who were present during the occurrences or conversations in question. I sought to interview everyone directly involved whenever possible, but I also relied on correspondence, documents, e-mail, and other documentation related to the parchment's travels. Except where otherwise noted below, I obtained all of this documentation through court files generated during the course of the litigation that followed the FBI sting. These materials are on file in U.S. District Court and Wake County Superior Court, both in Raleigh.

INTRODUCTION
I relied heavily for this opening chapter on interviews with Charlene Bickford, Ken Bowling, and Bob Wittman, all of whom generously answered multiple rounds of questions. The Henry Stanley passage is from his book *How I Found Livingstone: Travels, Adventures, and Discoveries in Central Africa* (New York: Charles Scribner's Sons, 1913). The bird watcher anecdote comes from Dan Koeppel's article "Gone to the Birds," published in *Backpacker* magazine in September 2004.

1. A BREAK-IN
David Keough at the U.S. Army War College at Carlisle Barracks, Pennsylvania, helped me navigate through the vast jungle of Civil War resource material to find the most relevant stuff. He also first

advanced to me the highly credible theory that an Ohio infantry-man took the Bill of Rights—not a member of the cavalry, as many had speculated previously—and thus helped focus my research. Dale Talbert and Karen Blum of the North Carolina attorney general's office spent parts of several years researching the history of the document; they pointed the way through the federal and state court system to important documentation and endured multiple rounds of questions. I'm grateful for their help. Patrick Kennedy at the Troy-Miami County Public Library's Local History Library in Troy, Ohio, helped excavate details of the Shotwell family's Miami County tenure. For biographical material on Rue Hutchins, I relied on A. Donald Kelmers's self-published (in 1999) booklet about his great-grandfather, *Rue Pugh Hutchins*. (Hutchins, by the way, almost certainly did not take the Bill of Rights. By the time the Ninety-fourth Ohio reached Raleigh, he'd been reassigned to recruit "colored troops" in Charleston, South Carolina.)

In terms of recounting the last days of the Civil War, I found these books and articles useful:

William Anderson, "Sherman: The Occupation of Raleigh," *Philadelphia Inquirer,* April 26, 1865.

John G. Barrett, *Sherman's March Through the Carolinas* (Chapel Hill: University of North Carolina Press, 1956).

Mark L. Bradley, *This Astounding Close: The Road to Bennett Place* (Chapel Hill: University of North Carolina Press, 2000).

Forney's War Press, "North Carolina," April 15, 1865. This is the source of the "piruting" passage.

———, "Sketches of Sherman on His Great March," April 15, 1865. This is the source of the Sherman quote.

Record of the Ninety-fourth Regiment Ohio Valley Infantry in the War of the Rebellion (Cincinnati: Valley Press, 189?). This rare volume is available at the U.S. Army War College and Troy's Local History Library.

Whitelaw Reid, *Ohio in the War: Her Statesmen, Her Generals, and Soldiers,* vol. 2 (Cincinnati: Moore, Wilstach & Baldwin, 1868).

There are many resources available on the Bill of Rights' creation, including "The Bill of Rights: Milestone Documents in the National Archives," a booklet published for the National Archives and Records Administration by the National Archives Trust Fund Board in 1986. I also consulted:

Akhil Reed Amar, *The Bill of Rights* (New Haven: Yale University Press, 1998).

Charlene Bangs Bickford and Kenneth R. Bowling, *Birth of the Nation: The First Federal Congress 1789–1791* (Lanham, MD: Madison House Publishers, Inc., 1989).

Kenneth R. Bowling, "'A Tub to the Whale': The Founding Fathers and Adoption of the Federal Bill of Rights," *Journal of the Early Republic*, August 1988, 223–51.

Leonard W. Levy, *Origins of the Bill of Rights* (New Haven: Yale University Press, 1999).

2. The Natural

I interviewed Wayne Pratt for this book nearly a dozen times between January and June 2007. His wife, Sarah Shinn Pratt, his friend David Schorsch, his business partner, Marybeth Keene, and his sister, Cindy Pratt-Stokes, also cumulatively spent dozens of additional hours telling me about Pratt's life. Leslie Hindman spoke to me about her experience with the Bill of Rights and about referring Wayne Pratt to Charlie Reeder.

The following other sources added details and perspective, not only in this chapter but throughout the book:

Laura Beach, "Wayne Pratt, 64, Auction Force Who Built Large Business in American Furniture," *Antiques and the Arts Online*, July 30, 2007.

Jean Dunn, "Shops in Woodbury, Nantucket to Close: Wayne Pratt Remembered by Family, Friends, Colleagues," VoicesNews.com, August 22, 2007.

Thatcher Freund, *Objects of Desire* (New York: Penguin Books, 1995). The passage in which the author recounts Pratt's youth is on pages 194–95.

R. W. Stevenson, "A Lifelong Love Affair with the Past," *New York Times*, May 12, 2002.

For Pratt's appraisal of the television stand on *Antiques Roadshow*, see "Tulsa," hour 3, from the 2001 season. He can be seen appraising the maple bowl in hour 1 of the show's Denver stop, also in 2001.

3. THE $4 TREASURE

The following articles served as resources for the story of the flea-market Declaration of Independence:

Eleanor Blau, "Declaration of Independence Sells for $2.4 Million," *New York Times,* June 14, 1991.

Dorothy S. Gelatt, "The Legend of the Famous $4 Picture Frame," *Maine Antiques Digest,* September 2000.

Selwyn Raab, "Sotheby's Challenged in Selling Declaration," *New York Times,* June 4, 1993.

Rita Reif, "Declaration of Independence Found in a $4 Picture Frame," *New York Times,* April 3, 1991.

Despite obviously deep reservations about answering my questions, attorney Charlie Reeder shared what he could remember of his meetings with Pratt and Bob Matthews. I appreciate his cooperation.

4. THE GRAIN MAN

I gleaned many details of Charles Shotwell's life from the Indiana State Library and the Indiana Historical Society. Much of the Shotwell family history is taken from U.S. Census records; biographies of Grier M. Shotwell by the Citizens Historical Association of Indianapolis, on deposit in the Indiana State Library; Charles Roll's *Indiana: One Hundred and Fifty Years of American Development,* vol. 3 (Chicago: Lewis Publishing Company, 1931); and an obituary, "Shotwell, Long Resident of City, Is Dead in West," printed in the *Indianapolis Star* on May 31, 1937. Also see "Hoosier Profile: New Board Chairman Knows About Schools," by David Watson, in the *Indianapolis Times,* January 19, 1952. Grier Shotwell's daughter Sylvia Shotwell Long also helped fill in historical blanks. The Indianapolis city directory was the source of my 1880 information about the city's growth.

One footnote about Shotwell's 1924 letter: His mention of a vault in the North Carolina secretary of state's office is one of the few details that doesn't stand up to scrutiny. The only vault in the Capitol was located in the treasurer's office. But Shotwell's retelling of the day's events was bolstered by his mention of a nearby fire. Set by Confederates in a railroad depot, the blaze was not widely reported at the time and therefore would have been known only to people who were then in Raleigh.

For background on Miami County at wartime, I consulted Thomas Bemis Wheeler's "Miami County and the Civil War," a master's thesis written in 1964 at Miami University, on file at Troy's Local History Library.

Document collecting has been deemed a surprisingly book-worthy subject over the years. The following volumes were indispensable in terms of placing the Bill of Rights' story in a broader context and providing details about the intensity of the hobby's adherents:

Mary Benjamin, *Autographs: A Key to Collecting* (New York: Bowker, 1946).

Lady Dorothea Charnwood, *An Autograph Collection and the Making of It* (New York: Henry Holt, 1930).

Leo Deuel, *Testaments of Time* (New York: Alfred A. Knopf, 1966).

Charles Goodspeed, *Yankee Bookseller* (Boston: Houghton Mifflin, 1937).

Charles Hamilton, *Collecting Autographs and Manuscripts* (Norman: University of Oklahoma Press, 1961).

Adrian H. Joline, *Meditations of an Autograph Collector* (New York: Harper & Brothers, 1902).

Thomas F. Madigan, *Word Shadows of the Great* (New York: Frederick A. Stokes Company, 1930).

Allen Noel Latimer Munby, *The Cult of the Autograph Collector in England* (London: Athlone, 1962).

Kenneth W. Rendell, *History Comes to Life: Collecting Historical Letters and Documents* (Norman and London: University of Oklahoma Press, 1995).

Henry Thomas Scott, *Autograph Collecting: A Guide to the Collector of Historical Documents, Literary Manuscripts, and Autograph Letters, Etc.* (London: S. J. Davey, 1891).

Henry T. Scott and Samuel Davey, *Autograph Collecting: A Practical Manual for Amateurs and Historical Students* (London: Gill, 1894).

Colton Storm and Howard Peckham, *Invitation to Book Collecting: Its Pleasures and Practices. With Kindred Discussions of Manuscripts, Maps, and Prints* (New York: R. R. Bowker Company, 1947).

W. Thomas Taylor, *Texfake: An Account of the Theft and Forgery of Early Texas Printed Documents* (Austin, TX: W. Thomas Taylor, 1991).

Robert Williams, *Adventures of an Autograph Collector: An Introduction to Collecting, with Tips for Beginners* (New York: Exposition Press, 1952).

The section on neglect in public archives is drawn largely from the American Historical Association's annual report of 1900, vol. 2. Specifically, see the sections titled "Report of the Public Archives Commission" and "Historical Manuscripts in the Library of Congress." The AHA's research into the state of public archives continued for several years, and the 1901 and 1902 reports include equally shocking revelations regarding the absence of any systematic record keeping across much of the nation. I also benefited from two speeches published in the *American Archivist* in April 1939. Randolph G. Adams's talk was titled "The Character and Extent of Fugitive Archival Material"; Curtis W. Garrison spoke on "The Relationship of Historical Manuscripts to Archival Materials."

The Donald R. McCoy passage appears on page 4 of his book *The National Archives: America's Ministry of Documents, 1934–1968* (Chapel Hill: University of North Carolina Press, 1978).

5. BEST FRIENDS

I spoke to several people in Waterbury, including former mayor Edward D. Bergin Jr., to piece together Bob Matthews's Waterbury experiences. Some of them asked not to be identified. I relied on excellent reporting in several newspapers, particularly the *Hartford Courant*, for more on Matthews's background, particularly his early years. For deft and comprehensive coverage of Matthews's story, see Lisa Chedekel and Kim Martineau's "A Hotshot in the Hot Seat," published in the *Courant* on September 21, 2003. The quote "You know when things feel too good?" was among several borrowed from that piece. Also see Alison Leigh Cowan's "Amid Scrutiny, Intrigue Envelops Rowland Friends," in the *New York Times* on June 12, 2004.

Matthews's thoughts on the Bill of Rights were obtained from a deposition given on September 4, 2003, in Raleigh. The transcript can be found in U.S. District Court there: case 5:03-cv-204, document 75.

The following other articles and books were instrumental in this chapter:

Andree Brooks, "Waterbury Finally Coming into Its Own," *New York Times*, September 7, 1986.

Charles Monagan, *Waterbury: A Region Reborn* (Chatsworth, CA: Windsor Publications, Inc., 1989).

Christopher J. Sheehan, "At 31, Waterbury Developer Takes Up 'Second Career' as a Manufacturer," *Business Digest of Greater Waterbury*, December 1989.

6. THE DOCUMENT HUNTER

Ken Bowling spent many hours fielding my questions about his life and the world of historic documents; I'm indebted to him for his patience and fortitude. I learned more about his pursuit of the Biddle Sale letters through his article "The Biddle Sale of Rush Papers and Other Letters from Pennsylvania Members of the First Federal Congress to Their Constituents" in the journal *Manuscripts*, Summer 1972. Details about the theft from the Rosenbach museum were drawn from Douglas C. McGill's article "Museum Says Ex-Chief Sold Off 30 Rare Letters" in the *New York Times* on April 22, 1987.

The anecdote about Matthews's film-festival party first appeared in Julie Hatfield's article "The 'Other' Hollywood Celebrates" in the *Boston Globe* on June 23, 1997. My source for details of Matthews's Nantucket estate, including quotes about the possessions inside, was the article "Nantucket Getaway" in the Summer/Fall 2001 issue of *Antiques & Fine Art*. There was no byline on that piece. For a more detailed description of the Clintons' visit to Matthews's estate, see Bob Hohler's article "Islands Get Full View of the Hillary Era" in the *Boston Globe*, August 21, 1999.

For the passage on the Sheldon Peck painting, I consulted an unsigned story by the Associated Press published on January 19, 1998. It appeared in the *New York Times* under the headline "Card Table, a $25 Garage-Sale Bargain, Is Sold for $541,500."

Matthews's comments about his and Pratt's Bill of Rights tactics are taken from his aforementioned deposition.

One final note: I was unable to resolve a dispute over who came up with the idea of telling Reeder that Matthews was no longer interested as a way to drive down the price of the Bill of Rights. Pratt told me that on the flight to Indiana, Matthews had suggested the tactic. But Matthews, in his deposition, testified that "Wayne wanted to use [this ploy] to be able to get the price down—look, Bob won't be able to invest."

7. THE LEAVES OF THE SYBIL

The North Carolina State Archives maintains the 1897 correspondence quoted in this chapter. I located it in the Secretary of State file, Series I, "Correspondence."

My source for the Cyrus Thompson passage was Josephus Daniels's memoir, *Editor in Politics* (Chapel Hill: University of North Carolina Press, 1941).

General Order 100—also known as the Lieber Code—is available online, thanks to the Yale Law School's Lillian Goldman Law Library; see http://avalon.law.yale.edu. The W. Hays Parks and Joseph Glatthaar opinions are taken from affidavits in the state of North Carolina's amended memorandum of law in support of its motion for summary judgment, filed in January 2008. Similarly, much of the information regarding North Carolina's history with regard to sovereign documents—including the quotes from Governor Morehead—came from the state's sourced court filings. The John J. Metzgar Papers—which include descriptions of the documents the soldier took from Raleigh—are on file at the University of North Carolina's Southern Historical Collection, Manuscripts Department, Wilson Library. My source for the Wheelock passage was the state of North Carolina's memorandum for summary judgment.

For the Scharf passage, I consulted the *Dictionary of American Biography*, vol. VII (New York: Charles Scribner's Sons, 1935), edited by Dumas Malone. Leo Deuel's *Testaments of Time,* cited previously, informed the material on Giovanni Belzoni and E. A. Wallis Budge. Other theft information came from the aforementioned American Historical Association's annual report from 1900.

The unsigned article in the Raleigh *News & Observer* of October 5, 1897, is titled "A Revolutionary Relic: Copy of Original Articles to the Twelve Amendments." That piece included a reprinting of the October 1 *Indianapolis News* article also mentioned in this passage.

For background on the Mecklenburg Declaration of Independence, I consulted Colton Storm and Howard Peckham's *Invitation to Book Collecting*, referenced previously. The Public Library of Charlotte & Mecklenburg County maintains an excellent website with background on the enduring debate; see http://cmstory.org/meckdec.

Finally, I obtained input for this chapter from George Stevenson Jr. and Jeff Crow of North Carolina's state archives. I'm grateful for their cooperation.

8. STRANGERS

The sales documents mentioned in this chapter are located in the aforementioned court files. An invoice from Alan Firkser that briefly outlines his conservation work on the Bill of Rights is also available there.

In recounting the Sotheby's auction of the Dunlap Declaration of Independence, I relied on two articles: James Barron's "For 1776 Copy of Declaration, a Record in an Online Auction," in the *New York Times* on June 30, 2000; and Kris Axtman's "The Price of Independence: $8.1 Million," in the *Christian Science Monitor*, July 3, 2000.

9. THE ART DEALER

Peter Tillou agreed to speak to me for this book despite a clear disinclination to do so. I'm grateful for his time and his efforts to remember as many details as possible. Also, thanks to Bill Reese for his help facilitating the interview.

Additional background on Tillou came from the following articles:

Alex Beam, "John Kerry Cashes In on Art," *Boston Globe*, April 20, 2004.

Frances McQueeney-Jones Mascolo, "Portraits Snapped Up by Conn. Collector," *Boston Herald*, June 14, 1998.

Vivien Raynor, "Folk Paintings at UConn Mix Mystery and Allure," *New York Times*, July 17, 1983.

Rita Reif, "Auctions," *New York Times*, October 18, 1985.

Lita Solis-Cohen, "The Winter Antiques Show," *Maine Antiques Digest*, March 1999.

Peter Tillou, "My Love Affair with Dealing and Collecting," *Antiques & Fine Art*, March/April 2000.

Judd Tully, "A Bull Market," *Washington Post*, January 21, 1999.

Antiques dealer Wayne Mattox fielded several rounds of questions about his industry and about Wayne Pratt. The anecdote about the Boston Queen Anne card table came from Frances McQueeney-Jones Mascolo's article, previously cited.

For the passage about John Hobbs, I turned to an article by Christopher Mason and Christopher Owen, "Furniture Restorer's Allegations of Deception Shake Antiques Trade," published in the *New York Times* on May 22, 2008.

My source for the Manuscript Society passage was *Autographs and Manuscripts: A Collector's Manual* (New York: Scribners, 1978), by John F. Reed; Edmund Berkeley Jr., editor. And A.S.W. Rosenbach's anecdote about Oscar Wilde's stolen papers appeared in his book *A Book Hunter's Holiday: Adventures with Books and Manuscripts* (Boston: Houghton Mifflin Company, 1936).

10. THE BOOKSELLER

Bill Reese spent numerous hours describing not only his experiences with the Bill of Rights but also the wider world of rare, historic documents. He has remarkable spot-on recall for names and details. I drew additional biographical details, and a couple of direct quotes, from two of Nicholas A. Basbanes's books: *Among the Gently Mad: Strategies and Perspectives for the Book-Hunter in the 21st Century* (New York: Henry Holt & Co., 2002) and *Patience & Fortitude: Wherein a Colorful Cast of Determined Book Collectors,*

Dealers, and Librarians Go About the Quixotic Task of Preserving a Legacy (New York: HarperCollins, 2001).

The *Rare Book Review* passage I quote came from Reese's column, "A Letter from America #4: Secrets in the Rare Book Business," dated May 2002.

For the information on South Carolina's Bill of Rights, I consulted the South Carolina Historical Commission report for fiscal year 1944–45. Thanks to archivist Rodger Stroup for furnishing that, and for his additional input. In addition to learning of Georgia's Bill of Rights mystery from Greg Jarrell, I gathered information on his Declaration of Independence discovery from Moni Basu's January 19, 2007, article in the *Atlanta Journal-Constitution,* "Archivist Discovers Historic Document." For background on Delaware's Bill, I consulted "Shared Custody Keeps Delaware's Bill of Rights Right Here at Home" by Robin Smith, in the Wilmington-based *News Journal,* September 18, 2007.

The quote about the carpetbagger from Pennsylvania came from Charles Hamilton's previously sourced *Collecting Autographs and Manuscripts.* The New Jersey Bill of Rights fiasco turned up in two articles on September 18, 1944, neither of which includes a byline: "Bill of Rights Is Found: Jersey's Copy of Ancient Document, One of 10 Extant, Twice Lost," in the *Newark Evening News;* and "State's Copy of Bill of Rights Found—Was 'Lost' Seven Years," in the *Trenton Evening Times.*

Thanks to John Kaminski for his detailed recollection of his encounter with New Hampshire's original Bill of Rights.

11. THE BUYER

Seth Kaller was yet another participant in this story's telling who had little to gain, and I appreciate his participation. He related his experiences with the Bill of Rights in as much detail as possible over the course of several interviews and assisted me in my research on several other fronts: He led me through the winding and insular corridors of the document-collecting and -dealing communities and loaned me copies of hard-to-find tomes on the trade.

It's worth noting that Kaller still declines to reveal the identity of the person who contacted him about North Carolina's Bill of Rights in the 1990s—though he did say the person was trying to broker a deal on behalf of Wayne Pratt and John Richardson, which he himself didn't know at the time.

The section on the National Constitution Center was chiefly the result of interviews with Joe Torsella, Steve Frank, and Steve Harmelin. The museum officials also furnished a timeline of events related to the museum's dealings with the Bill of Rights that proved critical in sorting through the flurry of events leading up to the FBI sting.

Buzz Bissinger's book *A Prayer for the City* (New York: Random House) was published in 1997. For more background on the National Constitution Center (www.constitutioncenter.org), see:

Frederick Cusick, "Constitution Center President to Resign in Dec.," *Philadelphia Inquirer,* August 22, 2003.

Kathryn Levy Feldman, "The House That Joe Built," *Pennsylvania Gazette,* November/December 2003.

Stephan Salisbury, "A 21st-Century Vision: Constitution Center Strives to Tell 'a Story about You,'" *Philadelphia Inquirer,* June 29, 2003.

———, "Philadelphia Does History Right: So Far, So Good at the National Constitution Center," *Philadelphia Inquirer,* June 13, 2006.

———, "Rendell Chairs Constitution Center," *Philadelphia Inquirer,* December 10, 1996.

For background information on Richard Gilder and Lewis Lehrman, I consulted:

Douglas Martin, "Benefactor Wants Private Group to Manage Central Park," *New York Times,* January 17, 1997.

Robin Pogrebin, "Historical Society Shifts Focus with Its Shift in Leadership," *New York Times,* June 25, 2004.

Robin Pogrebin and Glenn Collins, "Shift at Historical Society Raises Concerns," *New York Times,* July 20, 2004.

Stephanie Strom, "$75,000 a Record Gift for Yale? Here's How," *New York Times,* June 1, 2004.

Also see www.gilderlehrman.org and www.nyhistory.org. Finally, I viewed a 2005 C-SPAN interview with both men. Go to www.qanda .org and search for *Gilder Lehrman.*

John Estey, Governor Ed Rendell's first chief of staff, provided context for what was happening in Harrisburg as the Bill of Rights emerged as an issue.

12. A Revelation

Laura Beach's article "The Winter Antiques Show," in *Antiques and the Arts Online,* January 21, 2003, helped me construct the back-drop for the meeting between Pratt and Tillou.

My chief source on the Malcolm Forbes sale was Bill Reese's column for the *Rare Book Review,* "A Letter from America #5: The Malcolm Forbes Sale," June 2002.

Paul Bass's reporting in the *New Haven Advocate* was invaluable in helping me piece together Bob Matthews's years in that city. Bass elaborated on his work in an interview. The two articles I quote from are "Welcome to the Sausage Factory," June 11, 1998; and "That's What 'Friends' Are For: Poor Bob Matthews Gets Swept Up in Rowland-gate," July 3, 2003. Also see "Friends Like These: From Mansions to Subpoenas of Rats and Robbers," April 1, 2004.

The article I reference in *Business New Haven* was titled "To the Rescue: Developer Matthews Acquires New Haven Manufacturing" and published on September 22, 1997. There was no byline.

The information about Naegele and Hughes came from reporting in the previously sourced pieces in the *Hartford Courant* (by Chedekel and Martineau) and the *New York Times* (by Alison Leigh Cowan). I also went to Superior Court in Waterbury, Connecticut, to review the lengthy court file generated by the legal struggles between Robert Hughes and Bob Matthews; an affidavit provided by Hughes during that litigation factors later in the story.

13. Time Runneth Not Against the King

The letters from Pratt to Tillou and from Richardson to Pratt (with billing information) were among the aforementioned files in the Wake County Superior Court case involving the Bill of Rights.

Rubin Weiner furnished a detailed recollection of his Bill of Rights research and involvement in the drama involving the FBI and John Richardson.

There are several proximate translations of the Latin word *re-plevin;* mine came from the previously sourced book *Invitation to Book Collecting*.

For background on the B. C. West case, I consulted two articles published in *Carolina Comments*, the bimonthly newsletter of the North Carolina Division of Archives and History: Thornton W. Mitchell's "Another View of the West Case," November 1981; and William S. Price Jr.'s "Toward a Definition of Public Records: North Carolina's Replevin Action," November 1977.

The "buyer beware" quote from the Manuscript Society came from the aforementioned book *Autographs and Manuscripts*, by Reed and Berkeley.

Roxanne Patel's article in the July 2003 issue of *Philadelphia Magazine*, titled "The Paper Chase," was a useful resource; two direct quotes in the recounting of the Yale Club meeting come from that story.

Part of the passage about *Antiques Roadshow*, including the quote from Dan Elias, was drawn from "On the Road with Dan Elias," in *Tufts On-Line Magazine*, Summer 2001. Pratt's appraisal of the whale-bone dominoes came on *Antiques Roadshow*'s Tucson stop during the 2002 season (hour 2).

Finally, a note about the fee Richardson was to be paid for his services: Though Richardson's own math added up to $1.89 million, Pratt told me the attorney was actually in line for $2.6 million, though he offered no documentation to account for the discrepancy. (It's hard to imagine expenses adding up to $700,000, even for a D.C. lawyer.) If Richardson indeed had $2.6 million coming, Pratt and Matthews's share would have dropped to $500,000 each.

14. THE JOY OF ILLEGITIMATE POSSESSION

The correspondence generated during Charles I. Reid's attempt to sell the Bill of Rights in 1925 is on file in the North Carolina State Archives, Director's Office, General Correspondence, I-M, Box 53, "Manuscripts" folder. Biographical information about Robert House came from the North Carolina Office of Archives and History website: www.history.ncdcr.gov/centennial/features/nchr.htm.

The mention of the "interesting deposit" came from the Indiana State Library *Bulletin,* May 1907, in the *Twenty-seventh Biennial Report of the Librarian of the Indiana State Library, for the Fiscal Years Ending September 30, 1907 and September 30, 1908 and Bul letins December, 1905–September, 1908.* Biographical details involving Grier Shotwell came from the sources referenced for chapter 4.

My sources for Reid's plane crash were a series of Associated Press reports. One that ran in the Hagerstown (MD) *Morning Herald* on November 21, 1929, was titled "Airman Killed in Plane Fall atop Building: Charles I. Reid Loses Fight with Balky Motor in New York." A follow-up appeared in the *Brownsville (TX) Herald* the same day under the headline "N.Y. Seeking Pilots' Rule." Neither article included a byline.

15. NOWHERE FAST

This chapter was built on interviews with as many of the relevant parties as I could reach (Joe Torsella, Steve Harmelin, John Estey, Jeff Crow) and the timeline provided by the National Constitution Center. I was partly able to make up for the lack of participation within Governor Mike Easley's office by obtaining notes kept by Reuben Young, Easley's legal counsel, through North Carolina's Open Records Law.

That said, the decision of Easley and his staff to decline interview requests for this book left questions unanswered. For example: Easley told reporter Mark Johnson of the *Charlotte Observer* that when he first got the call from Pennsylvania Governor Ed Rendell about the Bill of Rights, "My first thought was, 'Wait a minute, I'd be receiving stolen property if I got this thing. I'm not going to call him back. I'm going to try and figure out a way to get this document.'" This mirrors the state's long-standing reluctance to buy back the missing parchment and fits neatly with what came next. But this sentiment wasn't delegated along with the orders to follow up. In fact, the Constitution Center's internal notes show that Dellinger's initial reaction—in his first conversation with the museum—was to let museum officials buy the document with North Carolina's blessing.

Young's notes indicate that it took a couple of weeks to come around to the idea of trying to get the document back through legal intervention and strongly suggest there were differing opinions about the best way to proceed—which mirrors the impression the governor's office left with the Constitution Center.

In declining an interview request, Easley cited ongoing litigation—though that didn't prevent him and various staffers from recounting the story to various North Carolina–based media over the past few years. That left the impression that the governor's office wants to let stand the oversimplified version of the story that was reported locally. Dellinger, too, declined to be interviewed because of continuing litigation. After Easley left office, however, he wrote a feisty account of the affair in the Spring 2009 issue of the *North Carolina State Bar Journal.* This version—in which he claims credit for almost every step of the document's recovery—is filled with swashbuckling claims of derring-do (in addition to the passage about Easley being confused about when the Bill of Rights would be recovered). "After I received the initial call from Governor Rendell," he wrote, "I decided it was time to bring these offers [to sell the Bill of Rights to North Carolina] to an end"—after which he claims to have called his legal team to organize a sting of his own devising. Asked to comment on this, a federal official directly involved with the sting scoffed, calling much of the article a fiction. "This thing continues to infect the egos of so many people," he said.

The *Charlotte Observer* article mentioned above—"How N.C. Located Its Bill of Rights," published July 4, 2004—was my source for the circumstances of Easley's call with Rendell.

An official summary of the Rowland condo deal appeared on a March 18, 2004, press release titled "Woodbury Man Pleads Guilty to Federal Misdemeanor Tax Charge" issued by the U.S. attorney's office, District of Connecticut. Further information came from interviews with Pratt and from in-depth reporting in the *Hartford Courant* and *New York Times.* Specifically, see:

Dave Altimari, Edmund H. Mahoney, and Jon Lender, "New Issue: Rowland Condo Deal," *Hartford Courant,* January 6, 2004.

Keith M. Faneuf, "Impeachment Inquiry Breaks Down Condo Sale," Manchester *Journal Inquirer,* June 9, 2004.

Edmund H. Mahoney, "The Worst Setback Yet: Pratt Pleads Guilty to Federal Tax Charge," *Hartford Courant,* March 19, 2004.

Mike McIntire and Alison Leigh Cowan, "Rowland Property Sale Raises Questions amid Ethics Inquiry," *New York Times,* January 6, 2004.

Mark Pazniokas, "Evidence of Deception: Hearings Open with Details of Condo Deal," *Hartford Courant,* June 9, 2004.

16. THE SKY'S THE LIMIT

My resources for parchment making are primarily found online. For a concise description of the process, see *Bookbinding and the Conservation of Books: A Dictionary of Descriptive Terminology* (http://cool.conservation-us.org/don/don.html) by Matt T. Roberts and Don Etherington.

The *Indianapolis Star*'s unsigned obituary for Grier Shotwell is titled "Attorney Grier Shotwell Dies; Civic and Educational Leader," May 14, 1972.

For the sections on Sotheby's and Leslie Hindman, I relied on a source within the federal government who shared findings from the FBI investigation that I was unable to access through more conventional means. Sotheby's chose not to make David Redden and Selby Kiffer available for interviews. When I asked the firm to comment on my reporting, spokeswoman Lauren Gioia responded by e-mail that my account did "not seem to fit the recollection of many of our staff members who were involved back then." Given several opportunities over the course of more than a year, however, she was unable or unwilling to elaborate. The following articles and books were useful in terms of background on the auction house:

James Barron, "Public Lives; He's Auctioned the 1776 Declaration, Twice," *New York Times,* July 4, 2000.

Michelle Osborn, "For $4, a $1M Piece of History," *USA Today,* April 3, 1991.

Richard Perez-Pena, "Notes Reveal 'Profoundly Humane' Whitman," *New York Times,* February 19, 1995.

Rita Reif, "Arts/Artifacts; For One Born to Sell, Not Even the Sky's the Limit," *New York Times,* August 20, 1995.

——, "Einstein Paper Sets Auction Record," *New York Times*, December 3, 1987.

——, "What's the Bid? Sky's the Limit," *New York Times*, February 4, 1993.

Christine Sparta, "Auction Offers Intimate View of Einstein," *USA Today*, June 23, 1998.

Peter Watson, *Sotheby's: The Inside Story* (New York: Random House, 1997).

Simon Worrall, *The Poet and the Murderer* (New York: Plume, 2003).

Tom Taylor's case against Sotheby's in the 2004 sale of Texana documents appeared on the Antiquarian Booksellers Association of America website; for a full reading of his arguments, see http://cool.conservation-us.org/byform/mailing-lists/exlibris/2004/06/msg00059.html.

My source for the passage about Hindman's request for a larger commission from the Shotwell family was FBI agent Paul Minella's affidavit, submitted with the state of North Carolina's motion for summary judgment, September 10, 2003. For background on Hindman beyond what I learned in a couple of interviews with her, I consulted these articles and books:

Associated Press, "Other 'Masterpieces' Surface After van Gogh Find," January 12, 1991.

Leslie Hindman with Dan Santow, *Adventures at the Auction* (New York: Three Rivers Press, 2002).

Steve Kloehn, "Celebrity Auction Mania Is Nothing New," *Chicago Tribune*, April 30, 1996.

New York Times, "Sotheby's Buys in Chicago," June 27, 1997.

Michelle Osborn, "Regional Auction Houses Taking Action from New York," *USA Today*, March 7, 1991.

Elliot Spagat, "Van Gogh Painting Sells for $1.43 Million," Associated Press, March 11, 1991.

17. JUST A REGULAR GUY

I constructed the scenes in Raleigh through interviews with Frank Whitney, Bobby Higdon, and Paul Minella. Most biographical information about Bob Wittman came from several lengthy interviews. However, the following books and articles were also helpful in terms of filling in the details of a colorful career:

Roger Atwood, *Stealing History: Tomb Raiders, Smugglers, and the Looting of the Ancient World* (New York: St. Martin's Press, 2004).

Kelly Crow, "From the Art World to the Underworld," *Wall Street Journal*, August 22, 2008.

John Schiffman, "FBI Unit Here Patrols the Art World," *Philadelphia Inquirer*, October 25, 2005.

Bradley Vasoli, "Philly Home to FBI's Top Expert on Art Crimes," (Philadelphia) *Bulletin*, August 15, 2008.

For the passage about the 1995–96 interactions between John Richardson and North Carolina, I relied on interviews with David Olson. One fascinating question still lingers over the two Richardson letters, which served as the underpinnings for the FBI's seizure: On whose authority was Richardson acting? Charlie Reeder, the Shotwell family lawyer, told me he'd had no idea such correspondence even existed; more than a decade after the fact, he said, he had yet to even see the letters. Wayne Pratt, too, claimed to know nothing about the missives. "I never had anything to do with those letters," he said. "Nor did I ever see them." That leaves us to conclude that Richardson was acting alone—a seemingly unlikely eventuality. Unfortunately, Richardson declined to be interviewed for this book.

18. DECEPTION

For the passage on Charles Merrill Mount, I relied on the following articles:

Karlyn Barker, "Rare Documents' Vulnerability Comes to Light," *Washington Post*, August 20, 1987.

Victoria Churchville and Saundra Saperstein, "D.C. Author Arrested with Rare Letters," *Washington Post*, August 14, 1987.

——, "The Fall from Grace of an Artist, Author: Trail of Debts, Lawsuits Ends at Jail Cell," *Washington Post*, August 16, 1987.

Herbert Mitgang, "Reacting to Document Thefts, Libraries Move to Add Security," *New York Times*, August 20, 1987.

Ed Bomsey not only recounted the Mount case but also thought-fully described his life as a collector and dealer. The sources on the spate of document thefts are:

Robert Gavin, "History Sold to Highest Bidders? Archivist Charged in Theft from State Library," *Albany Times Union*, January 29, 2008.

Buford Green, "Document Thief Sentenced to Four Years" *(Springfield, IL) State Journal-Register*, November 3, 1998.

Carol D. Leonnig, "Archives Thief Gets Two Years," *Washington Post*, May 27, 2005.

Beth Musgrave, "Louisville Man, 70, Caught Stealing Historic Letters," *Lexington Herald-Leader*, December 9, 2005.

Joseph A. Slobodzian, "Archivist Given 21 Months in Thefts of Historical Items," *Philadelphia Inquirer*, August 1, 2002.

Sarah Vos, "4 Lexingtonians Indicted in Theft of Rare Books," *Lexington Herald-Leader*, March 4, 2005.

Yilu Zhao, "Man Stole Rare Items at Yale, Police Say," *New York Times*, December 7, 2001.

Several articles provided background details for the Richardson bi-ographical passage:

Patrick Butters, "Clinton, Rawlings Exchange Laughs, Stories at State Dinner," *Washington Times*, February 25, 1999.

Serge F. Kovaleski, "Agency Payment Called a 'No-No': D.C. Sports Funds Went to Campaign," *Washington Post*, April 27, 2003.

———, "Chairman of Sports Agency Resigning," *Washington Post*, June 19, 2003.

———, "D.C. Sports Panel Probed for Hiring Chair's Law Firm," *Washington Post*, May 5, 2003.

———, "Sports Agency's Spending Criticized; Expenditures Soared as Funds Declined," *Washington Post*, April 22, 2003.

19. SPECIAL DELIVERY

Bob Matthews's activities circa 2000 were scrutinized by a number of newspapers. I consulted the following:

John Christoffersen, "2 High-Energy Guys or a Money Connection?" *(Manchester, CT) Journal Inquirer*, March 23, 2004.

Alison Leigh Cowan, "Years Later, the Way a Rowland Friend Profited Is Criticized," *New York Times*, August 9, 2004.

Jon Lender, Dave Altimari, and Edmund H. Mahoney, "House Panel Tracks Funds for Rowland Friend," *Hartford Courant*, March 24, 2004.

Mike McIntire and Jon Lender, "Family Ties and Hefty Profits: As a Food Company Seeks State Aid, Investments in Its Stock Benefit Some Close to the Circle of Power," *Hartford Courant*, April 13, 2003.

Mark Pazniokas, "Focus Is on Timing of Favors: Governor, Matthews Helped Each Other," *Hartford Courant*, June 10, 2004.

Paul Bass's "Jay Gatsby" line came from the previously sourced article "Friends Like These" in the *New Haven Advocate*.

The *New York Times* quote about Rowland being "perhaps unbeatable" comes from Paul Zielbauer's November 7, 2002, article "The 2002 Elections: Connecticut; Rowland Steers to the Middle, Keeps His Eye on the Voters and Wins."

The passage about Joe Constantino primarily came from his statement to the FBI, a précis of which is in court files in Wake County Court. The background on his relationship with Pratt came from Constantino's speech at Pratt's memorial service on September 1, 2007.

20. THE THUMP ON THE DOOR

This chapter was almost entirely constructed through interviews and visits to the site of the sting. I obtained additional details through depositions of Bob Wittman, Joe Torsella, and Steve Harmelin, all taken on September 3, 2003, and available on file in U.S. District Court in Raleigh.

The Mark Bowden quote is from "So, Saddam Is Dead . . ." in the *Wall Street Journal*, January 2, 2007.

21. BLOW-BACK

I consulted dozens of stories about the sting and its aftermath. These pieces figure into this chapter:

Jeffrey Gettleman, "One of 14 Original Copies of the Bill of Rights Has Resurfaced, but Who Owns It?" *New York Times*, August 11, 2003.

Anna Griffin, "1789 Copy of the Bill of Rights Recovered," *Charlotte Observer,* March 20, 2003.

David Hewitt, "Bill of Rights Seized by FBI," *Maine Antiques Digest,* May 2003.

Patrik Jonsson, "A Bill of Rights, Looted Long Ago, Is Stolen Back," *Christian Science Monitor,* April 22, 2003.

Dan Majors, "A Bill of Rights Wronged," *Pittsburgh Post-Gazette,* March 25, 2003.

Paula Peters, "Nantucket Dealer Tied to Stolen Document," *Cape Cod Times,* April 5, 2003.

Joseph A. Slobodzian, "Sting Nets Stolen Piece of History," *Philadelphia Inquirer,* March 20, 2003.

Jim Smith, "FBI Recovers Stolen Copy of Bill of Rights," *Philadelphia Daily News,* March 20, 2003.

I also used a line from a press release issued by Governor Mike Easley's office on March 19, 2003, titled "Gov. Easley Announces Safe Recovery of N.C. Bill of Rights."

Bob Matthews did not respond to multiple interview requests for this book; his version of post-sting events is drawn from two sources: his deposition of September 4, 2003, previously sourced; and from an interview I conducted with him in April 2003 for an article for *Connecticut Magazine.*

Not surprisingly, his version of events is disputed. Marybeth Keene said Matthews never screamed at her, and Pratt could not recall a single instance in which Matthews confronted him. Pratt contended that Matthews made these allegations in order to distance himself from the deal, and thus avoid trouble with the FBI.

22. THE GREAT DIVIDE

The first part of this chapter draws on Matthews's previously sourced deposition. Michael Stratton's legal briefs of September 11 and 12, 2003, are on file in U.S. District Court in Raleigh (see documents 82 and 84 in the previously cited civil case). Paul Newby did not respond to a request to comment on Stratton's accusations.

Sources for the condo deal and other Matthews issues are detailed in notes for chapters 15 and 19. Also see the previously sourced

Chedekel/Martineau story (September 21, 2003) in the *Hartford Courant* and the Cowan piece in the *New York Times* (June 12, 2004).

Matthews's quote regarding the condo sale appeared in the previously cited *Courant* article published on January 6, 2004.

Robert Hughes's deposition is on file in Waterbury Superior Court.

My source for the passage involving Matthews and Joe Santopietro was a *Courant* article by Edmund H. Mahoney, Jon Lender, and Dave Altimari, "Scandal Figure Gave Before," April 10, 2004. The piece on Matthews's estate in Washington came from a story by Dave Altimari and David Owens, "Mountaintop Dream Ends," in the *Hartford Courant,* December 18, 2004.

Karen Blum described to me her revelation concerning the wording in the Bill of Rights. Other information about experts' attempts to verify the Bill of Rights came from the state of North Carolina's aforementioned memorandum in support of its motion for summary judgment.

23. ANOTHER WAY

My source for the Boturini, Kingsborough, and Shapira passages was Leo Deuel's previously sourced *Testaments of Time.* The Joline quote comes from his previously sourced book, *Meditations of an Autograph Collector.*

For the passages on Rosenbach, I consulted the exhaustive *Rosenbach: A Biography,* by Edwin Wolf II and John Fleming (Cleveland: World Publishing Company, 1960). All correspondence quoted in this section involving the bookseller and the Bill of Rights is on file at the Rosenbach Museum & Library in Philadelphia. My sources for the dedication were an unsigned *New York Times* article from December 16, 1943, titled "Observance Held Here: Original Copy of Bill on View at Ceremony at Subtreasury." I also consulted an undated U.S. Department of Treasury press release titled "'Bill of Rights' Manuscript to Nation," which is on file at the Rosenbach Museum & Library.

The Ernst Posner quote came from the Council of State Archivists report, "The State of State Records: A Status Report on State Archives and Record Management Programs in the United States," released in January 2007. Other parts of this chapter were informed by a supplement to that report titled "Profiles of State Archives and Records Management Programs." The Hamilton and Benjamin quotes are taken from their previously sourced books.

My source for the paragraph on Thomas Phillips was the previously referenced book by Storm and Peckham, *Invitation to Book Collecting*.

Everett Wilkie shared his thoughts with me on the complexities of public archives, collectors, and historic documents. My sources for the dispute involving the John Carter Brown Library were Bill Reese and an article, "Exeter Still in Legal Limbo over 2 Historical Documents," by Marilyn Bellemore, in the *North Kingstown (RI) Standard Times*, October 16, 2003. For the passage on institutional skirmishes over documents, I talked to Joe Klett at the New Jersey state archives and consulted Christine Schiavo's article in the *Philadelphia Inquirer*, "Historians Have at It over North Jersey Deed," on July 30, 2006.

The Thornton W. Mitchell quote comes from his article "Another View of the West Case," cited previously.

The article quoting Price, "Prospects Dim for Recovering State's Copy of Bill of Rights," appeared in the Raleigh *News & Observer*, December 16, 1991. No author was listed.

POSTSCRIPT

For information about Rowland's sentencing, I consulted Avi Salzman's *New York Times* piece, "Rowland, a Year and a Day Later," dated February 12, 2006.

The *Palm Beach Post* item about Bob Matthews, "Social Climb or 'Blitz' to Shift Attention?" was written by Jose Lambiet and published on March 5, 2006. Information on the Palm House came from the company website, www.palmhousehotel.com.

For the latest on the vicissitudes of Matthews's real estate empire, I turned to Jose Lambiet's reporting in the *Palm Beach Post* and on his website, www.Page2Live.com; Lambiet was one of very few journalists Matthews spoke to in the post-Rowland era. Specifically, see "Socialite Has County's Largest Delinquent Tax Bill," posted on the site on May 19, 2009. For developments in Massachusetts, I consulted two stories: "Bank Seizes Point Breeze," by Peter B. Brace, in the July 1, 2009, *Nantucket Independent,* and Jason Graziadel's story in the *Mirror and Inquirer,* "Bank Takes Control of Point Breeze," July 2, 2009.

My source for the passage on Sean Combs was Lola Ogunnaike's article, "Politics and Partying Meet in the Hamptons," in the *New York Times,* July 6, 2004.

The *New York Times*'s praise for the National Constitution Center appeared in an article by Witold Rybczynski, "More Perfect Union of Function and Form," on July 8, 2003.

My source on the story of Michael Sparks and the thrift-store Declaration of Independence was "Declaration Moves from Rags to Riches," by Andrew Marshall, in the *Deseret (UT) News,* June 22, 2007.

Sarah Koonts at the North Carolina state archives answered numerous questions about the condition and storage of the Bill of Rights and the state's future plans for it. For more on the parchment's tour of North Carolina during 2007, see "State's Copy of Bill of Rights Finishes Tour Sunday," by Jim Schlosser, Greensboro *News & Record,* December 1, 2007.